The Meanings of
Marital Equality

SUNY series in the Philosophy of the Social Sciences
Lenore Langsdorf, editor

The Meanings of
Marital Equality

Scott R. Harris

State University of New York Press

Published by
State University of New York Press, Albany

© 2006 State University of New York

For information, address State University of New York Press,
194 Washington Avenue, Suite 305, Albany, NY 12210-2384

Production by Michael Haggett
Marketing by Anne M. Valentine

Library of Congress Cataloging in Publication Data

Harris, Scott R., 1969 Sept. 16–
    The meanings of marital equality / Scott R. Harris.
        p. cm. — (Suny series in the philosophy of the social sciences)
    Includes bibliographical references and index.
    ISBN 0-7914-6621-3 (hardcover : alk. paper) — ISBN 0-7914-6622-1
    (pbk. : alk. paper).
    1. Marriage. 2. Equality. 3. Interpersonal relations. I. Title. II. Series.

HQ734.H3253 2005
306.81—dc22

                                                                    2005006026

ISBN-13: 978-0-7914-6621-6 (hardcover : alk. paper)
ISBN-13: 978-0-7914-6622-3 (pbk. : alk. paper)

10   9   8   7   6   5   4   3   2   1

This book is dedicated to Jenine

Contents

Preface

"There is no adequate definition of social problems within sociology, and there is not, nor has there ever been, a sociology of social problems." Almost thirty years ago, Spector and Kitsuse (1977, p. 1) helped launch the constructionist approach to social problems with this introduction to their book *Constructing Social Problems*. This opening line appears at first glance to be an outrageous, if not absurd, statement. At the time (and continuing to this day), the sociological literature was replete with descriptions and analyses of social problems. Sociologists had already written much about poverty, crime, discrimination, divorce, and a plethora of related issues. What could Spector and Kitsuse have meant by this ridiculous assertion?

Their argument only made sense if one read further and discovered that they were proposing a fairly radical reconceptualization of the nature of social problems, from objective properties of social life to socially created definitions. If social problems only existed when people defined them into being, then to study those problems was to study definitional practices, not the "actual" extent, causes, and consequences of social ills. Thus, the absence of a "sociology of social problems" that Spector and Kitsuse decried was actually the absence of a sociology of social problems-*as-interpretive-claims-making*, as "the activities of those who assert the existence of conditions and define them as problems" (Spector and Kitsuse 1977, p. 74).

Naturally, this opening line—designed (arguably) to capture interest and provoke debate—was polemical and needed subsequent qualification. In later chapters, Spector and Kitsuse noted that although value conflict theorists (Fuller and Myers 1941) and other scholars had already approached social problems from somewhat definitional perspectives, a thoroughly and rigorously constructionist perspective had not been developed. Since the publication of *Constructing Social Problems*, a healthy tradition of research has been inspired by Spector and Kitsuse's

book, though not without continuing debate over the proper way to proceed[1] (Best 1993, 2000; Holstein and Miller 1993; Ibarra and Kitsuse
1993; Loseke 1999; Schneider 1985; Woolgar and Pawluch 1985).

In a sense, what I am attempting to do in this book is paraphrase
Spector and Kitsuse and argue similarly that *there is not, nor has there ever
been, a sociology of inequality.* To be sure, there are innumerable sociological
studies of inequality. Actually, a strong case could be made that inequality
is "public enemy number one" for sociologists. Inequality is perhaps
becoming the central, organizing theme of the field. When sociologists
think about economics, they think inequality (Morris and Western 1999).
When they think environmental decline, they think inequality (Foster
1999). Similarly for crime (Hagan and Peterson 1995), social control
(O'Brien and Jacobs 1998), education (Mehan 1992), health (Bartley
2003), family (Lareau 2002), religion (Maines and McCallion 2000), the
self (Anderson and Snow 2001), gender (Lorber 2001), and so on. Yet
with all the attention that has been paid to inequality, I would argue that
not enough has been given to inequality-*as-an-interpretively-constituted-
phenomenon.* The vast majority of sociologists assume that inequality is an
objective reality and that it is their job—rather than members' practical
tasks—to define, find, measure, and explain "it." Even qualitative, interactionist scholars tend to conform to this conventional wisdom. Inequality is
simply given; it is out there waiting for the researcher to find it. For example, Maines (2000, p. 257) describes inequality as "one of the most significant and decisive facts of human societies" while Schwalbe et al. (2000, p.
421) begin with the assumption that inequality is "endemic to and pervasive in late capitalist societies."

Just as there were precursors to Spector and Kitsuse's perspective on
social problems, there is interpretive research on inequality—such as
work that looks at competing definitions of and diverse experiences
with "poverty," "class," "status" (S. Collins 1996; R. Collins 2000;
Kingston 2000). But these sorts of studies are not couched in or seek
the development of an overarching theoretical orientation that casts
inequality *in general* as a socially constructed interpretation. Social
problems scholars have not attempted to develop a coherent body of
work that puts claims-making about inequality at the center of the
analysis, *an approach that attempts to bracket the "truth" about the existence and meaning of inequality in order to better study how people convert
indeterminate states of affairs into inequalities of some or another variety.*
This neglect is surprising, given the prevalence of interest in both
inequality and constructionism.

In this book it is not my intention to argue that important differences in wealth, income, power, prestige, health, and quality of life do or do not exist between particular individuals and groups. What I want to argue is that more sociologists should scrutinize the constructed nature of *all* claims-making about those kinds of differences—even social scientific claims. Otherwise, sociologists will have an underdeveloped appreciation of the diversity of "inequality" as well as the interpretive work that underlies any manifestation of that phenomenon. In order to demonstrate how this sort of understanding may be lacking and why it is essential, I will focus primarily on the subfield of marriage, but the implications for the study of inequality in general should be clear. Although this is a simple study in marriage, it is also more broadly a critique of sociologists' (and other social scientists') tendency to reify inequality and obscure the diverse meanings that "equal" and "unequal" situations may have for people in everyday life.

OVERVIEW OF THE BOOK

In the first chapter I outline four tendencies that traditional approaches to studying equality and inequality have in common, despite differences in theoretical orientation or substantive topic. Then I critique these tendencies and propose an alternative approach. I develop this alternative by returning to four founding figures in interactionist, social constructionist thought: Herbert Blumer, Alfred Schutz, Harold Garfinkel, and John Dewey. I select and explain key concepts from each author and apply these ideas to the subject of equality, creating what I think is a coherent and useful perspective.

In chapter 2 and 3 I begin to apply this perspective to the specific issue of equality in marriage. In chapter 2 I attempt to summarize and critique the past forty years of quantitative research that uses explicit procedures for distinguishing equal marriages from unequal ones. By taking a close look at the methodologies that cut across these studies, I show how different scholars (or even the same scholars in different publications) have used contradictory definitions and measurement strategies to classify couples. Moreover, I suggest that all of these idiosyncratic measurement systems probably have very tenuous connections to the ways that married persons define and measure equality in their marriages.

Some readers may leave chapter 2 with the impression that I am merely advocating qualitative methods in a "quantitative versus qualitative" debate.

Chapter 3 should clearly convey that this is not really the case. In this chapter, I explain that I am calling for the de-reification, not simply the de-quantification, of the equal/unequal dichotomy. Qualitative researchers tend to be more sensitive to their respondents' points of view, but even among ethnographers there is still a marked tendency to approach the issue of marital equality from a conventional, objectivist perspective. I borrow Gubrium and Holstein's (1997) distinction between *naturalist* and *constructionist* ethnography to highlight the distinctive assumptions, methods, and findings that the latter can bring to the study of equality and inequality in marriage.

Chapters 4 and 5 draw on my own research on equality in marriage. I use my interviews with a small but diverse sample of married individuals to demonstrate (not necessarily "prove") what might be missed if researchers stick with an objectivist approach. In chapter 4, I present the stories of respondents whose narratives resembled—*somewhat*—the themes that marital scholars have propounded. The details of my respondents' stories of (for example) "dividing housework" and "sharing power" do not necessarily mesh with the ways scholars have operationalized those issues. Then in chapter 5 I discuss respondents whose narratives differed more dramatically from mainstream definitions of marital equality. Some of these respondents told tales that relied on religious conceptions of equality or that highlighted other idiosyncratic issues that haven't been the subject of mainstream quantitative surveys or qualitative interviews on equality in marriage. But in both chapter 4 and 5 the point to keep in mind is that—regardless of whether my respondents' narratives sound "familiar" or "unfamiliar"—their stories are all *interpretive accomplishments* rather than reality reports.

In chapter 6, I return full circle to the broader theme of this study. Although they are couched within the subfield of marital equality, I believe that many of the ideas I discuss here are applicable to any area of social life in which equality is a concern. To demonstrate, in this concluding chapter I compare my own study with three recent articles on nonmarital inequalities. While I could have selected easier targets—such as quantitative research that disavowed any interest in subjects' viewpoints—I chose to focus on three programmatic articles that call for more qualitative, interactionist research on inequality. As I show, even in these papers the assumption is that inequality is an objective fact and that it is primarily the researcher's prerogative to define, locate, and explain it. Thus, I argue, studies similar to my book could and should be done on other substantive topics to challenge the conventional wisdom across the field of sociology and the other social sciences. Such work is necessary if researchers are to escape the confines of their own preconceptions. Conventional approaches to studying equality/inequality limit our understanding of the diversity of equality-meanings and the interpretive processes that create them.

Acknowledgments

Thanks go first to my respondents, who graciously shared their time with me. I also feel a sense of gratitude to many of my teachers, colleagues, friends, and family who either commented on my papers or simply gave me some encouragement: Mitch Berbrier, Anne Carle, Ken Collier, Dan Earles, Jim Fletter, Michael Flaherty, Jay Gubrium, Vik Gumbhir, Patricia Gwartney, Andy Harris, Bob Harris, Colleen Harris, Jenine Harris, Karen Harris, Jocelyn Hollander, Jim Holstein, Meg Wilkes Karraker, Russell Kelley, Lenore Langsdorf, Phil Lewin, Ken Liberman, Doni Loseke, Doug MacBeth, David Maines, Charles Marske, Nancy Newman, Peter Newman, Robert O'Brien, Joel Powell, Scott Pratt, Bob Prus, Pam Stirling, and Worth Summers. Obviously, people included in this list don't necessarily agree with everything I've written, and should not be blamed for any shortcomings that readers find in the book.

Over the past several years my research and writing were supported by a Charlotte W. Newcombe Dissertation Fellowship from the Woodrow Wilson National Fellowship Foundation, a Research Support Grant from the University of Oregon's Center for the Study of Women in Society, and a SLU2000 Research Leave from Saint Louis University.

Parts of this book are based on my earlier publications. I am grateful to the following publishers of my previous articles for their permission to reprint material in this book:

- "The Social Construction of Equality in Everyday Life." *Human Studies* 23:371–393. 2000. Reprinted with kind permission of Springer Science and Business Media.

- "Meanings and Measurements of Equality in Marriage: A Study of the Social Construction of Equality." Pp. 111–145 in *Perspectives on Social Problems*, vol. 12, edited by J. A. Holstein and G. Miller. 2000. Stamford, CT: JAI Press. Reprinted with permission from Elsevier.

- "What Can Interactionism Contribute to the Study of Inequality? The Case of Marriage and Beyond." *Symbolic Interaction* 24:455–480. 2001. Reprinted by permission of the University of California Press.

- "Studying Equality/Inequality: Naturalist and Constructionist Approaches to Equality in Marriage." *Journal of Contemporary Ethnography* 32:200–232. 2003. Reprinted by permission of Sage Publications, Inc.

- "Challenging the Conventional Wisdom: Recent Proposals for the Interpretive Study of Inequality." *Human Studies* 27:113–136. 2004. Reprinted with kind permission of Springer Science and Business Media.

1

Equality as a Social Construction

The goal of this book is to conceptualize a "radical" way of studying equality in social life: an interactionist, interpretive approach. The book is not "radical" in the sense of espousing an explicit political position, but because it attempts to go to the "root" of equality, to understand how and why equality and inequality are experienced features of the world.

My thesis is that equality is not an independent, objective, or self-evident characteristic but is a socially constructed phenomenon. By (1) synthesizing the theoretical perspectives of Herbert Blumer, Alfred Schutz, Harold Garfinkel, and John Dewey, (2) critically reviewing and analyzing a portion of the literature on equality, and (3) conducting a focused inquiry on the issue of equality, my book challenges conventional understandings of equality and attempts to demonstrate the utility of an interactionist approach to the subject.

TRADITIONAL AND INTERACTIONIST APPROACHES TO STUDYING EQUALITY

Generally, sociological treatment of the concept "equality" has taken four forms. First, sociologists have attempted to conceptualize and operationalize equality in a clear, logical, and rational manner. Such efforts are based on the reasonable belief that the quality of their work on equality depends upon whether the concept is carefully defined and measured. Second, sociologists have attempted to determine whether (or to what degree) equality exists in a situation, and to identify those factors that

1

promote or inhibit equality. The central goal here has been to discover what variables are requisite to equal or unequal states of affairs. Third, sociologists have tried to identify the beneficial and malignant effects that result from the presence of equality and inequality. Almost always, inequality is found to be associated with numerous negative consequences. Fourth and finally, sociologists have recommended various courses of social reform in order to ameliorate inequalities and their negative effects. This last approach to the topic of equality is reflected in the phrase "Inequality and Social Policy," the theme of the 1998 Annual Meetings of the American Sociological Association.

This brief typology of the sociological treatment of equality may not be an entirely exhaustive one; however, it accurately characterizes the vast majority of work on this subject. Indeed, considering the prominent role that equality plays in sociology, the typology may also reflect sociology as a whole. As Cancian (1995) has noted, much sociological work in recent decades has been devoted to the moral tasks of discovering and reducing inequality, wherever inequality may be found.

In pointing out the centrality of equality in the field of sociology, I want to show that there is still, remarkably, an immense and untapped line of inquiry that remains to be pursued. It is my contention that sociologists have not yet developed a symbolic interactionist (Blumer 1969), social constructionist (Berger and Luckmann 1966; Garfinkel 1967) approach to studying equality. In what follows, I hope to demonstrate that contention and illustrate the manner in which an interactionist or constructionist approach might proceed.

The Neglect of Interactionism

None of the traditional approaches to equality that I listed is distinctly interactionist. On each and every count, interactionism requires a different stance.

Symbolic interactionism contradicts the first form of analysis because it requires that sociologists give priority not to their own formal definitions and operationalizations of equality but to the meanings and measurements of equality that emerge and are actually used by people in the course of their everyday lives. If the goal of one's research is to understand and explain the behavior of human beings, then the first task should be to investigate the meaning things have *for them*, because it is on the basis of those meanings only that they will act (Blumer 1969, p.

2). Sociologists' definitions and measurements of equality may be completely foreign to the people they study, especially if no attempt is made to acquire an intimate familiarity with the lives of those people.

Interactionism contradicts the second and third forms of analysis because it eschews a deterministic approach to social life that would view equality as a definitive independent or dependent variable (Blumer 1969, ch. 7). The difference between traditional and interactionist approaches here is subtle yet vast. It is the difference between making notions of equality *the basis* of one's research and making such notions *the subject* of one's research (cf. Zimmerman and Pollner 1970). The former approach tends to take for granted what the latter investigates— the interpretive practices that bring equality into being.

Finally, while interactionism is certainly not against social reform, this perspective does imply that efforts to promote a just world must be accompanied by an awareness of how inequality is reflexively constituted by those who seek to "discover" and "reduce" it. This "de-reification" (cf. Berger and Luckmann 1966) of equality both clarifies and complicates the process of deliberate social change.

Neglect by Interactionists

Traditional sociologists are not alone in their neglect of interactionist principles when studying equality. Interactionists themselves have not systematically investigated this topic from their own point of view. Occasionally, interactionists do make passing references to "equality" as a subject amenable to their approach. However, they have not committed themselves to the kind of sustained, rigorous, and comparative inquiry that might lead, say, to a grounded theory (Glaser and Strauss 1967) of equality *as an interpretation*. In the 1960s, for example, Howard Becker (1973, p. 130) briefly described equality as a vague notion that is difficult to relate to concrete behavior. In the early 1980s, Berger and Kellner (1981, p. 170) called for studies of the "ever-changing meanings" of equality. More recently, well-known interactionists have argued that there are "a diversity of alignments to American values" like equality (Strauss 1995, p. 11), and that sociologists need to recognize that they do not possess "an authoritative definition of justice" (Best 2004, p. 158).

Bold claims like these are striking and provocative. However, they are also extremely underdeveloped. Despite the appeal of investigating the diverse meanings of such an interesting and ubiquitous concept as equality, interactionists have not followed up on the leads offered by these passing references. Those interactionists who do extended research and theorizing about equality tend to do so from "naturalist" or "conventional" perspectives (as I show in chapters 3 and 6). Given the important role that notions of equality play in social science research, political discourse, and everyday life, perhaps it is time to remedy that neglect. This book attempts to articulate a more comprehensive theoretical framework for future studies of "the social construction of equality," the interpretive practices by which people define situations as equal or unequal.

I believe the heading "the social construction of equality" could serve as a general rubric for bringing together a number of distinct approaches united by their focus on the interpretive aspects of equality in social life. Studies collected under this rubric need not limit their theoretical base solely to traditional interactionism and its pragmatic heritage of James, Dewey, and Mead. Complementary insights can and should be drawn from related constructionist traditions. Consequently, in the first three sections of this chapter, I will attempt to inform and inspire research on the socially constructed nature of equality by incorporating key ideas not only from (1) the symbolic interactionism of Herbert Blumer (1969), but also (2) the social phenomenology of Alfred Schutz (1964) and (3) the ethnomethodology of Harold Garfinkel (1967).

Although it may be possible to treat the social construction of equality as if it were a "purely" technical or theoretical interest, studies in this area can be shown to have serious implications for issues of social reform. Equality is, after all, an extremely popular moral ideal. In a fourth section of this chapter, then, I will draw upon John Dewey's (1989) ethical theory to show how interactionist research in this area might be used to assist efforts to promote a just society.

SYMBOLIC INTERACTIONISM AND EQUALITY

Herbert Blumer, it is well known, first coined the phrase "symbolic interaction" (Blumer 1937) and became the most influential advocate of the perspective. Over a period of six decades he clearly, consistently, and persuasively articulated an alternative to traditional deterministic sociologies. Following his teacher, G. H. Mead (1934), Blumer conceived of human beings as *minded* creatures who actively construct meaningful worlds of objects in the course of their interactions with each other. Blumer also went beyond Mead by articulating the methodological implications of a sociology that adopts this perspective. His writings still repay a close reading, at least as a very useful starting point.

Blumer's Basic Premises

My explication and application of Blumer will focus on his succinct formulation of interactionism's three fundamental premises (1969, p. 2). I will do so, however, through a slightly indirect route. I will begin by naming and numbering what I see as his most provocative assertion, but one that is not made explicit in his list. I would like to call it the zero premise (rather than the "fourth" premise), because it underlies each of the others. This premise simply says: *The meaning of things is not inherent.* This notion is central to Blumer's thinking, as references to it can be found throughout his book (e.g., 1969, pp. 3, 4, 11, 12, 68–69). However, the main reason I would like to accentuate it is because I believe it can provide the basis and impetus for studying the social construction of equality. There is good reason to think so. The zero premise has already borne fruit in hundreds of interactionist studies, especially in the fields of deviance and social problems. Clearly, these two traditions of constructionist research grew out of the insight that the meaning of things is not intrinsic to them (cf. Goode 1994, p. 100; Schneider 1985, p. 226). Becker's famous book on deviance, for example, begins with the oft-cited observation that no act is inherently deviant (1973, p. 9). Deviance is not inscribed in certain behaviors; it arises from the way groups create and apply rules to those behaviors. Similarly, constructionist work in the field of social problems is built on the assumption that no conditions are automatically problematic for a society (Blumer 1971; Spector and Kitsuse 1977). Instead, social problems are contingent on the process of collective definition that brings them into being.

　　The claim that the meaning of things is not inherent often seems shocking or silly to some. Common sense may suggest, in the manner of realism, that "of course" a chair is just a chair, or a cow a cow. Blumer, however, argues that the meaning of such things is not self-evident. Things do not speak for themselves. It is entirely possible for the "same" object to be interpreted very differently by different people: "To one with no experience with the use of chairs the object would appear with a different meaning, such as a strange weapon" (Blumer 1969, p. 69). Even where there is superficial agreement (e.g., that an animal is a "cow"), such agreement may belie vast divergences in perspective. A cow would likely mean very different things for a butcher, a vegetarian, a Hindu, and an executive at McDonald's. The zero premise can thus be justified quickly if one merely imagines the various purposes and perspectives that different groups might bring to a single object.

With this discussion in mind, I turn to Blumer's original three premises and their import for studying equality. Clearly, the notion that meaning is not inherent is reflected in each of them. It is reflected in Blumer's first premise by the words "for them": *Human beings act toward things on the basis of the meaning things have for them* (Blumer 1969, p. 2). If the first premise merely read, "Human beings act toward things on the basis of the meaning things have," it would be much more open to a realist rather than constructionist reading. The "for them" is more consistent with Blumer's view of meaning as perspectival and not inherent. Blumer's first premise also goes beyond (what I have called) the zero premise, however. It indicates the central place meaning holds in human behavior. That is, meaning is not a minor or irrelevant concern, but is at the very heart of what people do. A simple "stimulus"—noticing someone eating a hamburger, for example—may elicit a variety of reactions, depending on the meaning that event holds for its observer. It may be defined as an "unremarkable event," "a cruel and unnecessary act," "sacrilege," or "another satisfied customer." Meaning will be a crucial component of the observer's response to seeing someone eat a hamburger. The methodological implication is that "one has to get inside the defining process of the actor in order to understand his [or her] action" (Blumer 1969, p. 16).

Blumer's second premise is also concerned with meaning. It is, in fact, a direct response to what I have listed as the zero premise. Since meaning is not inherent, yet human beings live in worlds of meaningful objects, an obvious question arises: Where does meaning come from? Blumer argues in this premise that the source of meaning is human interaction: *The meaning of things is derived from, or arises out of, the social interaction that one has with one's fellows* (Blumer 1969, p. 2). Human beings learn from each other the significance of things. People learn, for example, that a chair is something to be sat in, or that a cow is a sacred animal, from the communities into which they are born. As Blumer puts it, "The meaning of a thing for a person grows out of the ways in which other persons act toward the person with regard to the thing" (Blumer 1969, p. 4). Such socialization is not merely a childhood process. Everyday interaction with significant others tends to confirm what people already know and helps them make sense of new, ambiguous situations. It is not unheard of, for example, for adults to decide to convert to vegetarianism and change their view of those who eat meat.

Thus, although we learn the meaning of things from others, those meanings are never fully or finally settled. This suggests another key idea of symbolic interactionism—the central role of self-interaction, or thought. To assume that the meaning of things is essentially automatic amounts to cultural determinism, an indirect way of making meaning inherent (Blumer 1969, p. 5). Blumer's third premise avoids this pitfall by emphasizing the importance of a reflective self: *These meanings are handled in, and modified through, an interpretive process used by the person in dealing with the things he [or she] encounters* (Blumer 1969, p. 2). This premise asserts that people are in fact *active*. They think. They point things out to themselves through self-interaction. They must do so because at any given moment there are millions of stimuli to which they might attend (James 1890, p. 402). People are selective with their attention because they couldn't possibly respond to their whole environment at once. To return to my earlier example, whether and how a chair is relevant is contingent on the ongoing behavior of the actor. In certain situations, a chair may be deliberately sat on. In others, it may be deemed a valuable commodity or source of firewood. In still others, it may be a barely noticed shape in the background. Human beings, one might say, fashion their own environments according to the various projects they pursue and perspectives they take (Mead 1934, pp. 278, 333).

To summarize, Blumer's three premises, including the "zero premise" implicit in them, portray human beings as living in worlds of meaningful objects that are always "under construction." His premises thus place human action and interpretation at the center of the sociological stage. The job for interactionists is to investigate the usefulness of these premises for understanding human behavior. I believe that the subject of equality is an important topic with which such studies can be conducted.

Interactionism on Equality

The four premises I have just discussed can be used to generate four parallel premises for studying the social construction of equality. In particular, the insight contained in the zero premise should provide a provocative starting point for the development of a distinctly interactionist approach to equality. The zero premise, when applied to the topic of equality, suggests that we entertain the "preposterous" notion that no situation—no trade, marriage, gender, economic system, race, species, and so on—is inherently equal or unequal. The quality of *equality* does not exist independently, absolutely, or objectively in any given state of affairs. The zero premise for studying the social construction of equality is simply this: *Nothing is inherently equal or unequal.*

To many, this will appear to be a shocking or ridiculous claim. It is in fact diametrically opposed to the stance that sociologists and the general public alike have traditionally taken toward this topic. Typically, people take the meaning and existence of equality for granted. Equality is "reified," or treated as residing in the "nature of things" (see Berger and Luckmann 1966, p. 89, on reification). By regarding equality as a preexistent fact rather than an interpretation, sociologists and the general public routinely ignore the contingent, definitional processes that bring it into being. Consequently, the concept of equality operates as an unquestioned resource in frequent discussions over such issues as the causes, effects, and extent of various social inequalities.

A symbolic interactionist approach, in contrast, would sidestep debates over, say, what factors inhibit an equal marriage or whether one "race" is somehow inferior to another. It would focus attention instead on the interpretive processes by which *any* situation comes to be labeled in those terms, for assertions of equality will always depend on the purposes and perspectives of the people who make them. Interactionism suggests that equality and inequality can be profitably understood as labels applied to situations rather than self-evident, universal characteristics inscribed in the nature of things.

If equality does not inhere in any given situation, then one cannot assume that all people "see" equality in the same way. Indeed, one cannot safely assume even that equality will arise as a relevant concern in any particular situation. This leads directly into my application of Blumer's first premise to the topic of equality. I believe the first premise for studying the social construction of equality should be the following: *People act on the basis of their perceptions of equality, if and when equality is a relevant concern for them.* Most human beings are probably not as concerned with equality as sociologists are, but when the issue does arise, interactionism predicts that people will act on the basis of their understanding of what equality means. People may of course act in a variety of ways—for example, they may express satisfaction with or approval of congenial inequalities (such as rewarding superior performance or "excellence") or they may express outrage and pursue remedies for problematic inequalities—but such expressions will occur with reference to the particular understandings of equality to which the actors themselves are oriented.

An interactionist approach to research on equality in social life would thus respect and study the various ways people interpret and act toward "equal" and "unequal" situations. This does not mean that "it is forbidden" for sociologists to construct their own "objective" definitions of equality—"objective," that is, from the perspective of a particular community of researchers. But researchers should take care not to ignore the actual lived experience of the people whose behavior they hope to understand. To that end, the *primary* concern of an interactionist approach to equality should be the meanings and measurements of equality around which members of society orient their actions.

So far I have only discussed *what* people know about equality. I have not mentioned *how* people know what they know. In other words, not only the substance but the source of "equality meanings" are amenable to interactionist analysis. Paralleling Blumer once again, the second premise of a constructionist approach to equality can be stated briefly: *Equal and unequal situations are defined as such in the course of interaction.* An interactionist approach thus directs our attention to what people's understandings of equality actually are as well as to how those understandings are formed. Regarding the latter, interactionism suggests that the things considered equal or unequal are defined as such by people as they relate to one another. People may learn as children, for example, that it is appropriate to kill and eat animals but not human beings. By watching what people do and listening to what they say, children are socialized to believe that animals are morally unequal to human beings. Much of this socialization is of course implicit. People's actions may intentionally or unintentionally "operate to define the thing for the person" (Blumer 1969, pp. 4–5). However, such socialization may also be explicit, as when a child is told in so many words that inferior human beings can be identified by the color of their skin.

As with Blumer's second premise of interactionism, my second premise should not imply that socialization is merely a childhood process that establishes the meaning of things once and for all. Perspectives on equality can shift and change drastically over the course of one's life, especially as one acquires new affiliations with new reference groups. Moral entrepreneurs (Becker 1973), in addition, can play an important role in "raising consciousness" about new or ignored equalities and inequalities. "Generational inequality" is one social problem that has recently been "discovered," amid concerns about the kind of environmental and fiscal difficulties that an older generation can bequeath to a younger one. Getting others to see an inequality like this one, and to see it as a social problem, involves a process of socialization.

Like Blumer's third premise, the final premise of the social construction of equality accentuates the fact that, although people may be "raised" to define certain things as equal or unequal, people are best conceived as *using* those perspectives rather than blindly following them. It reads: *The meaning of equality is modified by, or handled through, an active, interpretive process.* This last premise does not deny the usefulness of identifying general cultural and subcultural differences in perceptions of equality. However, it does encourage researchers to attend to "what is taken into account and assessed in the actual situations in which behavior is formed" (Blumer 1969, p. 89). Cultural rules about equality will always contain some ambiguity that must be "remedied" by people (cf. Dewey 1988, p. 74; Garfinkel 1967). Active, minded human beings must always decide just when and how beliefs about equality actually apply. Vague prescriptions like "friends should be treated as equals" must be related in a creative way to the intricate complexities of daily life (Harris 1997).

In short, my Blumerian principles for studying the social construction of equality suggest that sociologists treat equality as a trait ascribed to situations, as something people act toward based on the perspectives they develop and use in the course of their interactions with each other. These premises implore sociologists to respect and study the definitional processes by which people identify equal and unequal situations as such. Fortunately, interactionist research will not need to "start from scratch." Work by phenomenological and ethnomethodological sociologists can also provide insightful leads for inquiry, as I hope to show in the next two sections.

PHENOMENOLOGY AND EQUALITY

Probably the most important resource available for the development of an interactionist approach to equality is Alfred Schutz's (1964) paper "Equality and the Meaning Structure of the Social World," a rich analysis of the concept of equality as it operates in the commonsense thinking of social groups. As a phenomenologist, Schutz is acutely aware of the interpretive ambiguity that pervades social life. His writings in general are thus in many ways complementary to symbolic interactionism, as others have noted (e.g., Flaherty 1987, p. 154; Prus 1996, p. 87). During the many years since Schutz originally published his paper on equality (Schutz 1957), interactionists have neglected its valuable insights.[1] In what follows, I will extract what I believe are the most useful ideas that can be gained from reading Schutz's discussion of this topic. Because his analysis is built on his larger phenomenological approach, I must first review two of his more basic concepts.

Schutz on Typification and Relevance

According to Schutz (1973, pp. 7–10), a fundamental feature of all socialized human beings is that they experience everyday life in the mode of typicality. The various things people notice are not perceived as merely one new and unique phenomenon after another, but as *types*—as instances of "desks," "dogs," "teachers," "birthday parties," "having fun," and so on. Though each manifestation of an object or situation can be shown to have unique features, the validity of the labels people use is rarely questioned. Generally, it suffices to refer to something as, say, a "desk," even though each appearance of that object differs from other things called "desk" and from itself on other occasions. Unless motivated by a special reason, human beings tend to take for granted the adequacy of the meaning and applicability of the labels they give things.

An interesting aspect of the relationship between types and their referents is (what I call) its non-exclusivity. Any pairing of type-to-object can be adulterated, for at least two reasons. First, typological labels can be—indeed, are meant to be—applied to other manifestations of the "same" thing. To typify is, after all, to say "*this* is another instance of *that* phenomenon." Second, and more important, the "same" typified object can always be redescribed by subjecting it to further typification. Any strip of reality can be cast in numerous (potentially infinite) different lights. A married couple, for example, may characterize a pile of clothes simply as "the laundry." However, it is also possible that the couple will typify the clothes as "flammable," "made of cotton," "store bought," "factory made," "imported," "old," "cheap," "durable," "work clothes," "dyed," "embarrassing," "a big job," "physical objects," "atoms and molecules," and so on.

How is it that the same thing ("a pile of clothes") can be typified in so many different ways? Schutz says that the manner in which typification occurs depends on our interests, on what is deemed *relevant* to our ongoing at action. In his words,

> All types are relational terms carrying, to borrow from mathematics, a subscript referring to the purpose for the sake of which the type has been formed. And this purpose is nothing but the theoretical or practical problem which, as a consequence of our situationally determined interest, has emerged as questionable from the unquestioned background of the world just taken for granted. (1964, p. 234)

Thus, during a discussion of household chores, a pile of clothes may in fact be labeled "dirty laundry." Alternatively, if the discussion were about leaving flammable things near the fireplace, the clothes might be characterized as "a fire hazard." The pile of clothes—if noticed at all—may be typified in a multitude of ways depending on the problem at hand.

Schutz makes it clear that types tend not to be employed in an isolated manner but in conjunction with other related types and subtypes. For instance (to push my banal example even further), consider the practice of distinguishing "white" clothes from "dark" ones or perhaps "delicates" from "durables" when washing the dirty laundry. A series of types thus frequently converges around a common ("well-circumscribed") problem, constituting what Schutz calls a "domain of relevance."

> The well circumscribed problem can be said to be the locus of all possible types that can be formed for the sake of its solution, that is, of all problem-relevant types. We may also say that all of these types pertain, by the very fact of their reference to the same problem, to the same *domain* of *relevance*. (1964, p. 235; emphasis in original)

Of course, as Schutz notes, how "well circumscribed" a problem may be is always an open question. Every problem has potentially infinite inner and outer horizons of unexplored meanings and implications. Inwardly, one might further refine the problem of "doing the laundry" by distinguishing between things that are worn (e.g., clothes) from things that are not worn (e.g., towels and rags). Outwardly, one might frame "doing the laundry" as merely one part of a larger set of concerns, such as "practicing good hygiene" or "doing housework."

In sum, Schutz shows how the world people take for granted is given intelligible shape by the sets of typifications they use to accomplish their practical activities. The world does not by itself determine which of its "aspects" will be relevant, and just how. Clearly, typification and domains of relevance are such fundamental aspects of social life that Schutz's understanding of them has implications for all areas of sociological inquiry. These two concepts, however, are especially applicable to the subject of equality, as I illustrate next.

Schutz on Equality

The utility of Schutz's treatment of typification and domains of relevance begins to become evident when one considers the way people refer to various kinds of equality and inequality, such as marital, economic, and legal. The terms equality and inequality always seem to be accompanied—explicitly or implicitly—by a qualifier of some kind. To be meaningful, it appears, equality must be related to *some particular area of interest*. Moreover, these domains of relevance will tend to contain a series of types that are thought to constitute equality. For example, if the problem at hand is to compare the wealth of two people, one might do so by examining their "income," "investments," and "possessions."

Using the concepts of typification and domains of relevance in this manner, Schutz makes a number of significant claims. For the sake of clarity, I would like to list and examine these as four succinct propositions. The first proposition I can extract from Schutz is: *All typification involves equalization (but not equality)*. As I noted earlier, Schutz argues that to typify is to say "Here is another instance of [X]." Typification involves singling out an object of attention and declaring it "the same" as certain other things. To call an animal a "dog," Schutz explains, is thus in some sense to declare it equivalent or "equal" to other phenomena belonging to that category.

> By recognizing Rover as a dog and calling him so, I have disregarded what makes Rover the unique and individual dog he means to me. ...In so far as Rover is just a dog, he is deemed to be equal to all other dogs.... [Therefore,] all typification consists in the equalization of traits relevant to the particular purpose at hand. (Schutz 1964, p. 234)

In this limited sense, all typification can be described as a process of "equalization," the positing of a certain "sameness." But Schutz also believes that equalization by typification is separable from occasions when people determine equality by comparing various factors, such as IQ or grade point average. The terms equality and inequality are not used to merely to posit sameness and difference, but to compare a finite number of "goods" and "bads"—positive and negative aspects of people, relationships, or situations (see chapter 2). Two "pinch hitters" are made "the same" by typifying them as such; their respective batting averages, however, may be equal or unequal, depending on their respective records (e.g., hits, strikeouts, walks, etc.).

Schutz proposes to focus on instances where equality or inequality is posited based on the comparison of such elements:

> In order to avoid semantic confusion it might be better to call all objects, facts, events, persons, [and] traits, falling in the same type and so pertaining to the same domain of relevance, *homogeneous*....We propose to reserve the terms equality and inequality for the relationship of elements pertaining to the same domain of relevance. (1964, p. 239)

Thus, in Schutz's terminology, two undergraduates are made homogeneous when typified as "freshmen." They become equal or unequal if someone evaluates them on the basis of their grade point averages or their scores on the Scholastic Aptitude Test.

The example of comparing undergraduates is also helpful for understanding Schutz's second proposition: *Equality is determined by criteria that are specific to a particular domain of relevance.* Or, in his words,

> Height cannot be measured against wealth, nor can both be measured against freedom. Only within ... domains of relevances can degrees of merit and excellence be distinguished. Moreover, that which is comparable in terms of the system of one domain is not comparable in terms of other systems, and for this reason the application of yardsticks not pertaining to the same domain of relevances leads to logical or axiological (moral) inconsistencies. (Schutz 1964, p. 240)

For Schutz, then, GPA and SAT scores constitute separate domains of relevance for comparing students because different measurement procedures are used to stratify students. While GPA is determined by compiling one set of typified components (i.e., the letter grades of "A," "B," "C," "D," and "F"), SAT scores are measured by another (i.e., "right" and "wrong" answers to a list of questions).

Schutz's second proposition does not deny that people can and *do* make comparisons that take into account different domains of relevance. College administrators, for example, use GPA and SAT scores *together* when deciding which applicants are "the most promising students." Additionally, it is very likely that administrators will not only take both

GPA and SAT scores into account, but will consider one score to be more important than the other. Thus, not only are the elements within domains comparable, but the different domains themselves can be weighed one against the other. Schutz notes this in (what I will call) his third proposition: *Domains of relevance are ranked hierarchically* (Schutz 1964, p. 241). The fourth proposition I can extract from Schutz is directly related to the third. Since domains of relevance are cultural products, Schutz simultaneously suggests the following: *Domains of relevance are ranked differently by different groups* (Schutz 1964, p. 241). We might expect to find, for example, that administrators favor the SAT over GPA when determining scholarly potential, because it is "a standardized measure." Students, on the other hand, might view GPA as the more important indicator of their abilities, since the SAT is only a three-hour test, while grades "represent years of hard work." Each group might choose to weigh the two domains differently if they both had a vote in the admissions process.

Implications of Schutz

At first glance, Schutz's propositions each contain a high degree of plausibility. Each deserves careful examination and critique. Given the near complete neglect of Schutz's paper on equality, all of his intriguing ideas on the subject remain an untapped source of interactionist research questions. Perhaps the most striking implications I can derive from Schutz's work are methodological: If sociologists want to understand the role "equality" actually plays in people's lives, they must respect and study

- The various domains of relevance with which people may be concerned.
- The various ways that different people may rank those domains of relevance.
- The various kinds of typifications that people may use within diverse domains of relevance.

Conventional sociological approaches to studying equality have not been attentive to the implications I have drawn from Schutz's paper. Nor are traditional approaches especially compatible with Schutz's perspective. An interactionist approach, however, could incorporate and develop many of Schutz's ideas into a striking new research program.

ETHNOMETHODOLOGY AND EQUALITY

Originating with the work of Harold Garfinkel (1967), ethnomethodology is a third sociological tradition that can provide a wealth of insights and inspiration for future constructionist research on the subject of equality. Garfinkel drew heavily on the phenomenology of Husserl and Schutz, but he went much further by demonstrating and advocating a detailed, empirical study of people's everyday reality-making practices. In particular, *ethno-methodology* focuses on *people's-methods* for sustaining and enacting a sense of social order, wherever that order may be found. Garfinkel recommends that we investigate *all* "social facts" as the ongoing situated accomplishments of people. Ethnomethodology's relentless attention to the local, ad hoc, definitional efforts of people thus makes it a valuable resource (or strategy) for studying the social construction of equality. In what follows, I will attempt to illustrate how an ethnomethodological understanding of language use can help us to gain access to how people "see" or experience equality in everyday life.

The Reflexive and Indexical Properties of Language Use

If, following Schutz, all "things" can be typified in potentially limitless ways, then it becomes apparent that our use of language has a "reflexive" character. We do not passively "report" about a self-subsistent reality. Whenever we discuss and describe things, we are reflexively creating the matter that we are talking about. To return to my earlier example, how we characterize a pile of clothes is not a process of observing an obvious, self-evident trait. Observation is not automatic. It is a creative act in which we construct an intelligible sense of reality out of a multitude of possible senses. The nature of any situation we inhabit thus depends reflexively on our very own procedures for understanding it. Simply put, reflexivity means "To describe a situation is to constitute it" (Coulon 1995, p. 23).

    The reflexivity of language use is, however, only one-half of the dialectical relationship between our words and the contexts in which they are embedded. The other half is indexicality. Descriptions are not only reflexive in that they are context-shaping, they are indexical in that their meaning is context-dependent (Heritage 1984, pp. 140, 242). Indexicality refers to the fact that "the understandability of any utterance, rather than being fixed by some abstract definition, depends upon the circumstances in which it appears" (Maynard and Clayman 1991, p. 397).

A simple way to begin to illustrate the pervasive role that indexicality plays in social life is to consider the variety of meanings that can pertain to a simple word like "ball." In its singular or plural form, the word "ball" can mean (among other things)

> a formal dance
> a good time
> a part of one's foot
> a collection of string
> to form or gather up into a spherical shape
> a football
> a baseball
> a baseball that is pitched outside the strike zone
> to be intelligent, aware, or competent
> testicles
> to have sex
> to be bold or "macho"

Despite the variety of meanings this word can have, somehow we comprehend sentences like "She's a great worker, she's really on the ball" and "Pass me the ball!" Amid the flow of the spoken or written discourse, people somehow discover what sense of "ball" is being invoked at the time.[2] Communication thus involves much more than the exchange of self-subsistent linguistic signs, when individuals are required only to mentally access the precise, complete definitions of the words that they speak, read, or hear. Even in the dictionary, words can have many possible definitions. Rather, the recognizable sense of our concepts depends on "the socially organized occasions of their use" (Garfinkel 1967, pp. 3–4). Their meanings consist of what individuals do with or make of them. (A sarcastic tone, for example, can actually reverse the usual meaning of a term.)

How is it possible that the statement "I'm having a ball!" can be considered an intelligible thing to say? To consider the procedures by which people make passable sense of such a sentence is to encounter the kind of phenomena in which ethnomethodologists are interested. Garfinkel in fact refers to ethnomethodology as "the investigation of the rational properties of indexical expressions and other practical actions *as contingent ongoing accomplishments of organized artful practices of everyday life*" (Garfinkel 1967, p. 11; emphasis added).

Ethnomethodology on Equality

How does the reflexivity and indexicality of language use relate to the study of equality? It should be clear. The concept of reflexivity indicates that equality does not "speak for itself." It does not demand people's attention on its own. Assertions of equality invoke that quality as an important concern, rather than an as-yet-to-be-explored topic. Equality is *made* a salient feature of settings by the actions of people. Reflexivity indicates that when states of affairs are recognized as equal or unequal, that recognition is an *accomplishment*. Ethnomethodology directs us to recognize and investigate the various ways that accomplishment takes place (Garfinkel 1967, pp. 9–10).

The concept of indexicality, in turn, indicates that we should recognize and investigate the local, contextual meanings that are achieved through people's creative application of the term "equality." The definition of equality is not determined by what the dictionary says about it. From an ethnomethodological perspective, even the most rigorous, formal definitions of equality will *always* possess ambiguity and incompleteness (Garfinkel and Sacks 1970). There is thus no single "equality," but "equality-in-this-context" and "equality-in-that-context." The concept of "marital equality," for example, will probably mean very different things when it is used in a sociology course, a church sermon, and a divorce trial. The academic, religious, and legal settings may provide completely different issues and resources through which the notion of marital equality can be construed.

Consider, in the interests of clarity, a hypothetical example. Imagine you (the reader) and I are casually eating lunch in a restaurant. Next, suppose I notice a married couple sitting at a table, and say, "Now that seems like a relationship based on equality." In this instance, my utterance and the context it describes become co-constitutive. My words give some sense to the scene around us, while you search that scene for evidence of the meaning of my words. (Did the husband refrain from presumptuously ordering for his wife? Or do the spouses possess the same level of attractiveness, personality, and intelligence? Are they both listening attentively to each other without offering heavy-handed advice? What is meant by my utterance?) My description and the scene it describes are each meaningless without the other; moreover, their connection is not automatic or self-evident. It takes work on our part to bring the account and the scene into meaningful relation, to breathe intelligibility into each of them. Of course, it is also possible that in the context of a casual lunch the "real" meaning of my statement may make no difference to you, leaving you content to "gratuitously concur" (Liberman 1980) or to "let it pass" (Garfinkel in Heritage [1984], p. 124).

Future ethnomethodological research could examine the reflexive and indexical nature of the social construction of equality as it takes place in social situations. Such studies would be attentive to people's experienced sense of equality, rather than presuming a stable or idealized meaning for that term. To do an ethnomethodology of equality is to study equality *in use*. The challenge is to find contexts in which people regularly employ the concept "equality" as a part of their everyday routines (or else one could encourage them to do so in the context of a research interview).

DEWEY ON MORALITY, EQUALITY, AND SOCIAL REFORM

A typical interactionist review would probably end at this point. I have already brought three constructionist traditions to bear on my topic, laying (I hope) the theoretical groundwork for researching equality in a new and innovative way. My discussion thus far has been primarily intellectual—an exercise in constructionist sociology with the goal of improving my field's "understanding" of social life. There are, however, some obvious and important questions one could ask about my project: Why do it? What good could come of it? What benefit or harm may result if other sociologists join me in studying the social construction of equality? All these questions urge me to address the moral—rather than merely intellectual—implications of my argument.

Perhaps the best way to approach the "ethics" of studying the social construction of equality is through the work of John Dewey. Dewey is a forerunner of symbolic interactionism, but his writings on moral theory have been neglected by interactionists in favor of his "purely" social-scientific ideas. This neglect is strange, given that Dewey was profoundly concerned with morality, even in works ostensibly on social psychology (e.g., Dewey 1983). In this fourth section, I will attempt to draw on Dewey to explain the positive role that studies of the social construction of equality could play in the pursuit of a just society.

Dewey on Moral Theory

Dewey's conception of morality hinges on a distinction between two types of moral conduct: customary and reflective. Customary morality, he says, "places the standard and rules of conduct in ancestral habit" while reflective morality "appeals to conscience, reason, or to some principle which includes thought" (Dewey 1989, p. 162). Individuals abide by customary morality when they unquestioningly conform to the traditions and values of their social group. Right and wrong conduct are taken-for-granted aspects of social life, as people merely apply the received wisdom of their culture. Reflective morality, on the other hand, occurs when one is perplexed ("*What is the correct thing to do?*") and must take an active role in deciding on a solution. Reflection is likely to arise when one has reason to doubt the legitimacy or applicability of one's inherited traditions (e.g., in novel situations, in cases involving contradictory customary precepts, or when diverse cultures meet).

It is important to note that for Dewey the distinction between customary and reflective morality is not a sharp one. Instead, he says the difference between the two forms of moral judgment is "relative," not "absolute" (Dewey 1989, p. 162). Blind conformity to customary dictates is impossible because it takes at least *some* thought to select and apply the appropriate traditional standards. Similarly, any notion of "pure reflection" is also problematic. It is not Descartes's isolated ego but the community that supplies perspectives through which people are able to define reality (Dewey 1929, ch. 5; Mead 1934). Individuals *can* think creatively and critically, but only by using the tools (language, values, etc.) they have inherited from custom.

Still, even though the difference between customary and reflective morality is not "hard and fast," the distinction is a useful one for Dewey. He definitely favors the reflective side of the customary reflective spectrum. Strict adherence to customary codes represents stagnation to Dewey. Instead, his vision for humanity is of ceaseless progressive activity, the remaking of society in an increasingly democratic and purposeful manner. He advocates experimentalism, rather than dogmatism, for science *and* for morality (Dewey 1929, pp. 353–54). From Dewey's perspective, attempts to establish absolute moral doctrines would be like constructing scientific theories that could never be tested or criticized. Moral prescriptions should be open to examination and revision, just as scientific theories are. Dewey's vision thus requires that the reliance on fixed beliefs give way to *tolerance*, the "positive willingness to permit reflection and inquiry to go on in the faith that the truly right will be rendered more secure through questioning and discussion, while things which have endured merely from custom will be amended or done away with" (Dewey 1989, p. 231).

Dewey does not claim that the process of collaboratively reflecting on, discussing, and testing out moral beliefs will eventually yield flawless solutions to moral problems. In fact, he suggests we give up the quest for absolute certainty (Dewey 1988). There is no independent, rock solid foundation on which we can "finally" build a perfect code of conduct, one forever beyond criticism. But human beings *can* attempt to intelligently and collaboratively construct workable solutions to felt social problems. In the face of material and cultural conflicts, people can choose to attempt to "harmonize" as many competing interests and values as possible. Intelligent reconstruction seems at least as viable as other methods of moral problem solving, such as relying on established doctrines, on authority, or on whim (Dewey 1929, pp. 353–54).

Dewey on Equality

Dewey is well aware that moral concepts like equality are vague and multivocal. Everybody may agree that "people should be treated justly," he notes, but disagree over which situations are actually "just" (Dewey 1989, pp. 177–78). He decries the common tendency to treat conceptual distinctions, such as equal/unequal, as if they were inherent in things. Our "clefts and bunches" should not be assumed to "represent fixed separations and collections *in rerum natura*," he says; they do not mark "things in themselves" (Dewey 1983, p. 92). Instead, Dewey argues, scientific and moral concepts are more properly understood as instruments for negotiating reality rather than as mirrors of reality. Words are tools, and they should be treated as such. That entails removing them from their pedestals and submitting them to inspection; it does not mean banishing them as failures if they provide something less than absolute certainty (Dewey 1983, p. 168).

Dewey's view of concepts as tools brings me to the role that studies of the social construction of equality can play in people's efforts to bring about a "just" or "good" social order. The main function such studies can perform is to clarify the kinds of interpretive variability and ambiguity that are likely to arise any time a problematic situation is framed around the notion of equality. Studies in the social construction of equality can make people aware of a wide range of considerations that are likely to be relevant any time that equality is employed as a scientific concept or moral ideal. Sociologists can identify and describe differences in perspectives on equality and recommend that such differences be taken into account as a significant factor in the cooperative resolution of moral problems.[3]

The anger people experience when faced with an apparent inequality is a strong motivation for social action. Adopting Dewey's perspective, however, requires that such emotions should also inspire an examination of the (often implicit) criteria that give rise to them.[4] On what basis is one outraged? What underlying assumptions make it feasible to characterize the situation as one of inequality? Do others involved in the situation perceive it differently? What other moral principles, besides equality, might also apply? How do these alternative principles and perspectives coincide or conflict with one's initial response?

For Dewey, moral judgment is less arbitrary and more intelligent—in short, "better"—to the degree to which such matters are considered:

> To give way without thought to a kindly feeling is easy; to suppress it is easy for many persons; the difficult but needed thing to do is to retain it in all its pristine intensity while directing it, as a precondition of action, into channels of thought. A union of benevolent impulse and intelligent reflection is the interest most likely to result in conduct that is good. (Dewey 1989, p. 298)

Studies in the social construction of equality may present us with a similar "difficult but needed" challenge: to take seriously the interpretive aspects of equality as we try to co-construct a just social world.

CONCLUSION

In this chapter I have attempted to outline the theoretical assumptions of a radical approach to studying equality: a social constructionist perspective with strong ties to the sociological and philosophical traditions of symbolic interactionism, phenomenology, ethnomethodology, and pragmatism. The goal of this approach is *not* to think up new and improved definitions of equality, to treat equality as yet another causal variable, or to advocate a preconceived policy for achieving equality. Instead, the central preoccupation is to discover how *people* define states of affairs as equal or unequal, and to study the role those definitions play in ongoing interaction. The findings of such research should not only prove interesting and enlightening, but could potentially aid the reflective resolution of problematic inequalities.

I have used the phrase "the social construction of equality" as a way to integrate the perspectives of Blumer, Schutz, Garfinkel, and Dewey and apply them to the topic of equality in everyday life. In doing so, I have highlighted the complementarity of these scholars' work. By neglecting discrepancies, I do not mean to imply that no differences can be found in the thought of these figures (e.g., see Psathas 1980). However, I believe that at a fundamental level Blumer, Schutz, Garfinkel, and Dewey all share a deeply held commitment: to respect and understand the experiences and viewpoints of "others." That common commitment makes it possible to draw eclectically from each scholar to develop what could be an intriguing and useful program of research—as I hope to illustrate over the course of this book.

2

Quantitative Research on Marital Equality
Inter-Researcher Discontinuity and Researcher-Subject Divergence

One sociological subfield in which the issue of equality plays a central role is the area of marriage and the family. For several decades, family scholars have been concerned with the possible existence, causes, and consequences of equality in marriage. Pronouncements of the birth and rise of the egalitarian marriage, as well as claims to the contrary, are quite profuse. Equality is a popular variable in studies on a plethora of topics, such as marital satisfaction, extramarital affairs, dual employment, and mental health.[1] Yet nowhere in this literature does one find a rigorous, critical, and *constructionist* analysis of how the term is defined and used. This chapter and the next represent my attempt to conduct that missing analysis.

Unfortunately, the literature on equality in marriage is so vast that some limits must be set on my review. A comprehensive summary and critique of *all* the existing materials that address the topic of equality in marriage would probably be impossible. Scholars from a wide range of disciplines have studied the subject through a variety of theoretical and methodological approaches. Moreover, in many books and articles, marital equality is discussed in a vague or tangential manner. Consequently, rather than attempt to locate every offhand usage of the concept "marital equality," in this chapter I will focus on mainstream quantitative research that employs explicit methodological procedures to systematically identify equal and unequal marriages. This research frequently appears in top journals and is often cited in textbooks, handbooks, and encyclopedias on the family. Next, in chapter

3, I will summarize and critique the literature that takes a more qualitative approach.

The body of this chapter consists of two main parts. In the first section, I identify and summarize four major traditions of quantitative research on equality in marriage. In each case, I briefly describe the various meanings ascribed to marital equality as well as the wide array of methodological procedures developed to measure it. In the second section, I critique the approaches taken thus far. Here my argument is twofold: I suggest that there is not only a large degree of discontinuity between researchers' idiosyncratic studies but that, in all likelihood, there is also a vast divergence between researchers' meanings (and measurements) and subjects' meanings of equality. I believe that my review and critique of this literature justifies a turn away from preconceived, scholarly approaches to marital equality and toward the equality-concerns of married people themselves.

FOUR TRADITIONS OF QUANTITATIVE RESEARCH

Equality as a Fair Exchange

The first approach to the study of equality in marriage stems from exchange theory, which was developed by George Homans, among others (e.g., Blau 1964; Homans 1958, 1974; Thibaut and Kelley 1959). In this tradition, human interaction is seen as an exchange of goods between individuals who, as rational hedonists, attempt to reap benefits and avoid costs (Homans 1958, p. 606). Even close relationships, such as those among dating and married couples, are portrayed as individuals coming together to trade behaviors and resources. These exchanges are not limited to more tangible items such as money, car repairs, sexual relations, and housework, but include less palpable considerations such as displaying deference and affection or possessing a keen intellect and jovial sense of humor.

Scholars who take this particular view of social life tend to conceptualize equality in terms of how fair a marriage is to each spouse. If one were to try to identify a single question underlying this work, it would be *"Who gets what?"* The emphasis in the exchange tradition is on counting up the costs and benefits that a couple acquires by their association and determining if one comes out "ahead" or if both are getting their due.

The most prominent manifestation of this approach is the strand of research that has been conducted under the rubric of "equity theory" (Walster, Walster, and Berscheid 1978; Hatfield et al. 1985; Sprecher 1995). For these researchers, an equitable relationship exists only when "both participants' relative gains are equal" (Hatfield et al. 1985, p. 92). This means that, after considering everything that is exchanged in the marital relationship, the ratio of costs/benefits must be the same for each spouse.

Moving from theory to research presents something of a problem for scholars who define all interaction in terms of exchange. If this is the case, then there are potentially innumerable costs and benefits that need to be taken into account before equity can be determined (Walster, Walster, and Berscheid 1978, p. 233). Equity scholars developed two methodological strategies in light of this concern. One asks subjects to make a single, overall evaluation of their relationships. Perhaps the most frequently used equity scale (Sprecher 1995, p. 223), the Hatfield Global Measure, uses this technique. The scale is brief enough to quote in full (Hatfield, Utne, and Traupmann 1979, p. 112; see also Walster, Walster, and Berscheid 1978):

> Considering what you put into your relationship, compared to what you get out of it...and what your partner puts in, compared to what s(he) gets out of it, how would you say your relationship stacks up?
> +3 I am getting a much better deal than my partner.
> +2 I am getting a somewhat better deal.
> +1 I am getting a slightly better deal.
> 0 We are both getting an equally good...or bad...deal.
> −1 My partner is getting a slightly better deal.
> −2 My partner is getting a somewhat better deal.
> −3 My partner is getting a much better deal than I.

The second methodological strategy for measuring equity is to collect data on a short list of costs and benefits believed to be important in all dating and marital relationships. In the Traupmann-Utne-Walster scale (Walster, Walster, and Berscheid 1978; Traupmann et al. 1981), subjects describe their own and their partners' level of inputs and outputs in four general areas of the relationship. Twenty-four items are organized under the headings "personal concerns," "emotional concerns," "day-to-day concerns," and "opportunities gained or lost." For example, one "personal concern" item reads: "Intelligent Partner: Having a partner who is intelligent and informed" (Walster, Walster, and Berscheid 1978, p. 239). In response to these prompts, subjects indicate how highly rewarded they and their partners are. The existence or absence of equity is then determined by adding up the numerical values that researchers have assigned to these responses.

There is, within the general exchange framework, a second strand of literature on dating and marital relationships. These scholars have focused on other exchange factors in close relationships besides equity. For example, some theorize that an equality of outcome, where individuals receive the same amount of rewards regardless of their contributions, may be more important to close relationships. Another view is that individuals who feel highly rewarded in their relationships will be very satisfied and will not be affected by the existence or absence of either equity or equality of outcome (Cate et al. 1982).

A number of studies thus examine the relative impact of three variables—"equity," "equality," and "rewards"—on close relationships (Cate, Lloyd, and Henton 1985; Martin 1985; Michaels, Edwards, and Acock 1984; Reynolds, Remer, and Johnson 1995). These three constructs typically are based on original scales, as well as scales borrowed from equity researchers. The most popular "rewards" scale is derived from Foa and Foa's (1974) list of resources all human beings are thought to exchange. In seven questions, subjects are asked to report how highly rewarded they feel in the areas of love, status, services, goods, money, information, and sex.

Power Equality

A second, and extremely prolific, approach to the study of equality in marriage focuses on the "family power structure." Although some studies in this area examine children's power along with their parents, the bulk of the literature compares the relative power of husbands and wives (Kranichfeld 1987, p. 43; McDonald 1980, p. 841).

In this research tradition, power is frequently (but not unanimously) defined as the ability to influence another person's behavior (Blood and Wolfe 1960, p. 11; Straus and Yodanis 1995, p. 437). Such a definition could feasibly include quite a large array of behavior. In practice, though, the principal focus for the majority of research on this topic has been limited to *"Who decides what?"* By far, the predominant method of measuring power egalitarianism in marriage has been to collect survey data on marital decision-making patterns (McDonald 1980, p. 848; Mizan 1994, p. 85; Safilios-Rothschild 1970, p. 547). Consequently, when researchers speak of "egalitarian" marriages in this literature, they usually mean relationships in which each spouse has the same amount of "say" regarding what goes on in their family.

The earliest inspiration and most prominent exemplar for family power research was the study conducted by Blood and Wolfe (1960). With data collected from a large sample of urban and rural Michigan wives, Blood and Wolfe's survey raised several interesting questions that captured the attention of family scholars for decades (McDonald 1980; Safilios-Rothschild 1970). First, Blood and Wolfe suggested that the American family was changing from a situation of patriarchy to one of power-egalitarianism. Others strongly disagreed with this claim (e.g., Gillespie 1971). Second, a provocative explanation for the egalitarian thesis could be garnered from Blood and Wolfe's exposition. This was the supposition that the transition to egalitarianism was due not so much to evolving norms but to women's recent economic and educational gains. The skills and resources wives were beginning to bring to their marriages, especially through work, were perhaps giving them more power in those relationships. Scholars would later elaborate this argument and, based on cross-cultural research, posit an "interaction" between normative and resource bases of spousal decision-making power (Cooney et al. 1982; Rodman 1967, 1972).

Blood and Wolfe's method for measuring spouses' relative power was brief and easy to administer. It consisted of an eight-item scale designed to cover important issues that ranged from "typically masculine" to "typically feminine" concerns (1960, p. 20). In an interview format, the subjects were asked, "Who usually makes the final decision about":

1. What job the husband should take
2. What car to get
3. Whether to buy life insurance
4. Where to go on vacation
5. What house or apartment to take
6. Whether or not the wife should go to work or quit work
7. What doctor to have when someone is sick
8. How much money the family can afford to spend per week on food. (1960, p. 19)

In response to each item, subjects could choose between "husband always," "husband more than wife," "husband and wife exactly the same," "wife more than husband," and "wife always." By assigning numerical values to these responses and tabulating the results, Blood and Wolfe were able to discern three groups of marriages: husband-dominant, wife-dominant, and egalitarian.

Blood and Wolfe's methodology came to be known as the "final say" approach to measuring marital power. The technique is an appealing one, and has been adopted by numerous scholars. The exact questions vary, but Blood and Wolfe's basic format is for the most part retained (e.g., Blumstein and Schwartz 1983; Centers and Raven 1971; Safilios-Rothschild 1967; Shukla 1987).

A smaller group of studies eschews the survey approach and uses intricate observational methods to assess the "power structure" or "leadership structure" in families. Noting that husbands' and wives' self-reports on decision making tend to disagree, and that subjects may select traditional or egalitarian responses due to normative expectations, observational researchers aspire to provide a more "objective" view of familial power distribution, untainted by spouses' perceptual biases (Gray-Little and Burks 1983, p. 526; Olson and Cromwell 1975, pp. 143–44). In this research, data collection usually takes place in laboratory settings, where spouses—often with one or more children present—complete some sort of game or task. In one such game, when subjects roll balls toward wooden targets, family members must try to figure out the rules as they play (Straus and Tallman 1971). When one family member makes a suggestion ("*Try this!*") and another complies, researchers record the event as an indication of power. Two other observational measurements of power include counting interruptions and noting who spends more time speaking, where "more interrupting" and "more speaking" are coded by researchers as indicating "more power" (Gray-Little 1982, p. 636). The degree to which power is equally distributed is determined by adding up the numerical values assigned to its putative behavioral manifestations.

Equality as Sharing the Labor

The third approach to marital equality focuses on the amount of work spouses perform during their everyday lives. The increase in wives' paid employment outside the home has fueled much of the research in this area. There is widespread concern that, though wives are increasingly sharing the traditionally male role of breadwinner, husbands have not responded by sharing more household tasks at home. Thus, many wives are faced with a "second shift" (Hochschild 1989) or may experience "role overload" (Pleck 1985).

The principal focus for this tradition can be described as *"Who does what."* Equal marriages, accordingly, are considered to be those in which each spouse regularly performs the same amount of work as the other. Distinctions are usually made between three types of spousal labor: paid labor, housework, and child care (Pleck 1985, p. 15). The emphasis in this research is on the latter two categories of household labor, where husbands have consistently been found to do less work than their wives (Shelton and John 1996).

The technique most frequently used to measure the degree to which the household labor is shared is the "relative distribution method" (Warner 1986, p. 180). This is the strategy employed by Blood and Wolfe (1960), who (as with marital power studies) have had a significant influence on this area of inquiry as well (Pleck 1985, p. 28). Like power, Blood and Wolfe measured the division of household labor via a brief scale that taps a sample of traditionally masculine and feminine tasks. Here again, subjects are required to answer eight questions by choosing between the fixed responses of "husband always," "husband more than wife," "husband and wife exactly the same," "wife more than husband," and "wife always":

1. Who repairs things around the house?
2. Who mows the lawn?
3. Who shovels the sidewalk?
4. Who keeps track of the money and the bills?
5. Who does the grocery shopping?
6. Who gets the husband's breakfast on work days?
7. Who straightens up the living room when company is coming?
8. Who does the evening dishes? (1960, p. 49)

Researchers have varied the specificity, type, and number of tasks, but the general format has been replicated many times (e.g., Bird, Bird, and Scruggs 1984; Ross, Mirowsky, and Huber 1983; Smith and Reid 1986; Twiggs, McQuillan, and Ferree 1998).

The approach fostered by Blood and Wolfe has been criticized for giving equal weight to tasks that take different amounts of time to complete. For example, paying the bills may take less than one hour per week while doing the dishes every day may require a total of four hours of weekly labor. Warner (1986) has identified four strategies used by researchers to overcome this weakness. The first technique requires researchers to assign weights to various tasks, based on the expected frequency and duration of the tasks (e.g., Kamo 1988; Model 1981). These weights act as multipliers against the values assigned to responses such as "husband always," "both equally," and "wife more than husband." The other three techniques—the reconstruction approach, the activity log approach, and the diary approach—require subjects to estimate or systematically record how much time they spend on various activities during a specific or average day or week (Warner 1986, p. 181).

Status Equality

The fourth tradition of research on marital equality originates with the writings of Talcott Parsons. As the leading advocate of the functionalist school of thought, Parsons has stood at the center of a number of controversies. Here, the source of inspiration for all the studies in this final area is Parsons's singular claim that it is functional for wives *not* to pursue careers (1940, p. 853; 1959, p. 265).

Parsons' argument hinges on a social psychological assumption regarding an emotional element in close relationships: relative status. Within the sociological literature, the word "status" is used in many different senses. In the literature reviewed here, however, status generally refers to an instance of "differential valuation" that affects the level of prestige an individual possesses. There are, as Parsons himself points out (Parsons 1940, p. 848), many potential sources of differential status, such as one's personal qualities, possessions, and achievements. Curiously, Parsons limits his attention almost exclusively to matters of occupationally derived prestige when discussing status equality in marriage. This is perhaps because he believed that employment was the most crucial source of self-respect for the American male (1959, p. 265). In any case, the line of researchers following Parsons have reacted and remained attentive to this particular focus.

Parsons believed that status comparisons—whether between siblings, between parents and their children, or between spouses—can disrupt the solidarity of close familial relationships. When family members compete for higher status, the one who loses may experience negative emotions. Consequently, Parsons thought that factors inhibiting such comparisons provided a functional service in maintaining important social bonds: "So long as lines of achievement are segregated and not directly comparable, there is less opportunity for jealousy, a sense of inferiority, etc., to develop" (1954, p. 192). It is as an extension of this rationale that Parsons makes the controversial claim that inspired this tradition of research.

As one might expect, Parsons's argument encountered considerable resistance, and many opposing points of view have since emerged. Oppenheimer (1977), for instance, has argued that it was inaccurate to portray husbands and wives as competitors; in her view, spouses should be seen as partners in competition with other family units. Thus, she stresses the importance of status competition at an interfamilial rather than intrafamilial level. Simpson and England (1981) propose another alternative hypothesis that they call "role homophily." Their claim is that, rather than being a disruptive element, similarity in occupational status brings spouses together. Husbands and wives who possess similar jobs are predicted to have more in common, which is thought to foster intimacy and communication. Richardson (1979, p. 70), on the other hand, suspects that the Parsonian thesis has merely perpetuated a myth that corresponds to widely held sex-role expectations for husbands and wives.

In order to measure spouses' occupational prestige, these researchers have taken two approaches. The first relies on prestige score rankings obtained from previous survey research. In Richardson's study (1979), for example, he determines status equality by dividing prestige scores into high, medium, and low categories and then assigning spouses to these groups based on their occupations. Only those husbands and wives who fall into the same prestige category are labeled equal.

The second methodological approach is to develop a typology of occupations that is ranked hierarchically (e.g., Hiller and Philliber 1980; Oppenheimer 1977; Smits, Ultee, and Lammers 1996). Generally, scholars place the "professional" occupations at the top of the list while jobs requiring clerical or manual labor fall near the bottom. Based on these stratified typologies, researchers are able to locate each subject within a particular status level. Husbands and wives whose occupations are similarly ranked are found to be status equals.

Given researchers' focus on occupationally derived prestige, the view of marital equality taken in this last tradition might best be summed up as "*Who ranks higher?*"

CRITIQUING THE LITERATURE: DISCONTINUITY AND DIVERGENCE

In the preceding discussion, I briefly summarized four traditions of quantitative research on the subject of equality in marriage. This literature is quite large. With the exception of status equality, the various lines of research have already been subjected to numerous reviews. Why conduct yet another one?

First, notice that these research traditions tend to receive *separate* reviews. Even the *Encyclopedia of Marriage and the Family* (Levinson 1995) delegates research on equity, power, and division of labor to distinct chapters. A better question to ask might be: Why is this the case? Aren't each of these traditions merely different ways of approaching the same phenomenon—namely, equality in marriage? On the one hand, giving specialized treatment to each area of research makes it easier for scholars to perform a detailed review. On the other hand, such segmentation may prevent the sharing of insights and development of new ideas through the process of cross-fertilization (Prus 1987, p. 264). The time is ripe for discussions that endeavor to treat spousal equality more generally and inclusively.

Second, it is also important to note that the individuals who conduct periodic reviews are generally recognized practitioners within a particular tradition of research. As practitioners, they are more likely to make some (within-paradigm) criticisms and then offer a list of potential "remedies"; they are less likely to conduct their reviews with an eye toward developing a completely different perspective on their subject. In contrast, demonstrating the viability of an alternative approach is the main goal of this chapter and book.

The following section contains two parts, reflecting the dual thrust of my purposeful critique. In the first half, I show that within each of the four traditions there is a surprising lack of consensus regarding the proper meaning and measurement of equality. Thus, even though scholars write as if they are researching the same phenomenon (e.g., "equity" or "power equality"), the nature of that phenomenon varies dramatically from study to study. This discontinuity undermines the cumulative impact of their work.

In the second half of this section, I suggest that previous research is flawed for a related, but more fundamental, reason: All of the varied, inconsistent meanings and measurements that researchers have collectively employed to date are probably—if not, logically speaking, necessarily—different from and incompatible with the particular meanings and measurements actually used by married people in specific situations. Such divergence is significant if researchers are striving to produce findings that accurately portray, resonate with, or "tie back into" the lived experiences of the people they study.

Thinking about inter-researcher discontinuity and researcher–subject divergence will be instrumental in developing a social constructionist approach to equality, as I hope to show.

Inter-Researcher Discontinuity

Studies of Equity

On a superficial level, equity scholars display a high degree of consistency. There is unanimous agreement that their topic of inquiry is the issue of fairness in who gets what. A small number of scales have been developed, and those measures have been used repeatedly. Generally, there is some convergence around three types of classifications in equity research: the overbenefited, the underbenefited, and the equitably treated.

Closer examination of this tradition, however, reveals a fundamental problem: scholars have not established a shared, standard procedure for separating equitable from inequitable relationships. Specifically, the range that constitutes equity, the set of scores that passes as "good enough" or "close enough" to be considered equity, varies from study to study. The result is that the phenomenon of equity is highly "method dependent" (O'Brien 1985). That is, the same research subjects would be classified differently depending on which idiosyncratic technique researchers choose to employ.

A relatively straightforward instance of this can be demonstrated by examining two publications that were generated from the same sample of 118 subjects. In the first article (Traupmann, Petersen, Utne, and Hatfield 1981, p. 472), respondents were classified based on the statistical benchmarks of +1.0 and −1.0. Those subjects whose scores fell within this range were considered equitably treated, while those who scored above or below this range were considered overbenefited and underbenefited, respectively. The second report (Utne, Hatfield, Traupmann, and Greenberger 1984), however, employed a stricter range for equity—this time it was those scores that fell between +0.1 and −0.1. The result is that the classification of subjects shifts dramatically. In the first article (p. 472), researchers found 87 equitably treated, 105 overbenefited, and 44 underbenefited. In the second publication (pp. 327–28), the findings changed to 123, 89, and 24, respectively. (Readers may wonder how more cases of equity can be found when a stricter range is employed. This seems to be the consequence of another complicating factor involving the use of different coding procedures.)

This example is by no means the only instance of divergent classification; it is just the simplest to understand. Many other idiosyncratic procedures have been used, and their relation to one another is ambiguous at best. For example, and in contradiction with the two articles earlier, some studies only consider those individuals who score *exactly* zero to be equitably treated (Hatfield, Greenberger, Traupmann, and Lambert 1982; see also Cate, Lloyd, and Henton 1985; Cate, Lloyd, and Long 1988). Sometimes (Hatfield, Walster, and Traupmann 1979) researchers set benchmarks to discern between the "slightly overbenefited" (0.1–0.5) and the "greatly overbenefited" (0.51–31.0); on other occasions, the "slightly," "somewhat," and "very much" overbenefited are grouped into the same statistical cell (Hatfield, Traupmann, and Walster 1979; Hatfield et al. 1982).

Equity theory is concerned with identifying a phenomenon—perceptions of fairness—and determining its impact on other important aspects of close relationships. However, the precise procedures used to identify that phenomenon change from study to study. This makes it difficult to assess whether or how one scholar's findings relate to another's. It is unclear how replications can confirm or deny causal relationships when the shape of the equity "billiard ball" is one time round, one time oval, another time square.

Studies of Power

The literature on familial power is vast. It already has received many critical overviews (e.g., McDonald 1980; Mizan 1994; Safilios-Rothschild 1970). A crisis occurred in the early 1970s, when some scholars seriously questioned the viability of the concept of "power" and the methods used to measure it (Sprey 1972; Turk 1975). When Turk and Bell (1972) applied nine survey and observational measures to the same sample, none of them was found to be highly correlated with each other; whether the husband, wife, or child of a given family was found to be the "dominant" member depended on which particular technique was used. Since then, power research has continued, with many "basically unresolved" dilemmas (Mizan 1994, p. 89) either ignored (e.g., Blumstein and Schwartz 1983; Shukla 1987) or mentioned as an item requiring further research (e.g., Straus and Yodanis 1995).

Though much has been said and could be said about power research, my attention here will be restricted to issues that are most basic to the topic of defining and measuring equality. As with the equity literature, we find no uniform standard among power scholars for demarcating the statistical point at which the power-egalitarian marriages can be separated from those that are not. Blood and Wolfe's work (1960) best illustrates the confusion on this issue. The range of equality for this landmark study was constructed, in an ad hoc manner, around the *sample mean* score rather than the "absolute" or "true" point of exact equality. The effect of this is that scores that might otherwise have been taken as indicating husband dominance are grouped in the egalitarian category. Blood and Wolfe justify their decision in this manner: "Though slightly skewed to the husband's side in absolute terms, it seems preferable to label these as relatively equalitarian" (1960, p. 23). The reason "it seems preferable" is unclear. However, the procedure yields a symmetrical distribution of cases—22% husband dominant, 46% egalitarian, and 22% wife dominant—that does facilitate statistical analysis.

A decade later, Turk and Bell (1972) replicated Blood and Wolfe's study and found very similar results. When employing the same scale and following the same classification procedure, they found 21% husband-dominant, 42% egalitarian, and 28% wife-dominant marriages. However, when they centered the egalitarian category around the absolute point of equality, the method identified five times as many husband-dominant (42%) as wife-dominant marriages (8%).

Marital equality is thus contingent on the particular techniques used to assess it. Yet, scholars have failed to establish a common procedure or a theoretical rationale for classifying couples. Scattered recognition and discussion of this issue exists, but consensus has never been reached or even seriously sought. Consequently, researchers continue to rely on idiosyncratic procedures within their separate studies of the "same" phenomenon, power equality. One review of the literature summed it up this way:

> A major source of distortion in examining the association between the egalitarian pattern and marital satisfaction has been the lack of a coherent system for classifying couples. The goal of obtaining groups of equal size often seems to guide the classification of subjects as much as does the goal of meeting conceptual requirements. (Gray-Little and Burks 1983, p. 534)

The problem of inconsistent classification, these authors suggest, "could easily be remedied by instituting standard practices" (p. 526).

Researchers have not come any closer to reaching such consensus. In fact, many scholars are still debating the correct definition of the term "power." Kranichfeld (1987), for instance, has considered past research and concludes that women's sources of influence have been largely ignored by traditional meanings and measurements:

> If power is defined as the ability to change the behavior of others intentionally, then power is at the core of much of what women do. In fact, women do not just change the behavior of others, they shape whole generations of families.... Women's power is rooted in their roles as nurturers and kinkeepers, and flows out of their capacity to support and direct the growth of others around them throughout the lifecourse.... Women are the lynchpins of family cohesion and socialization, and this is certainly a position of power. (p. 48)

Kranichfeld's paper illustrates how quickly the balance of "power" can shift from one spouse to the other if a researcher merely takes a slightly different stance toward the meaning of the concept.

Studies of the Division of Labor

Researchers in this third tradition also lack consensus on how to satisfactorily distinguish between equal and unequal marriages. Hochschild (1989, p. 282), for example, considers husbands to be adequately sharing when they do between 45% and 55% of the household labor. Other scholars are more generous and use a range of 40% to 60% (Haas 1980, pp. 290–91; see also Smith and Reid 1986). Piña and Bengtson (1993, p. 905) deem an equitable division of household labor to exist if husbands' and wives' contributions fall within seven hours per week of each other. Benin and Agostinelli (1988, p. 353), in one of their categories, treat as equal those spouses who both do between sixteen and twenty hours per week. Blumstein and Schwartz (1983, pp. 144–45), on the other hand, compare spouses' efforts by using a category with the parameters of eleven to twenty hours per week.

The full discontinuity of these five approaches can be demonstrated by examining three hypothetical marriages. Suppose a particular sample and methodology produced three couples, and each spent a total of thirty-two hours on housework. In the first marriage, though, the husband did only twelve hours while the wife did twenty; in the second marriage the husband did somewhat more—fourteen hours to his wife's eighteen; in the third marriage the husband did more again, fifteen hours to his wife's seventeen. In each case, these couples would be considered "close enough" for some studies but not for others. The first marriage would be considered "close enough" only for one of the studies (Blumstein and Schwartz); the second marriage for three of the studies (Blumstein and Schwartz, Piña and Bengtson, and Haas); the third marriage for all of the studies but one (Benin and Agostinelli).

These discrepancies may seem trivial, especially when coupled with a hypothetical scenario. Far more serious than such methodological contradictions, however, are researchers' disagreements over the nature of the phenomena they are studying. For many people, "the essential fact of housework...is that it stinks" (Mainardi 1970, p. 448). For them, every type of household "task" is just that—an undesirable chore. Thus, playing with the children, cooking the evening meal, and cleaning the bathroom are regarded in research as homogenous "domestic work items" that differ only in the amount of time they take to complete (e.g., Kamo 1988, p. 185).

Not all researchers, though, agree with such a conception. Some grant certain exceptions to the classification of all household tasks *as* tasks—usually by excluding child care from analysis because it "cannot clearly be categorized into its 'work' and 'leisure' dimensions" (Blair and Lichter 1991, p. 96). Other scholars think the problem is more pervasive, that there may be much more "inter- and intraindividual variability of attitudes...toward the various tasks that constitute housework" (Valadez and Clignet 1984, p. 818). Many household tasks can be described as work, leisure, a combination of work and leisure, or neither work nor leisure (Shaw 1988). Some argue that the "niceness versus nastiness" quality of various household tasks complicates researchers' attempts to merely count up and compare spouses' work loads in simple, hourly terms (Coleman 1988). (Does ten hours of "nice" housework equal ten hours of "nasty" housework?) Additionally, researchers note that certain types of labor, such as emotion work (Erickson 1993) and thought work (Devault 1991, pp. 55–57), are ignored by existing methodologies. (How much *time* do emotion work and thought work take?)

Studies of Status Equality
Status is the smallest tradition of research attempting to systematically discern equal from unequal marriages. However, even here no methodological consensus has been sought or achieved. Researchers (e.g., Smits, Ultee, and Lammers 1996, p. 102) often write their introductions as if building on a cumulative line of previous work on the causes and effects of "status inequality" in marriage. Yet, each study employs a unique

method for measuring that variable. Studies that classify spouses on the basis of three prestige levels (Richardson 1979) may yield different results than those that discern four (Hiller and Philliber 1980; Philliber and Hiller 1983), five (Smits, Ultee, and Lammers 1996), or eight (Oppenheimer 1977) status groupings. Finer distinctions will always tend to produce status inequality where looser distinctions do not (Harris 1997, p. 3). Thus, couples who are determined to be unequal by a more precise technique would likely be classified as equal by a more liberal one. Rather than studying a common variable, these researchers may be examining several different, idiosyncratically produced "equalities."

Researcher–Subject Divergence

My critique to this point has examined the extent to which researchers disagree on how to define and measure "marital equality." My goal in doing so has not been to create dissensus. The dissensus already exists, and it has significant implications for the cumulativeness of research findings.

The second half of my critique is much broader and, potentially, the more important part. It raises questions that may lead to new and potentially fruitful lines of study: How might researchers' meanings and measurements of equality compare to those of their subjects? Do the issues researchers have raised, and the techniques they have used to examine them, have very much to do with the way spouses actually think and act? Asking questions—even speculative ones—about researcher–subject divergence can help us raise taken-for-granted preconceptions to the level of awareness (Blumer 1969, p. 41).

As this review of the literature indicates, there have been a wide variety of approaches to the study of equality in marriage. The meanings and methods used by scholars are frequently quite different, if not emphatically incompatible. Readers may wonder how such a diverse array of research can collectively be compared to anything, let alone to the mysterious practices of married people. I would argue that such comparisons can be made, albeit tentatively. To do so, however, it is first necessary to unite the diversity of previous work into a coherent whole by identifying what is common across all the studies.

To begin with, each study previously described represents an exercise in the social construction of equality. All the researchers have in common the practical project of determining who is egalitarian and who is not. And, when I try to discern the generic form (Simmel 1971) that measurements of equality have taken, I find that *researchers' equality judgments have been made by identifying, compiling, and comparing a finite number of "goods" and "bads."* "Goods" go by many names, such as "rewards," "benefits," or decision-making "privileges." These can be many or few, big or small. Status equality, for example, has been treated as consisting of one "good," occupational prestige; prestige is sometimes high, sometimes low. "Bads" have the same properties as goods, but tend to go by different names. They are called "costs" or "domestic work items."

All the diverse scales and behavioral coding schemes used to measure marital equality, if analyzed formally, can be seen as merely different ways of locating and adding up a finite number of goods and bads. In each case, equality is found to exist only when the goods and bads thought to belong to each spouse can be treated, for the purposes at hand, as amounting to the same thing. The process parallels mathematics. Goods and bads are analogous to the positive and negative numerals that may be "rounded off" and placed on either side of an "=" or "≠" sign.

With this picture in mind, we can consider the issue of researcher-subject divergence. Specifically, how might the relevance, value, and nature of goods and bads be differently perceived by married people and by those who study them?

Relevance

In the literature reviewed here, scholars have mostly presumed that they share the particular relevance structures (Schutz 1970) of their respondents. However, the concerns that shape researchers' and subjects' respective experiences of reality may, or may not, have very much in common. Considering the fact that different sets of researchers have found some issues more interesting or research-worthy than others, the same may be true for spouses. *Are* all married people uniformly preoccupied with "Who decides what"? Or, do they focus on "Who does what"? Do spouses regard each type of concern to be just as important as the other or does one take precedence? Even more radically, is it possible that married people might view equality through a completely different framework, one not yet discovered by researchers? If family scholars truly are interested in understanding spouses' behavior, such matters cannot be swept aside.

Following Schutz (1964, p. 235), I believe each tradition of research can be seen as an attempt to demarcate a specific "domain of relevance" that typifies and delimits the "data" taken into account. Equality *can be*

calculated on the basis of costs and benefits, decisions, chores, or prestige—it just depends on one's interests at the time. If one's domain of
relevance centers around the question "Who decides what," then certain
"facts" will be collected while others are excluded. *The demarcation of a
particular area of interest* can thus have profound consequences. The
most obvious implication is that it *limits the number and kinds of goods
and bads that are considered in the process of determining equality.*

It is perhaps possible that some scholars have correctly guessed what
domain of equality most preoccupies their subjects. To date, however,
such a premise has only been assumed. It has not been investigated
through a rigorous examination of the empirical world (see Blumer
1969, pp. 27–28).

Value

The second possible occasion for divergence in the way researchers and
subjects might process goods and bads involves the value attached to
these items. How important or significant is a particular good or bad?
Researchers and their subjects may vary widely in their responses to
that question.

One illustrative practice that occurs within each tradition of research
is that of uniform weighting. Scholars generally have taken great liberty
in implicitly or explicitly applying a preconceived value to their particular equality indices. Frequently, all the items on a scale are simply treated
as possessing the same degree of importance. For example, "having an
intelligent partner" is given the same weight as "sexual fidelity" in some
equity research (Walster, Walster, and Berscheid 1978, p. 240). An
"extremely positive" response to one will cancel out an "extremely negative" response to the other, producing a finding of exact equity. Thus,
each of these items is assumed to be just as relevant and important as the
other. It does not tax one's imagination to see how this may not be the
case across all (or even many) marriages. Some people may feel extremely
unrewarded by a flagrantly adulterous spouse, no matter how intelligent
the philanderer is.

Research on power and on the division of labor similarly treats indicators as if they possessed the same level of importance. In power studies,
the ability to decide "where to go on vacation" has been given as much
weight as having the final say over "whether the wife should work." In
studies of housework, each chore has been regarded as just as bad as the
next, with no significant differences between them except the time they

take to complete. Thus, while all decisions are interpreted as equivalent goods, all household tasks tend to be considered equivalent bads.

Status researchers, in turn, treat their respondents as "cultural dopes" (Garfinkel 1967, p. 68) by assuming that all spouses uniformly internalize and robotically apply a predetermined set of prestige scores or occupational rankings. Not only may there be subcultural variations in the general perception of occupational prestige, but, more important, spouses are likely to take into account any number of intricate factors while evaluating their respective occupations: How the job was acquired ("nepotism" vs. "hard work") and whether the spouse is good at his or her job ("a real pro" vs. "incompetent") are just two of many possible factors that may affect spouses' perceptions of their relative occupational prestige. Relative status is not a static cultural artifact; it is an ongoing, interpretive, and interactive accomplishment (Harris 1997).

Nature
The third potential source of divergence in the handling of goods and bads is precisely the nature of goods and bads *as such*. Researchers regularly presume that the goods and bads that constitute equality always appear so to respondents. Yet it is easy to find instances when this may not be the case. For example, is intelligence always a reward or might some view it as a character flaw (Komarovsky 1946, p. 187)? Is making a decision always a great privilege or can it be a tedious (Safilios-Rothschild 1970, p. 543) or anxious experience? Does all housework stink or can it sometimes be a leisurely activity (Shaw 1988) if not a moral, nongendered calling (Ahlander and Bahr 1995, p. 65)? Do lawyers always have high occupational prestige or can their profession at times be stigmatizing (e.g., when they represent very unpopular clients)?

Goods and bads are not always obviously so, and married people may not necessarily agree with researchers' classifications of them. A good for one may be a bad for the other, assuming it is deemed relevant and significant enough to be considered.

CONCLUSION

In this chapter I have summarized and critiqued four traditions of quantitative research on equality in marriage. In doing so, I have made two main arguments:

1. There is very little consensus in the quantitative literature regarding how marital equality should be defined and operationalized. The various meanings and measurements scholars use to determine equality are discontinuous.

2. It is very likely that the various ways scholars have defined and operationalized equality do not reflect the lived experience of married people. Researchers' and spouses' meanings and measurements of equality are probably very divergent.

If my review of the literature is deemed correct, what should be done about it? My intention is not to convince scholars to quit studying such an important topic as equality in marriage. Social research is difficult, and all inquiry is fallible in one way or another. I am not saying that absolutely no progress has been made or that research on marital equality should cease until a "perfect" methodology can be developed. However, I would like to leave it to others to suggest procedures for "remedying" traditional quantitative approaches.[2] Instead, in this book I will focus on my main goal: articulating and demonstrating an alternative approach for studying equality in marriage, a constructionist approach. I believe my summary and critique of the literature indicates the possible utility of a significantly different way of studying the familiar topic of equality in marriage.

The primary source of difficulty in researching equality in marriage appears to stem from the interpretive aspect of social life. Marital equality (and all of its "signs") can mean different things to different people or even different things to the same person on different occasions. Since marital equality is subject to interpretive variability through and through, a potentially fruitful way to proceed is to make interpretations the central topic and concern. As I stated in my introduction, symbolic interactionists (Blumer 1969; Mead 1934), social phenomenologists (Berger and Luckmann 1966; Schutz 1970), and ethnomethodologists (Garfinkel 1967; Pollner 1987) have been acutely aware of the interpretive element in social life and have constructed their theoretical premises and methodological directives accordingly. In my study of marital equality, I tried to keep these premises and directives in mind as I investigated people's interpretations of equality in their own marriages.

3

Qualitative Research on Marital Equality
Naturalist and Constructionist
Approaches

This chapter continues my critique of the literature on equality in marriage by focusing on qualitative research on the subject. I compare *naturalist* and *constructionist* approaches to studying marital equality with respect to three aspects of qualitative inquiry: sampling, interviewing, and the analysis and presentation of data. In each area, I argue, naturalists tend to obscure the diversity and complexity of respondents' interpretations. The constructionist alternative is to make storytelling paramount by treating equality and inequality as situated narrative accomplishments. A constructionist approach—the kind of approach taken in this book—focuses on respondents' own ethnographic skills while still fitting "the data" into a larger analytical story about equality.

NATURALISM, SOCIAL CONSTRUCTIONISM, AND NARRATIVE ANALYSIS

In narrowing down the literature reviewed here and in chapter 2, I have somewhat self-assuredly relied on the common categories of "quantitative" and "qualitative" research. However, this distinction is a loose one. If taken for granted, the quantitative/qualitative dichotomy can conceal continuities *between* as well as internal variation *within* the two "camps." It is the second methodological nuance that I focus on in this chapter. The mere usage of a similar qualitative technique (such as interviewing or participant observation) does not necessarily make scholars equivalent

45

"qualitative researchers." Scholars' theoretical orientations may be as consequential for the findings that they create as the particular methodological procedures that they use. Background assumptions shape not just the selection of technique; they color the way any particular method is employed and the manner in which the findings are worked up. Theoretical language and methodological practice contribute together to the discoveries that we make (Gubrium and Holstein 1997; Richardson 1990).

Of the many different perspectives qualitative researchers can adopt, two major options are naturalism and constructionism (Gubrium and Holstein 1997). Naturalism aims to document lived realities—beliefs, behaviors, dilemmas, strategies, and so on—without questioning the facticity of the world. Firsthand observation and in-depth interviewing are viewed as procedures that can be used to try to capture the real experiences of individuals and groups. Although naturalists may acknowledge that people can interpret things differently, these variations in meaning are merely one feature to document among the numerous features of social worlds. When interpretive differences are noticed, it is the researcher's task to resolve discrepancies and incorporate the informants' divergent stories into some larger explanatory and descriptive scheme (Gubrium and Holstein 1997, p. 29). Naturalists aim to create a well-integrated text that exposes myths and accurately conveys what is going on (see also Atkinson and Coffey 2002).

Constructionists, in contrast, take less for granted. They treat the meaning of things *in general* as indeterminate. Constructionist approaches, especially phenomenology (Maso 2001; Schutz 1970) and ethnomethodology (Garfinkel 1967; Pollner and Emerson 2001), attempt to place more, if not all, of the world in brackets. Schutz (1970, pp. 58–59), for example, suggests it is possible to suspend "all the common-sense judgments of our daily life about the world out there" when making phenomenological inquiries. Garfinkel (1967, p. vii), in turn, recommends treating "every reference to the 'real world'" as a reference to a locally produced phenomenon. By so doing, even simple descriptions of a "public school" and its "teachers," "desks," "students," and "cliques" can be considered creative interpretive feats rather than reports of reality. It is people's sense-making practices that bring a knowable world into being (Pollner 1987). For qualitative scholars with these sensibilities, social order and social facts are treated as human accomplishments, and the resulting program is to study *how* the accomplishing takes place *indigenously*, while recognizing that one's own research practices play an active role in constituting "the field" under study (Pollner 1991; Pollner and Emerson 2001).

As tends to be the case with dichotomies, there is no absolute separation between naturalist and constructionist inquiry. Similarities do exist. For example, both naturalism and constructionism aim to be more sensitive to people's actual experiences than quantitative research. Both approaches advocate the detailed study of interaction and meaning. And both approaches make some assumptions about what is "out there" in the real world. Even "strict" constructionists cannot bracket everything, try as they might to leave all definitional activity to the individuals they study (Best 1993; Woolgar and Pawluch 1985). The difference between naturalists and constructionists can thus be seen as one of degree. As I hope to show in this chapter, however, the degrees can be quite large and can have profound effects on the findings that two "qualitative scholars" create.[1]

The growth of narrative analysis has further highlighted the distinction between naturalism and constructionism. Of course, personal stories have long been a central concern in qualitative inquiry, but often for their value in assembling a more accurate portrait of a particular person, setting, or group (Gubrium and Holstein 1997; Plummer 2001). In contrast, recent work in narrative treats storytelling as a crucial means of reality construction in its own right. Informants' narratives are now seen as interpretive versions of events rather than as conduits of information about actual realities (Gubrium and Holstein 1995). Scholars in history, anthropology, psychology, communications, and sociology have turned to narrative analysis as a means of understanding how both lay and scholarly tales create order and coherence out of an indeterminate subject matter (Berger 1997; Bjorklund 1998; Bruner 1987; Cortazzi 2001; Cronon 1992; Maines 1993; Ochberg 1994; Ochs and Capps 1996; Polkinghorne 1988; Richardson 1990; Riessman 1993).

Like perspectives (Shibutani 1955), all stories are selective and transformative. Storytellers ignore certain aspects of experience while highlighting those that fit their current way of thinking (Berger 1963, ch. 3); they *actively* link otherwise ambiguous elements into meaningful patterns (Gubrium and Holstein 1997; Polkinghorne 1988). Narration is a process that is at once dialectical, flexible, and conditioned. It is dialectical in that the meaning of a story theme is shaped by the examples chosen to illustrate it while, simultaneously, the examples derive their sense from the pattern into which they are cast. Narration is flexible in that any given theme can be explicated through a diverse array of experiential particulars, and any single example could be used to illustrate a number of competing themes. This makes storytelling incredibly "artful" (Garfinkel 1967; Gubrium and Holstein 1997). Narration is conditioned, though, because in the social world not just any story will do. Creativity and indeterminacy are circumscribed by certain constraining factors. To be taken seriously, storytellers must be sensitive to their audience, responsive to the social task at hand, and mindful of the formula plot lines sponsored by the local and larger culture (Berger 1997; Bjorklund 1998; Gubrium and Holstein 2000; Loseke 2001).

Just as particular forms of excuses and justifications become socially acceptable in certain milieus (Mills 1940; Scott and Lyman 1968), some plot lines are socially favored over others. These vary by historical and interactional context (Bjorklund 1998; Gubrium and Holstein 2000). Some authorized tales emphasize free will and individual effort. Others point to external constraints in the environment (the economy, demographic trends, peer pressure, spirits, circumstance, coincidence). Still others implicate internal constraints (socialized values, self-esteem, the passions, alcohol, mental illness, demonic possession). Through subtle choice of language, storytellers position themselves as passive or active, victim or aggressor, in their social relations with others (Riessman 2002; see also Hopper 1993; Holstein and Miller 1990; Loseke 2001; Weinberg 2001). In so doing, they tend to align themselves with culturally approved ways of representing social life.

Narrators are not dopes, however (Garfinkel 1967). They are not bound to live by a single coherent narrative. In practice, it is not uncommon for narrators to self-consciously question, revise, and otherwise edit their own stories even as they tell them (Gubrium and Holstein 1998). A realist quantitative or qualitative researcher might try to assess the merits of the various accounts a respondent gives, resolve any discrepancies, and arrive at a more accurate depiction. Constructionist and narrative scholars, on the other hand, would bracket the accounts, studying how they are put together, the different meanings they convey, and the different consequences they may have.

Like naturalists, constructionists *do* assume license to describe the contexts that they study. However, they do so in a careful, minimalist way. Their appeals to ethnographic authority are more limited than naturalists (Gubrium and Holstein 1999). When constructionists characterize a context, the purpose more likely will be to investigate a situation's impact on interpretive processes (and vice versa), not to unequivocally "set the scene" that purportedly confronts every native member. Thus, a constructionist might incorporate some naturalist observation in order to compare how different institutional settings affect the stories that are told under their respective auspices, but be less inclined to reify those settings.

NATURALIST STUDIES OF MARITAL EQUALITY

What are the relevant themes that constitute marital equality? What causal factors promote and inhibit it? To date, qualitative scholars have made it primarily *their* prerogative to answer these questions. There are many books and articles that study marital equality by using a naturalist approach (e.g., Blaisure and Allen 1995; Deutsch 1999; Fox and Fumia 2001; Haas 1980; Hochschild 1989; Knudson-Martin and Mahoney 1998; Risman 1998, ch. 5). Each of them sets forth a conception of what an equal marriage "really" is. These conceptions, however, are not the same. Kimball (1983) and Schwartz (1994) provide the most thorough treatments of the subject. For them, equal marriages tend to have the following characteristics: Both partners share responsibility for breadwinning, housework, and child care; decision-making power is shared equally; communication occurs frequently and is not dominated by either partner; sexual relations are conducted fairly; mutual respect is exhibited; and spouses are best friends who put each other first (Kimball 1983, pp. xi, 71–72, 81, 83, 164–65; Schwartz 1994, pp. 13, 29, 76, 125, 194). These are not the only assertions Kimball and Schwartz make about equality, just some of the themes on which there is general agreement.[2] Moreover, the criteria highlighted in Kimball's and Schwartz's books are *not* universally endorsed by other qualitative social scientists as the qualifying characteristics of equal marriages. Haas's (1980; 1982) six-part conception of a "completely egalitarian" marriage, for example, neglects some of the themes (sex and communication) while including others that seem to overlap. Knudson-Martin and Mahoney (1998, p. 82), in turn, discern only four features of an equal marriage, but introduce even more terminology and categories (such as "accommodation"). A great many scholars, meanwhile, focus primarily on housework and child care in their research on marital equality (Blaisure and Allen 1995; Coltrane 1989; Deutsch 1999; Gerson 1993; Hochschild 1989).

In short, although many qualitative scholars provide very cogent and detailed depictions of marital equality, there is not complete consistency between them regarding the meaning of equality. There is instead a diverse array of competing scholarly definitions. I read this state of affairs as one good reason for turning away from researchers' meanings and toward the definitional activities of social actors. Another more important reason is this: From an interactionist perspective, what is significant about marital equality is not the various stories scholars tell, but the stories that people themselves might live by. Even if a particular scholar's conception were deemed the "best" characterization of equality in marriage, many questions would remain. How might the scholar's conception relate to the daily lives of married persons? Do many couples know about it? Do they agree with it? If people think "Here goes my spouse again, treating me like an equal/unequal," what is the specific meaning and context of that interpretation? Which theme are *they* referencing? Is it a theme frequently propounded by a certain scholar? Or could there be equality issues that are crucial to some married couples but are entirely missing from the scholar's conception? In either case, how do people complete the intricate work of assembling the raw materials of their lives into coherent narratives about marital equality? On what occasions, and for what purposes? How are their stories told, affirmed, contested, and acted on?

These are the kinds of questions that a constructionist approach would ask—questions that are different from the concerns of traditional social scientists. They are questions that require humility and curiosity, rather than a confident, outraged, or dogmatic pose. In order to ask them, scholars would have to be willing to listen to discover what equality means to specific persons in particular settings, as well as *how* it means, rather than positing what equality really is or ought to be.

Taking such a constructionist turn would also necessitate a different set of theoretically informed empirical practices. Some guidelines for future research might be helpful. In the following sections of this chapter, I discuss some of the ways that a constructionist methodology diverges from the naturalist approach to studying equality. For the sake of clarity, I have organized my remarks around three distinct areas: (1) sampling, (2) interviewing, and (3) analyzing and presenting the data. The issues, however, do overlap. The basic argument running throughout is that constructionist practices are better able to capture something that has been missed: the complexity of people's diverse situated interpretations of equality.

Naturalist Sampling

A qualitative social scientist who wants to learn about equality in marriage will likely do so by observing, interviewing, and/or interacting with egalitarian spouses. But the first task is finding those spouses. Where might they be located? One approach is to seek them in their presumed "natural habitats." A scholar might believe that some groups are more likely to practice equality in marriage and so tailor his or her sampling strategy accordingly. Feminists may come to mind as persons who may purposefully pursue marital equality. Consequently, the National Organization for Women has been a popular venue for finding egalitarian marriages (Blaisure and Allen 1995; Haas 1980; Kimball 1983). For those scholars who consider parenting essential to equality, research participants might be sought through schools or daycare centers (Deutsch 1999). Another technique that can be used is to run newspaper advertisements or make cold calls with the hope of recruiting potentially qualified people from the general public (e.g., Deutsch 1999; Haas 1980). Or, a scholar may contact couples he or she believes to be egalitarian or inegalitarian based on previous research experiences with them (Schwartz 1994). Whatever the source, once appropriate respondents are found they can be asked if they know anyone who has a similar marriage (Kimball 1983, p. ix; Schwartz 1994, p. 4). In this way, a snowball sample can be formed. Throughout all of these sampling processes, qualitative scholars rely partly on their own ability to locate egalitarianism and partly on participants' ability. Respondents are deemed capable—somewhat—of identifying their own and other marriages as equal or unequal.

The "somewhat" is key, and deserves elaboration; it points to an enduring tension in naturalist studies of equality and inequality in marriage. On the one hand, qualitative researchers have considered their research participants to be *expert informants* (Blaisure and Allen 1995, p. 7). Egalitarian couples in particular are said to have excellent advice to offer because they have succeeded in developing relationships that are "worthy of emulation" (Kimball 1983, p. ix; Schwartz 1994, p. 3). On the other hand, some respondents are thought to have better knowledge than others. Consequently, researchers frequently set selection criteria to limit their sample to those who can best speak about marital equality. For example, one qualifying characteristic has been the length of time that couples have been married. Blaisure and Allen (1995, p. 7) spoke only with couples married more than five years in order to exclude people in the "honeymoon phase" who might have an unrealistic understanding of equality. Rosenbluth, Steil, and Whitcomb (1998, p. 229), in contrast, purposefully sought persons married between one and ten years; their rationale was that younger couples would be *more* sensitive to "each partner's contributions and rewards." The presence of children at home is another trait that researchers have linked to competence. Risman (1998, p. 100) and Deutsch (1999, p. 239) excluded couples who did not have at least one child under eighteen living at home. Other scholars do not use that criterion to disqualify potential recruits (Blaisure and Allen 1995, p. 9; Haas 1980, p. 291).

Even respondents with presumed competence-generating traits, however, apparently cannot be trusted to know if they really have an equal or unequal marriage. Naturalists are wary of myths and mistakes (Deutsch 1999; Hochschild 1989). An initial screening device—based on the scholar's definition of equality—is sometimes used to exclude mistaken individuals or classify their relationships more accurately. These screening devices also vary by scholar. Deutsch (1999), for example, asked her potential recruits to estimate how parenting duties were split up in their marriages. Haas (1980, p. 290) asked about housework, employment, child care, and decision making. Risman (1998, pp. 99–100) inquired about the division of household labor, employment, child care, and the overall "fairness" of the marriage. All three authors employed unique strategies for including and (re)classifying respondents in order to "maximize the probability of selecting equal sharers who really are equal" (Deutsch 1999, p. 241).

Whether or not a stringent screening process is used, though, naturalist authors retain the right later on to discount respondents' inaccurate views. Listen to Schwartz as she explains how she uncovered the real truth about a particular couple by observing them over time:

> [Ian and Beryl] certainly consider each other their best friend, and it's hard to imagine that most observers would not agree. But after a long time with them, one comes to a slightly different conclusion. Beryl continually defers to Ian's opinions and almost always ends up capitulating to his argument.... There is no doubt they love each other.... But when Ian talks about Beryl, his tone is slightly paternalistic. (Schwartz 1994, p. 50)

Not only may a husband and wife be less equal than they think they are, the opposite may also occur. Hochschild (1989, p. 73) argues that couples adhering to traditional gender ideologies may be unable to admit to themselves just how equal their marriages really are.

Thus, while married people themselves provide valuable sources of information for naturalists, that information is viewed as potentially biased or misleading. It is ultimately the researcher who must separate fact from fiction in order to determine if respondents are really equal in practice. It is up to the researcher to decide who is qualified to speak and who among those is deluded.

Naturalist Interviewing

Once potentially egalitarian spouses are found, a qualitative scholar must decide how to acquire information about their married lives. To date, the main method of choice has been in-depth interviewing (Blaisure and Allen 1995; Deutsch 1999; Haas 1980; Kimball 1983; Schwartz 1994). In-depth interviewing fits well with the goal of learning from expert informants—those who can convey the hidden realities of marital equality. Naturalist scholars assume that, barring myths and mistakes, couples possess "authentic" knowledge of the "real" state of equality in their marriages. This practice is common among family scholars, who tend to treat household kin as "insiders" with privileged access to the actual happenings of family life (Gubrium and Holstein 1990). What the naturalist conception of interviewing underappreciates is the idea that *all* stories about marital equality are situated productions. All marital profiles are emergent interpretations sensitive to the context at hand, including autobiographical tales told by members of familial relationships (see also Atkinson and Silverman 1997). The research interview is an interactional context, and it is no more a neutral conduit of facts than any other situated social interaction. Like a legal deposition, a marital counseling session, or friendly banter at a party, a scholarly interview exerts an influence over the stories that people tell about their lives (Holstein and Gubrium 1995b).

One of the most obvious ways this occurs is through the prompts researchers use to generate marital storytelling. Succinctly put, naturalist researchers tend to formulate questions that reflect their own conceptions of equality. Whether or not they work from a preset interview guide (Deutsch 1999, pp. 243–45) or take a less formal approach (Hochschild 1989, p. 6), researchers encourage respondents to recall biographical instances that might appropriately be incorporated into the themes *the researcher* proposes as important.

Consider the following segments of an interview Gayle Kimball ("G") conducted with one of the couples she interviewed, Barbara ("B") and Slack ("S"). Very early in the interview (Kimball's second question),

Kimball raised the subject of housework and then asked more specifically about its presumed subcomponents.

> G: I'm interested in how you run your household. I imagine with your youngest being thirteen that you have a lot of driving and taxiing kids around. What are your tasks with the kids and how do you divide those up?

> B: Okay, the youngest two are from my previous marriage and they are pretty self-sufficient, but we do live in an area without public transportation and in the winter bicycles are pretty cold to ride around. They each ride school buses so we don't have a school transportation problem. With their social life, we do have transportation duties. Very often the two of us ride together, when taking the kids somewhere, mostly for the company of each other. [...]*

> G: What about the things like cooking and shopping?

> B: We do both things together too. Weekends are generally relaxed for us. We don't have a very heavy social life. Generally, we do the grocery shopping together on Saturdays. [...]

> G: What about cleaning the house? Washing clothes and all that stuff?

Later in the interview, Kimball again changed the subject. This time she encouraged her respondents to consider their interpersonal conflicts and how they resolve them.

> G: People talk about the need for communication skills in a relationship. Do you ever have those times when you get irritated with each other, resentful about the toothpaste in the basin or whatever? If so, how do you deal with those little frictions?

> B: It's hard to remember when things are going well. [*Laughter.*] I'm trying to remember back to the last irritation. [...]

---

* In the interview data I present in this book, I use ellipses (...) to indicate pauses and ellipses in brackets [...] to indicate that I have deleted portions of the talk. I also place hyphens at the end of words or partial words to indicate abrupt stops or starts.

S: We don't really have very many.

B: Oh, I can think of one. [...] When we're both in the bedroom dressing, it's an irritation to me when Slack goes out
and leaves the door open and the kids are out there.

(Kimball 1983, pp. 295-96, 303)

Notice how Kimball's preconceived definition of equality directed
the course of the interview. At her prodding, the discussion moved from
one issue to another: first housework (childcare, cooking, shopping, and
cleaning), then communicating about irritations or frictions. All the
while, Kimball assumed, instead of inquiring, that these were significant
components of equality for the couple. And, given the interactional
assignment of responding to these categories, Barbara and Slack graciously searched their biographies and transformed the raw data of past
experiences into pertinent examples. The two respondents told brief
anecdotes about their lives in relation to the concerns the researcher
raised, adopting the researcher's orientation toward married life as consisting of daily "tasks" and "irritations." If there are other issues or ways
of thinking about marital equality, they are less likely to arise in such a
format or be appreciated if they do.[3]

This is not to say that Kimball utterly controlled the stories that
emerged. Far more than in a quantitative survey where responses must be
selected from a small set of standardized possibilities, qualitative interviews allow much greater flexibility in the articulation of answers.
Respondents might talk virtually about anything. But though the
respondent can speak more freely in interviews like Kimball's, naturalists
share with quantitative approaches the tendency to view subjects as passively relaying information rather than actively constructing meaning
(Holstein and Gubrium 1995a). Even for marital scholars interested in
"misperceptions" of marital equality, interviewing is seen as an effective
tool for uncovering those potentially biased thoughts (Deutsch 1999;
Hochschild 1989). Survey research and naturalistic interviewing both
ignore the interpretive effort it takes to construct coherent life stories.
Neither approach treats respondents' narrative skills as noteworthy.

Naturalist Data Analysis

Along with locating potential egalitarians and conducting interviews
with them, two other crucial steps for naturalist researchers are analyzing

and presenting the data. These are complicated affairs. Interview transcripts can generate mountains of pages to look through (let alone any other data). Researchers must shrink the many stories they have heard down to workable size by employing concepts that summarize what they have learned. Based on what their respondents tell them, scholars have attempted to delineate the costs and benefits associated with egalitarianism, the factors that impede or facilitate achieving equality, and the central characteristics of equality (Deutsch 1999; Haas 1980, 1982; Hochschild 1989; Kimball 1983; Knudson-Martin and Mahoney 1998; Risman 1998; Schwartz 1994). Naturalist researchers have tended to collapse the data into those kinds of categories. In the process, they sift and file vast quantities of information, making it more manageable. All of this involves much interpretation, as is sometimes briefly acknowledged (Deutsch 1999, p. 248). Data so coded can then be used to write sections that are organized by theme and/or by marital couple, and researchers make different choices in this regard. Kimball (1983), Schwartz (1994), and Deutsch (1999) devote separate chapters to separate issues, such as "resolving conflict" for Kimball, "passion in a sexual democracy" for Schwartz, and "babies, breastfeeding, bonding, and biology" for Deutsch. Hochschild (1989), in contrast, presented her data more in the form of extensive, chapter-length marital profiles permeated by recurrent themes such as "gender strategies." All these authors, however, buttress the validity of the points they make by inserting brief quotations of respondents' own words.[4]

As with sample selection, data analysis rests firmly on the assumption that respondents are only *somewhat* capable of correctly identifying equality and the conditions associated with it. Scholars express much more confidence about their own abilities to develop and apply concepts that make sense of respondents' lives; they can tell respondents' tales more accurately than respondents themselves can. Consider Hochschild's and Deutsch's refutations of their respondents' explanations in favor of their respective scholarly versions:

> The Holts said that their upstairs-downstairs arrangement was an equal division of labor. The Delacortes said theirs was unequal. Both stories reflected what the couple *wanted* to believe[, which] clashed with some important reality in their lives, and created a tension.... For the Delacortes, the tension was between their joint traditionalism and the reality of both their pocketbooks and their personalities. (Hochschild 1989, p. 73; emphasis in original)

What this husband describes as a personality difference really reflects their different senses of entitlement. (Deutsch 1999, p. 68)

Employing a myth/reality distinction is an effective way to present a coherent ethnographic tale about marital equality. Dissonance between researchers' and respondents' accounts can be dismissed if one version is described as delusional or inaccurate. The same procedure can be used when a husband and wife disagree about the state of equality in their own marriage—the researcher merely sides with one or the other person (Deutsch 1999, p. 80). Even inconsistencies between a single respondent's accounts can be dealt with by averaging them, by endorsing a statement made at one particular time over earlier or later statements, or by persuading the respondent to rethink his or her viewpoint (Deutsch 1999, pp. 241–42, 246). Conflicting versions of reality are thus subsumed within an orderly, more "factual" account.

And what is the point of the coherent scholarly tale? What is its larger import? Qualitative researchers present their findings not as isolated islands of knowledge but as linked to larger sets of conditions, issues, and concerns. Haas's (1980; 1982) tale is most minimalist, a strictly scientific account that merely implies the importance of studying, endorsing, and practicing marital equality. Hochschild (1989), in contrast, couches her research in a lengthier historical account about a stalled revolution: Women have changed by entering the work force in greater numbers, but related societal components (workplaces, men, marital norms) have not changed. A dangerous social strain has emerged, as divorce rates indicate; the strain will likely continue unless large-scale social change occurs (Hochschild 1989, pp. 12, 267). Kimball's and Schwartz's stories overlap with Hochschild in some respects but tend to draw more optimistic implications. They extol the 50/50 or peer relationship as a new kind of marriage, possible "for the first time in human history" (Kimball 1983, p. 1; Schwartz 1994, p. 43). They emphasize that though it is a rare phenomenon, and something that is difficult to achieve, marital equality *is* feasible. The authors predict that more and more couples will want to have an equal marriage in the future and will need models to emulate and advice for attaining equality (Kimball 1983, pp. ix, 207; Schwartz 1994, pp. 3, 5, 179). That is what Kimball and Schwartz aim to provide. Their books are cast as contributions toward the achievement of a more just social world: "Learning how best to achieve peer marriage and how to enjoy its fruits and negotiate its challenges is the next great challenge in our age of equality" (Schwartz 1994, p. 16; see Kimball 1983, pp. 207-208).

CONSTRUCTIONISM AND MARITAL EQUALITY

When approaching the subject of equality in marriage, constructionism faces many of the same issues as naturalism. How should research participants be selected? How might interviews be conducted? How should data be interpreted and written up? Not surprisingly, constructionist strategies for dealing with these dilemmas may closely resemble naturalist strategies. For instance, a constructionist and a naturalist researcher may both rely on interview transcriptions and use a literary reporting style that favors quotations over correlation tables. However, there are important differences between the two approaches. Some of the parallel practices can be shown, upon closer inspection, to be only superficially similar. As a result, the research stories that constructionists produce can be highly divergent from the naturalist variety.

Constructionist Sampling

A constructionist approach to marital equality would make different assumptions about the ontology of equality that would lead to different orientations toward locating "egalitarians" and "inegalitarians." To start with, equality would be seen as an interpretation, not an entity "out there" waiting to be found in one or another location. For constructionists, equality and inequality come into being when people describe or understand situations in those terms. Consequently, the natural habitat for egalitarianism would not be the gathering places of certain privileged groups, but any setting in which equality is made relevant by some individual or group. In naturalistic research, as I noted earlier, the goal is to locate *expert informants*—persons who can convey potentially verifiable facts about the inner workings of marital equality. For constructionists, the goal is to locate *expert practitioners*—anybody who can employ the concept of equality to make sense of everyday life in a locally comprehensible manner.

Expert practitioners, though skillful in their use of the term equality, do not necessarily exhibit extreme self-confidence. On some occasions they may make statements such as "I might be biased, but..." or "That's my opinion, anyway"; they may even express uncertainty about the "correct" definition of the term "equality." But those kinds of conversational practices are themselves features of effective storytelling (see Gubrium and Holstein 1998). Part of being an expert practitioner is to sustain intelligibility and pursue objectives even as one doubts one's grasp of the meaning-making tools. The constructionist alternative is thus to look for anybody—however confident—who can and does use the concept of equality, focusing not on the veracity of their interpretations but on how (and for what reasons) those interpretations are assembled.[5]

Competence and accuracy do enter the picture for constructionists, but primarily as members' concerns. As Gubrium and Holstein (1990) have found with family meanings more generally, people themselves propose various criteria for discerning who has the best information. Sometimes people argue that family members have the real facts because they have firsthand knowledge of secret household affairs; other times the argument is that outsiders know best because family members can't see the forest for the trees. Everyday folk, like researchers, make connections between a person's credibility and their personal characteristics—such as age, length of time married, employed or not employed, children or no children—just as traditional researchers have done when studying marital equality. There are thus two sets of interpretive processes that constructionists highlight but traditional qualitative approaches overlook: making, justifying, and countering *claims* about marital equality, and making, justifying, and countering assertions about *claimants*. In this sense, assigning competence changes from a researcher's prerogative to practitioners' ongoing practical task.

Still, even though a constructionist approach requires treating *anyone* who can relate the concept of marital equality to concrete experience as competent enough to be taken seriously in research, the knotty question remains: Whose stories should be heard? The National Organization for Women (NOW) would certainly be a legitimate organization from which to recruit storytellers, but no more so than any other group that exhibited concern over marital equality. While constructionist theory in itself cannot tell researchers whose stories should be sought out, it can encourage us to reflect critically on our selection criteria. Researchers might ask themselves, Why interview only newlywed couples? Why not elderly couples? What about individuals who are no longer married—might divorcees have worthwhile stories to tell about the equalities and inequalities they once experienced in their marriages? As a result of such questioning, constructionist scholars may develop an ever-expanding interest in new voices and perspectives. They would not find themselves suddenly able to make strong claims about what equality "really" is. They would, however, be able to say a great deal about what equality means to different persons and groups, as well as where and how those meanings are achieved. In the end, deciding who ought to be heard and which contexts ought to be studied remains a judgment call, one made more complicated because respondents and contexts are constantly changing—even right before our eyes.

As Holstein and Gubrium (1995a) have shown, sampling is not a simple matter of letting representatives of populations speak their respective points of view. Even a single person may wear many different hats during the course of an interview, giving different answers to a question depending on whether they are, say, "speaking as a mother" or as a daughter, doctor, patient, and so on. People can construct multiple stories about any particular subject as they consider it from different points of view. This is likely to be very frustrating for the researcher who wants to classify a marriage in one of two groups, "equal" or "unequal." In contrast, a respondent who tells numerous, contradictory, and/or evolving descriptions of equality does not present a problem for constructionist research. Instead, such telling *is* the data.

Collecting a diverse sample may be laudable, but in a constructionist study even that "diversity" is treated tentatively, reflexively (Holstein and Gubrium 1995a). In my research, for instance, I made an effort to gather "demographic" information about the people I interviewed. The brief questionnaire respondents filled out at the end of the interview helped ensure that I was collecting a sample that was diverse along a number of dimensions, such as income, education, and religion.[6] When respondents proved to be overwhelmingly white, attempts could then be made to solicit interviews from more racially diverse individuals. But while I relied on my sociological "common sense" to decide what kinds of summary characteristics were important to consider, I did not interpret respondents' stories as direct expressions or outcomes of those characteristics. Rather, I treated those attributes as potentially relevant aspects of experience that respondents may or may not incorporate into their stories. Some of my religious respondents, for example, discussed their faith as extremely important to the state of equality in their marriages. Other respondents did not even mention their faith in the course of my interview with them, even though they later described themselves as belonging to a particular religious tradition on my questionnaire. Moreover, I invited respondents to "talk back" to me about the assumptions built into my questionnaire. In response, some of my respondents told me that their "religion" was too complex to be captured in a simple word or sentence or that the term "religion" distorted what they saw as their "personal relationship with God."

The diversity of one's sample can thus be made richer and more complex as those diverse persons are allowed to challenge the researcher's attempt to formulate whom they are. Constructionism not only discourages us from presumptuously screening "unqualified" respondents, it also encourages us to give our selected respondents more freedom to construct their own identities and storytelling positions. A constructionist approach allows respondents to express unfolding, inconsistent views and to challenge the researcher's placement of them into a particular population category.

Constructionist Interviewing

A constructionist approach to interviewing looks similar to naturalist interviewing but again requires a different analytical orientation to the process. The naturalist fact-finding mission is replaced by a concern for the *whats* and *hows* of marital equality (see Gubrium and Holstein 1997). There is a greater sensitivity to the diverse meanings equality may have as well as an appreciation for the interpretive procedures through which those meanings are achieved. Thus, a constructionist approach builds on the strength of traditional in-depth interviewing—its attention to actors' points of view—without forgetting the interactional processes and social settings that contributed to the creation of the data.

In order to be more sensitive to the diverse *whats* of marital equality, a constructionist interviewer would set aside his or her beliefs about what equality "really" is. There would be no preliminary definitions to structure an interview guide. Instead, the researcher would ask questions aimed at discovering what equality means to people—that is, whether it means having a "50/50" division of labor, or sharing power, or something else entirely. In my research, I made a concerted effort to encourage respondents to describe the nature of the equality or inequality in their marriages as they saw it. I was purposefully vague, especially at the beginning of interviews, about what I thought "marital equality" might be taken to mean. Consider the following excerpt from my interview with a stay-at-home mom, Sally, who told me on the phone that she thought she had an equal marriage. Some researchers, of course, would disagree with Sally and would immediately disqualify her from their samples because she was not employed or looking for work (Deutsch 1999; Haas 1980). From a constructionist perspective, however, it is interesting to see how she constructs a sense of equality that is meaningful to her, irrespective of scholarly criteria.

> Scott: I'd just like to hear from you in your own words about your own marriage and um, what it's like, and in what way it's equal, how it works for you....
>
> Sally: Well...we've been married um, for four years, in July, July 10, and I'm a good bit older than my husband. He's twenty-three and I'm thirty-two. And in the beginning of the marriage, um...I worked like a dog to put him through college, and he stayed at-, went to school and then stayed at home and did whatever and then...I was always the primary breadwinner until I got pregnant quite unexpectedly. We were married two years when I got pregnant, and um, everything totally shifted, where he went to work and I stayed home. And um, so in that aspect it's been very equal. Each of us has gotten to take a turn doing what we wanted to do. You know, he wanted to go to school, so I worked; now I wanted to stay home be pregnant and have the baby, now he works. Even though it's a lot less money when he works, because he's younger, and so forth and so on. But it's OK, we never really cared about money anyway.

Given the interactional framework I provided with my question, Sally reflected on her marital biography and cut out two "objects" (Blumer 1969) from her biography, two situations: (1) She once worked so that her husband could stay home and attend school; (2) now he works so she can stay home with the baby. Sally characterized the two situations as outcomes of what one or the other person wanted; moreover, she treated them as equivalent "turns" in a sequence. While scholarly concerns about the division of labor can be seen in Sally's response, that issue was only a subtheme in the larger tale about she and her husband each taking turns doing what they wanted to do. This was her emerging depiction of the equality in her marriage. It was a locally adequate rendition, at least for current practical purposes. Sally could certainly have revised her story, perhaps even reinterpreting the turn-taking as unfair or irrelevant in light of new considerations. In a constructionist approach she would be given free rein to do so.

My opening question reflected my desire to encourage respondents to talk about equality in their marriages in ways that reflected their own perspectives and concerns. By asking vaguely about "how equality works" for them, I left it up to Sally and my other respondents to fill in "equality" with whatever content *they* deemed relevant. In short, I tried to discover the *whats* that concerned them. At the same time, though, I recognized that their "perspectives and concerns" emerged within the unfolding interview context, and that a different interaction would have likely evoked a different kind of story. I tried to remain aware, as I conducted the interviews and read my transcripts, of how I influenced the course of my interviews. One way to cultivate this awareness is to imagine the different actions I could have taken but didn't. At the end of the previous excerpt, for example, I could have asked any number of follow-up questions or made any number of comments. Whatever I said might have made Sally more or less confident about her story, perhaps encouraging or discouraging her from continuing along the same lines. Consider these potential statements I could have made, had I been inclined to do so:

- "That's terrific."

- "Tell me more about taking turns—do you do a lot of that in your marriage?"

- "You said you 'worked like a dog' when you were employed. Do you think your husband works as hard now that it's his turn to have a job outside the home?"

- "So first you put your husband through school, and then you gave up your own career in order to raise his child. Some people might think that's a very *un*equal arrangement. What would you say to them?"

Instead of making any of these comments, I chose to say nothing during the brief pause in her talk. My silence at this juncture, however, was far from "unprovocative." It was arguably just as consequential for the emerging story as any of these statements might have been. My lack of verbal input prompted Sally to switch to another topic rather than elaborating on what she had already said. As I smiled and nodded at her attentively, Sally proceeded in a new direction.

Sally: Um, he listens to me.

Scott: Does he?

Sally: Yeah. I used to think it was because I was older, but now I think it's just because he . . . values my opinion, he understands that because I'm older I may actually know more than he does, you know, it's not, he's not givin' in to his wife or being . . . whipped or whatever. Because I have, you know, the benefit of almost ten years more experience than he does. So he actually listens to me, and I listen to him because, you know, lot of things I try don't turn out too good. So if he's got a idea about something, then we'll go with that. Sometimes it works, sometimes it doesn't. We don't really get mad at each other if it doesn't, that's kind of the nature of life.

Scott: OK. So you think that's probably an aspect of the equality, how you kinda, you both listen to each other's opinions and-

Sally: Yeah. See, if, if he tells, if he sounds right, I'll, you know, we'll go with him. It depends on who has the most conviction, you know, kinda. If I really feel really strongly about something, and he's just kinda half-assed, you know, well, we'll go with what I want to do. If he has a really strong conviction about something, then we'll go with what he thinks. We're not real big arguers, you know.

Unlike the first excerpt, this time I verbally encouraged Sally to say more about one of her comments ("he listens to me"). I also brought her back to the topic of the interview by directly asking her if listening was an aspect of the equality in her marriage. In response, she discussed "conviction" as a recurrent factor in the way she and her husband made decisions. Thus, here my participation in the creation of Sally's story is even more obvious. Sally looked to me for cues about what constituted a full and satisfactory answer, and elaborated on the parts of her married life that appeared to interest me. She carefully framed her remarks so that they fit the theme of the interview, ultimately telling a habitual narrative (Riessman 1990) about recurrent communication and decision-making practices. In this way, Sally assembled her marital biography into an egalitarian pattern that was meaningful to her, but the image that emerged was still a collaborative portrait.

A sensitivity to the *whats* and *hows* of marital equality stands in stark contrast with traditional approaches. Qualitative naturalists hope to "mine the minds" (Holstein and Gubrium 1995a) of married people, gathering as much relevant information as possible while remaining alert for myths and misinterpretations. In contrast, a constructionist approach recognizes that the meaning of that "relevant information" is always an interpretive and somewhat improvisational accomplishment.[7] Moreover, it does not relegate that insight to a methodological footnote, but considers meaning-production to be part and parcel of the analysis. That is, both the meanings *and* the processes that create them are "the data."

Constructionist Data Analysis

The tendency in naturalistic research is to construct composite pictures. Scholars paint a comprehensive portrait of equality, complete with a formal definition and organized lists of associated benefits, impediments, and the like. Coherent marital profiles are assembled from the raw material of interview responses, questionnaire data, and/or field observations. These interpretive biographies-at-hand (Gubrium and Holstein 1997, p. 157) are presented as objective, authoritative descriptions of married lives. In contrast, the constructionist alternative to this is to try to understand and convey the coherence that already exists in *respondents' stories*. Taken separately, those diverse stories may appear to the naturalist as incomplete, illogical, or otherwise lacking. The constructionist maxim, however, is to try to "keep the diversity intact"—to respect and study each respondent's narrative as a meaningful and creative accomplishment. Individual responses must be studied within their larger spoken context, not quickly fragmented and re-formed within researcher-generated categories.

Just as professional ethnographers juxtapose examples and ideas to prove a point, so too do respondents. In the course of an interview, respondents themselves pare down the available biographical data, interpretively analyzing and presenting it. They may even place their stories about equality within a historical context, linking the import of their tale to their own family background, the feminist movement, or an ancient religious tradition. Thus, the sorts of interview snippets that traditional approaches rely upon can be re-placed in their larger conversational context and analyzed as components of a meaningful story built up by the respondent in concert with the interviewer. Researchers' questions might be included in the presentation whenever possible, so their influence could be apparent to readers. Respondents' hesitations, false starts, revisions, and expressions of doubt might also be included, so the evolving, improvisational aspects of their views could be detected. The end result is a tentative, revisable understanding of diverse equality meanings and the processes that produce them. A more humble "interpretive study of interpretations" is pursued as an alternative to a confident "sociology of error" approach.

A major analytical feature that both constructionism and naturalism do share is an emphasis on *contingency*. Both approaches claim that neither equality nor inequality is inevitable. The sense of contingency that is in play, however, is not identical. For naturalists, many social factors (such as dysfunctional cultural lags) affect the potential realization of equality (Hochschild 1989; Kimball 1983), as do the daily behaviors of married couples. Deutsch (1999) stridently accentuates the contingency of human agency, repeatedly asserting that spouses must *create* equality even within societal constraints.

> Couples create equality by the accumulation of large and small decisions and acts that make up their everyday lives as parents. Couples become equal or unequal in working out the details: who makes children's breakfasts, washes out their diaper pails, kisses their boo-boos, takes off from work when they are sick, and teaches them to ride bikes. (Deutsch 1999, p. 230; see also pp. 1, 12, 58–59, 134, 152–53, etc.)

The problem with this statement, at least from a constructionist perspective, is that it assumes too much. Why assume that equality means co-parenting and that the signs of equality (e.g., teaching one's children to ride bikes) are obvious? It appears that naturalist arguments about the contingency of equality can only be made by holding the meaning of equality constant.[8]

Constructionist analysis starts from a different and, arguably, deeper understanding of contingency: the idea that equality and inequality are *interpretive* accomplishments. The constructionist alternative is not to assume but to investigate what particular signs matter to different married persons, as well as how they combine those signs into intelligible patterns. *Work* is also the subject of constructionist inquiry, but it is a different kind of work: the work of actively constituting a sense of reality. Constructionism's superficial similarity to naturalism continues in that it does not view "work" as taking place within a world devoid of social patterns or constraint. People generally have much interpretive leeway, but not just any interpretation will do. Stories about marital equality must "make sense" and fit within an ongoing stream of interaction. Settings tend to condition, but not determine, the possible tales that can be told (Gubrium and Holstein 1995). Research interviews, courtrooms, group counseling sessions, and other discursive environments (Gubrium and Holstein 2000) tend to favor some plot lines over others and exert an influence on the way narratives are composed (Loseke 2001). Thus, both naturalists and constructionists study contingency and constraint, but not in the same way: the constructionist studies equality-meanings and the contingent factors affecting their creation; the naturalist studies the reality of "equality" and the contingent factors affecting its creation.

Constructionism is also deceptively similar to naturalism in that constructionist data analysis can also be linked in different ways to larger sets of concerns. In principle, there are an infinite number of constructionist tales that might be told. Current academic practices, however, encourage some plot lines over others. One basic story constructionists might articulate would position their research within in one or more segments of "the field." That is, a constructionist scholar can situate their research on marital equality within one or more ongoing academic "conversations." A point I have tried to make in my research, speaking to interactionists and mainstream family scholars, is simply "Traditional research practices are missing something." In this book and elsewhere (e.g., Harris 2001), I have made an effort to compare the meanings people give to marital equality with the meanings scholars have attributed to it. I draw on my interviews to raise troubling issues and contradict scholars' taken-for-granted definitions. I ask, What is to be done about my respondent who claims to follow a biblical model of equality, wherein the relevant categories are "submitting," "relinquishing," and "elevating"? What about my respondent who complains not about housework but about her spouse's intellectual inferiority? What about my respondent who casts biographical instances such as drug use, clothing, and demeanor as indicators of a major "lifestyle inequality" in her marriage? A naturalist might ignore those interpretations, dismissing them as mythical or inaccurate; I have chosen to analyze and present them as skillful narrative accomplishments that challenge and complicate the usual way of studying marital equality.

A second and slightly more ambitious point constructionist research might make is that "Interpretive differences matter, and should be taken seriously." This point builds on the first one by claiming that capturing what has been missed is itself a worthwhile endeavor. Why is it worthwhile? Here the rationale may be that divergent interpretations do actually play a crucial role in human affairs, and it is our "job," after all, to study those affairs (Blumer 1969). Respecting and studying the viewpoints of others makes for better sociology because it gives us a clearer sense of—or at least another way of thinking about—what's going on out there. Perhaps various persons could benefit from this enhanced knowledge: social movement activists who want to bridge their equality frames with those of their audiences (see Snow et al. 1986), therapists who want to help troubled couples construct more workable stories to live by (see Freedman and Combs 1996; Miller 2001; Parry and Doan 1994); and married couples who want to critically reflect on the criteria they use to decide whether their marriages are "equal enough" for them. Anybody who wants to bring about a better or more "equal" social world could benefit from a constructionist understanding of the interpretive nature of claims about marital equality: how claims are made, contested, changed, and so on. To avail themselves of constructionist insights, however, people would have to be willing to accept that equality and inequality are interpretations, not objective self-evident facts. They would have to appreciate the reflexivity of moral talk as an unavoidable feature of social problem resolution (see chapter 1; Blumer 1971; Dewey 1989; Loseke 1999; Miller and Holstein 1989).

A third story line within which constructionist research might be couched is the historical context of marital equality. This context, however, would not be the naturalist's context. It would not decry a stalled revolution that is impeding equality (Hochschild 1989) or praise marital equality as a brand new form of marriage (Kimball 1983; Schwartz 1994). For a constructionist, the historical context would have more to do with past occurrences of marital equality discourse. The presumption would be that current claims about marital equality are built upon or arise out of previous claims about equality, both in marriage and beyond marriage (see Condit and Lucaites 1993; Loseke 1999, p. 82; Spencer 2000). The big story of marital equality, from a constructionist perspective, is the history of the term "marital equality" as it has been used over time by different individuals and groups. To my knowledge, such a history has yet to be written in any detail (but see Trumbach 1978).

CONCLUSION

In this chapter I have attempted to develop further an interactionist, social constructionist approach to the study of equality and inequality. Focusing on the qualitative literature on marital equality, I have tried to illustrate some of the major differences between naturalist and constructionist research.[9] My argument throughout has been that a constructionist approach is more sensitive to meaning and its creation (Gubrium and Holstein 1997). Naturalism tends to ignore and obscure the diverse meanings marital equality may have for people, as well as the interpretive processes through which (and contexts within which) those meanings are assembled. One way constructionism can remedy this neglect is to focus on storytelling—that is, on everyday narratives and the scholarly tales in which they become embedded (Maines 1993). As a result, we might better understand how equality and inequality emerge as consequential objects (Blumer 1969) in different social worlds.

In the next two chapters, I will turn to storytelling by presenting extended excerpts from several of the equality narratives that were generated in research interviews I conducted with a small but diverse sample of married individuals.

4

Narrating Marital Equality
Familiar Domains of Relevance

In chapters 2 and 3 I argued that although much has been written about the nature, causes, and consequences of marital equality, researchers have not achieved (or seriously sought) consensus about the proper way to define and measure equality. True, various groups of scholars have focused their studies around common "issues" or "manifestations" of equality between husbands and wives, such as "power" or "the division of labor." But even among researchers with those common interests there is still a large degree of inter-researcher *discontinuity* in the methodological practices used to identify equality. Moreover, I argued, there is potentially a large *divergence* between the ways that researchers and married people think about marital equality.

It is the latter, more important source of difference that I highlight in chapters 4 and 5, by drawing on my own interviews with a small sample of married individuals. Chapter 5 will focus on respondents whose stories diverged fairly dramatically from the definitions of marital equality that researchers have endorsed. Here, in chapter 4, I will focus on respondents whose narratives more closely resembled—though only in a general sense—the themes that scholars have propounded.[1] These were the stories that seemed readily categorizable as tales about "power relations," "dividing the labor," and so on. However, though these individuals employed familiar domains of relevance, I argue that they drew on unique biographical particulars to construct their marital tales. The typifications these married people used to exemplify their (however familiar) domains of relevance were even more diverse than the multitude of indicators—such as,

71

scales, observational checklists, and structured interview guides—that researchers have developed over the years to measure equality in marriage. Social life tends to be more complicated than formulaic representations allow (see also Loseke 2001).

ACQUIRING "DATA"

Most sociological studies of marital equality skip the important step of investigating *whether* equality is relevant to married people. Is equality (or inequality) an issue that concerns researchers' respondents? No doubt for many sociologists the issue of equality is relevant at all times and places. But from an interactionist perspective, primary emphasis must be given to what is relevant from actors' points of view. Not just the particular definition of equality, but the very existence of equality and inequality *in actors' worlds* is something that must be investigated and not taken for granted or treated as unimportant. Between May and December 1999 I attempted to do this by soliciting interviews with people who already considered their marriages equal or unequal. In brief, I placed numerous advertisements in diverse newspapers, posted announcements in different locales, and distributed fliers to persons interested in my study (either as participants or recruiters). My solicitations read "Do you have an equal marriage?" or "Do you have an unequal marriage?" or some variation on that theme. The question was followed by "If so, I would like to hear about it," along with a brief statement about who I was and how to contact me. This approach resembles that used by some qualitative researchers. A crucial difference, however, is that I refrained from using an initial screening process based on my own preconceived definition of equality (cf. Deutsch 1999; Haas 1980; Risman 1998). For example, I did not exclude respondents based on whether they claimed to divide the housework within a range of 60/40. Anybody who believed their marriage was equal or unequal was eligible to participate, regardless of what they meant by "equal" or "unequal."

In total I interviewed thirty individuals who were diverse along a number of dimensions,[2] including their stances regarding the presence or absence of "equality" in their marriages: sixteen responded to solicitations for persons in an equal marriage (eight male, eight female), fourteen to solicitations for unequal marriages (seven male, seven female). I conducted loosely structured, in-depth interviews (lasting 1.0–2.5 hours) in which I encouraged respondents to tell me about their marriages in their own words—in what respect were their marriages equal or unequal, how long their marriages had been that way, what it would take for inequalities to become more equal (or vice versa), and how equal or unequal they perceived their relationships in comparison to their friends' and relatives' relationships. My questions were intended to promote respondents' storytelling, to encourage them to discuss matters that were important to them.

As true to life as their revelations may have been, however, the context of their telling inevitably shaped the stories I heard. Respondents were not "dopes" (cf. Garfinkel 1967). They were not restricted by reality or culturally programmed to tell a single coherent story about marital equality. If assembled in a different situation or in a different kind of interview, the various aspects of their biographies would likely be configured into different narrative patterns that either had nothing to do with equality or exhibited equality or inequality in ways significantly different from what emerged in their interviews with me. Consequently, even though respondents did most of the talking, the stories presented here are best heard as collaborations (see Holstein and Gubrium 1995a, 27–29) in which my own interests and conversational moves played a role in helping to structure the story itself—although in a far more self-reflexive and far less intrusive manner than what characterizes most studies of marital equality (see chapter 3).

What follow are respondents' interpretations of marital equality as told in the context of a one-on-one conversation with a researcher. Many other venues exist in which interpretations of marital equality should be studied. Familial interaction at home is certainly one possible venue, but not the only one (Harris 2000b, pp. 136–39). Due to the deprivatization of domestic life (Holstein and Gubrium 1995b), interpretations of marital equality may take place in innumerable public contexts far removed from the household: courtrooms, divorce support groups, women's shelters, and so on. Just as interpretations of what it means to be "family" occur in diverse public arenas (Gubrium and Holstein 1990), so too may interpretations of equality. These public interpretations may be as important and amenable to sociological inquiry as the interpretations spouses make in their homes. By focusing on the viewpoints of married persons, I do not mean to imply that they are the only people worth studying. Nor do I mean to imply that only married persons can provide "authentic" descriptions of the nature and degree of marital equality in their marriages. Even respondents themselves sometimes warned me not to take what they just said too seriously, framing it as "just their opinion" or "just one side of the story." Many respondents explicitly indicated that they did not hold clear or static views of the equality and inequality in their marriages. To the contrary, they often seemed unsure of what they thought, or seemed to be thinking things through for the first time as they spoke with me.[3] Sometimes they revised what they had earlier told me, acting as self-conscious editors of their own stories (Gubrium and Holstein 1998).

Although these stories can simply be read "reality reports," I encourage readers to approach them as creative renditions of indeterminate marital situations. Recall, from chapter 1, my conceptualization of domains of relevance as concerns that are mapped onto reality, and typifications as selective characterizations of phenomena within those domains. Borrowing from Schutz, I argued that domains of relevance and typifications are not direct reflections of reality but are constitutive of reality; they provide a means of carving out intelligible segments of meaning from an otherwise ambiguous and overwhelming flood of potentially germane information. Thus, when my respondents craft a story around the issue of power, for example, they delimit and shape "the data" that they will take into account. Interruptions—perhaps otherwise ignored, viewed as justifiable assertiveness, or considered bad manners— may become indicators of influence or control. Deciding what to cook for dinner—potentially interpretable as a household chore or an enjoyable part of a hobby—may become a decision making privilege. Other aspects—perhaps sexuality or relative occupational prestige—might be set aside as irrelevant (though such matters could always be incorporated into the domain of power at a later date).

Even though I do not take the time to highlight each and every instance of it, I trust that imaginative readers will be able to recognize the interpretive *work* each respondent put into building a sense of equality and inequality.[4] The idea to keep in mind is that everyday actions and events do not come with labels attached. My respondents, in concert with myself, actively linked together a series of occurrences so that they formed the comprehensible patterns that follow.

With those caveats and suggestions in mind, I turn now to the "familiar" sounding narratives of five persons from five different relationships: Wayne, Deborah, Lucy, Meg, and Eric.

THE DOMAIN OF "POWER"

As I noted in chapter 2, there are numerous reviews of the history of marital power studies.[5] The upshot that I took from all of them (especially

Turk and Bell [1972]) is that power has been defined and operationalized in many ways, with little hope for consistency or triangulation between the different approaches. This state of affairs itself seems sufficient justification for a turn away from predilections of analysts and toward the concerns of married people. Moreover, since people compose the subject matter of sociological analysis, their meanings and measurements of power deserve at least as much attention as scholars'. Ordinary folk may be as skilled as social scientists in identifying "power" in their close relationships.[6] It is toward this end that I present the narratives of two of my respondents who can be heard as defining their marriages in ways that imply asymmetrical power. In both cases, this inequality was depicted as a cause of missed opportunities and a serious source of discontent.

Wayne's Story: A Lack of Freedom and a Bossy Wife

At the time I met him, Wayne was a somewhat reticent fifty-four-year-old man who managed a hotel in a small town in Oregon. He and his second wife Tonya, whom Wayne described as both younger (age forty-four) and more attractive than him, had been married ten years. Given the small size of their community, they knew each other for a long time, if only as acquaintances during the years prior to their marriage. Then they had worked together closely at the hotel. On the day of the interview, however, Wayne and Tonya's relationship had a rather uncertain future. They had separated about three months before Wayne responded to my advertisement to speak with "husbands in an unequal marriage." Wayne believed "there's usually one dominant person" in a relationship, and in his case it was his wife. Over the years he had grown increasingly tired of always having to "give in" to Tonya, and he had finally decided to take control of the situation. He initiated the separation. Although nowhere in the interview did Wayne use the word power, he expressed concern continuously with the way his wife dictated what he could and could not do. Wayne wanted the same "freedom" Tonya had, and he wanted his "say" to be heard if he was going to be married to her. If power means getting your way even in the face of opposition, then that's what Tonya had in abundance, Wayne seemed to tell me.

As Wayne guided me to a vacant hotel room, where we spoke, he informed me that he was somewhat hesitant to call me—he initially got my answering machine but left no message. He was not sure if it would be worth the long drive I made to see him, he said, since he thought he might quickly "run out of steam." I expressed my gratitude for whatever time he could spare, and tried to take his hesitancy into account as best I could in the beginning of the interview. I started by asking an extremely open-ended question, and Wayne responded by focusing on a crucial factor in his marital problems—their children. Though Wayne regularly watched the front desk while Tonya visited her family, she was frequently unwilling to do the same for him.

> Scott: So whatever you feel comfortable talking about, I would just like to know what you think about your marriage, and maybe, I don't know a good place to start—maybe you could just tell me a little about it?

> Wayne: Well, let's see. Been married ten years. Uh, I've known her for about twenty-five years. Got married ten years ago. She has three children and I have three children. They're all grown. And that's pretty well part of the problem, is her freedom to do anything she wants to with her children at any time, and uh, I don't have the same privilege. [. . . I'm] having grandchildren born right now in fact and uh, my oldest son called me up and said his wife's gonna have the baby on Sunday. They're gonna induce labor. [. . .] But Sunday's a day that we work, so uh, I couldn't go [until I found replacements for both of us]. But normally what it is, is . . . she gets something planned on a Saturday, I work and she goes and does it. [. . .] And uh, you know, when uh, when her children would come to visit us, if it's our day to work, it was *my* day to work, so she could be with her children. When my children came to visit and it's our day to work, it's my day to work.

Though the issue of visiting family repeatedly arose, Wayne's story about "giving in" to Tonya encompassed many daily irritations.

> [It's] everything actually. Finances, um, when it comes to choices of what car, different purchases, uh, it's uh, I say "This is what I want" and this is what she wants, there's no meeting of any kind. Finally I give in and, in fact so I asked her the other day, "Why did it have to come this far, you know, me asking you to leave to get your attention?" And she said "Because I was able

> to get away with it." And with everything, it just
> kinda went down the list of, of uh, everything, from
> entertainment to, to uh, being able to go fishing, uh,
> wood cutting, whatever I wanted to do away from her,
> or away from here.

Wayne viewed Tonya's refusal to compromise or cover for him at work as particularly outrageous in light of her numerous vacations.

> And lately she's decided she wanted to travel so, within
> the last nine months, she's been to Hawaii twice, the
> Bahamas once, Orlando once, Seattle a couple times,
> you know just, and uh, I've been, I've been in the
> fridge. I may get to eat out once in a while.

Wayne discussed many points of contention in his marriage, too many to excerpt in full. In each case, though, Wayne found that he did not have as much freedom as he would like. While Tonya could just "decide" she wanted to do something, Wayne did not have the same "privilege." Sometimes he was prevented outright from doing what he wanted to do; other times he could do what he wanted, but only if Tonya accompanied him.

Wayne's portrayal of his marriage was fairly grim up to this point. It was an unequal relationship, one that clearly dissatisfied him. When I asked if it was always this way, Wayne reported that initially they "had a fantastic relationship." He then presented a causal theory that accounted for a change in Tonya's behavior: Her job at the hotel put her in a position of authority and prestige and it went to her head. Tonya became increasingly materialistic, and developed a harsh and bossy demeanor.

> I guess, it's kind of like, I don't know how to explain it
> uh . . . she didn't have anything, when we got married,
> so she was, I guess, happy with anything, and then just
> a little bit more and more and more and, and especially
> when we came here, and we were "The Managers of
> the Howard Johnson's in Rockville," you know, it's a
> little bit of prestige, you know. [. . .] [So] she got a little
> bit . . . everybody that works here called her the warden.
> And she chased off some of the best help we ever had.
> [. . .] And I'd tell her, you know, different things "I
> don't like the way you're treating me" or "I don't like

> the way you're treating someone else. I don't like the
> tone of your voice when you talk to this person."

Wayne buttressed his portrayal of his wife, evolving into a domineering
personality by claiming that others shared his perceptions; it was not just
a personal reaction on his part. By reenacting a conversation with one of
the hotel cleaners, Wayne presented his own treatment of the staff as that
of a friendly coworker and contrasted it to Tonya's overly authoritative
and antagonistic demeanor.

> And um, she's, she's chasing off your help today, well
> they still live here in town [which was awkward for
> Wayne]. [...] One of the last gals that- that left here, in
> fact she said uh, she said "I'd feel like I worked *with*
> you but I would feel like I worked *for* Tonya." And she
> said "No, I'm not gonna do that for minimum wage."

If their marriage was fantastic before Tonya changed and it became
so unequal, then it seemed sensible that the relationship could return to
the way it once was. When I asked Wayne about this possibility, the
answer again revolved around his desire to visit his family and to influence major purchases, both of which Tonya blocked.

> Scott: So, what would she have had to have done differently,
> to make it equal, would you say?
>
> Wayne: Um, just allowed me the same freedoms, especially
> with our children. Um, and...well we bought a travel
> trailer. Let's go back to that. About three years ago. I
> wanted a little travel trailer to go up to the high lakes
> here, between here and Bend, just be able to hook
> onto it and go, spend a couple nights or night, and
> come back home. So I wanted a little one....
>
> Scott: And of course-
>
> Wayne: She wants a huge one. [...] [We] kinda went back and
> forth and back and forth. Finally I said "Fine. But it,
> it won't go anywhere, it'll just stay in the yard. Cause
> it's too big." So we've got a ten thousand dollar trailer
> sitting over there in the yard. It's never been moved.
> It's never rolled a wheel.

I asked Wayne if he thought his situation was "pretty common in relationships out there," and the way he responded made it clear that his tale

was a story about power, and one that could be applied to other couples as well.

> Uh, I would imagine that there's usually one dominant person in the relationship and, uh...I- you know, it's just...I suppose some, either male or female, one or the other can always give in for years and years and years but, when a person finally starts digging their feet in, it's time for the other one to take notice.

In the end, Wayne revised his tale of relentless domination to include a subplot about resistance—his preferred framing of the causes for and nature of his failing marriage to Tonya.

Deborah's Story: Learning Your Limitations from a Husband on a Power Trip

Although his biographical particulars were unique, Wayne's general story about power was not. Another respondent, Deborah, also described her unequal marriage in terms of power. A twenty-nine-year-old courtesy clerk at a grocery store, Deborah met her husband Bill years ago when she was a teenager. Bill, a factory worker with a daughter from a previous marriage, was several years older. Deborah described him as a "control freak" who enjoyed making the rules and feeling like "the man of the house." As with Wayne, however, Deborah told me that the limitations she faced were coming to an end, that she too was starting to stand up for herself and refuse to be manipulated and controlled.

   Though Deborah and I first talked by phone after she responded to a solicitation for individuals in an unequal marriage, our conversation was brief. When we met in person, I began by giving her a chance to classify her marriage in either direction, equal or unequal. She described her marriage as completely unequal and, interestingly, gave the inverse of Wayne's rags-to-riches account of marital inequality: The fact that she started out in the marriage with very little made *Bill* more bossy, not her.

> Scott: Well, I think I told you on the phone that I'm interested in equality and inequality in marriage. And I'm interested mostly in how you think about it and how you see your marriage as being equal or unequal. Um...it might be kind of a hard topic to just jump into but uh....

Deborah: Well, let's see. I would say that probably in my marriage...I'd say equality doesn't exist....Does not
exist. And...I kinda knew that before I got married. And it's something either you live with or don't
live with. And I did have a problem with it. But I've
just come to realize that either you take it and live
with it or you stay in a marriage and you talk about
or you fight about what you believe in. And I
believe in equalism or equality. And my husband
don't. [...] We never discussed it until it started
bothering me. I just felt like something wasn't right.
And so I brought it up to him. [...] And I started
asking him questions why we weren't equal. And he
gave a lot of reasons why we weren't equal and it was
pretty much, well, I came into the relationship with
nothing, with nothing. And he pretty much put a
roof over my head. I was young, I was young, and
he already had a job, and pretty much he had everything I didn't have. And so therefore we weren't
equal. [...] [That's how he felt] even though I was
working and I had my own money. He's more of a
old-fashioned type of guy... that he's the man of the
house and that's how it goes.

I asked Deborah what being the "man of the house" allowed her husband to do, and she recounted how Bill yelled at her for not behaving as
he would like her to. She described two instances when Bill unfairly
made her feel she had done something wrong, and typified the disagreements as "power trips."

Well, pretty much he gets to make the rules. [...] He
will put you in a situation to make you feel like you've
done something wrong. It's called a power trip.
Because he's old-fashioned and for him to feel like he's
the man of the house he's has to put you in that position. [...] Well [for example], when you're married
you think you both have a right to the bathroom, you
know? You're a couple, you got married. Well, with
him it's like he's in the bathroom—and we've been
married almost three years—and I just go in and out
of the bathroom and it didn't bother him. Well, all of

a sudden it bothers him. And I go in and he says, "How many times do you have to open the door?" So he puts it like it's my fault. And I said, "We're married—can't I come into the bathroom?" and he says, "Well, I want privacy." And I'm like, "Well, why didn't you tell me?" So before it used to make me feel like "Oh my god I'm doing something wrong." Now I just say, now I just put it to him like "Stop playing head trips because I'm not doing anything wrong and I'm not gonna deal with it." And other examples like um, when we're working outside and he's doing the manly things with tools and wood, and he wants me to help but I cannot guess his next move. And he will scream at me and say, "Why can't you do that right?" I call it a power trip, and then by that time I'm in tears because I'm doing something wrong which I finally figured out that it's not me.

When I asked what it would take for the relationship to be more equal, the conversation briefly turned to communication styles and to Deborah's earlier naiveté.

It would be more equal if he talked to you like the other half, like your wife, or a friend. It would be more equal that way. I used to tell him he didn't treat me like his wife. And he always said, "Well, what do you mean?" and I said, "Because you yell at me for stupid little stuff when I don't even know what you want from me." And we know other married couples, and they communicate, they don't yell at each other, they don't play the little head games that we're playing. And so finally I brought that up to him and he pretty much denied it. So I just call him on it now.

Deborah next explained that Bill's controlling tendencies also extended to their division of household labor and her employment choices. Although some sociologists might treat these as independent aspects of inequality, Deborah's story linked these elements as she focused on the limitations Bill placed on her.

Like with our household it's kinda like he goes out and does all the manly stuff and I stay inside and do all the woman stuff. Well, I'm not old-fashioned and I don't like staying in the house in doing all the woman stuff. Like the cooking and the cleaning and folding clothes. I like to go outside and do the guy stuff too. But see he's really hard to work with because outside he's very controlling. And so therefore I don't do the outside stuff and I do just inside stuff. Which I feel really confined. And I only have so many limitations and I have a really hard time dealing with that. [...] Now see, OK, this is a good point of being equal. Um, I want to go out and get another job, I want two jobs. And he won't let me do that. Well, actually, if I wanted to I would. But see he likes dinner cooked when he gets home, he likes the fire built, and he likes it the old-fashioned way. He likes dinner on the table, he likes the house clean. Well I'm not old-fashioned. If I wanna go out and work two jobs or three jobs, I wanna be able to do that. And so therefore I don't think we see eye to eye, and he is ten years older you know, and so I just think his... values lay differently than mine. They're probably ten years older than I am [*laughs*].

Next I asked a follow-up question about Bill's not letting her work, and as a result the interview turned to money and purchases. Deborah described Bill as constantly questioning her financial decisions, making her second-guess herself. Much like Wayne, Deborah buttressed her story of power and control with a reconstructed conversation that involved other individuals outside the relationship, in this case her stepdaughter.

Scott: So when he said he won't let you [work], did he actually say

Deborah: No he didn't say it that way he just... it was weird because we were at the mall and his daughter, we were all in on the conversation, and his daughter's thirteen years old, and she came at her dad, "That's not fair. You're kinda telling her she can't have a job because you want dinner on the table." And I used to say it that way too. But anymore, it's like if I'm gonna go get a second job, I shouldn't have to stand up for myself. So I wanna make as much money as he does. Like "Oh my god!" you know [*laughs*]. That's kind of, that's how old-fashioned he is. He says, "Well, we have enough money." But see, "we." When it comes to just me, I make seven bucks and he makes eleven. And when I want something, I should, you know, I can go out and get it but then . . . when it comes to the credit card bill it's like, "Oh my god, you spent too much money," even though I pay off the bill. And so it's kinda . . . unequal that way cause when I want something it's like, "Oh my god, you spent more money," but then when we need something in the house—"Let's go get it!" [*laughs*] We just got done buying an electric blanket for a hundred and six bucks, but we didn't think twice about it did we, you know. But when I need to go get something, I need to think twice about it.

Deborah further linked the power imbalance in her marriage to the way her husband had discouraged her from pursuing her dreams and goals. Bill's old-fashioned beliefs and controlling behavior were connected in a heart-wrenching way to her present employment options.

There's times I wanted to go to school and he says I'm not smart enough, so I shouldn't go, or I shouldn't get another job because I don't have the skills that everybody else does at my age. And so in a way he has held me back. And when it comes to being equal when he wanted to go to school I said, "You know, you have your faults, but you know what? Anybody can do what they can do if they put their mind to it. So you go to school. You're gonna be an EMT." And he quit in the middle of it. But I didn't hold him back, I said, "Go ahead and do it. You wanna get another job, go ahead and do it." Because I believe in him, and I think having equality in a relationship you should believe in your partner, you should support them, no matter how smart, what they can do, what they can't do, you should still be there for them. [. . .] I mean when I was eighteen I had a chance to go to school. They gave me a grant of 3,000 dollars to begin with, and I just got

> out of high school. And he said, "Well, you know, you
> need to know your limitations." And I've had that
> thrown in my face for ten years. And I think that's
> what kept me from doing different things. And I gave
> the money back to the school. And I could kick
> myself in the butt today. At least I could have taken
> some basic classes, and ... gone from there.

I asked Deborah if Bill had used that same phrase ("You need to know
your limitations") on other occasions. In response, Deborah focused on a
personality difference and its relation to their behavior. She portrayed the
inequality in her marriage as here to stay, given Bill's temperament.

> Yeah, well see, he's old-fashioned that way, and ... he's
> afraid to take chances.... It's like ... I like to take
> chances, I'm a dreamer... I like to do different things
> in life. I'd like to get a different house, and to do all
> that kind of stuff you'd wanna do, sometimes you have
> to go in debt. And he doesn't like to go in debt. He
> likes to stay safe. Me, I would like to be on the edge of
> a cliff, and have a rope around me and somebody kind
> of dangling me on the edge. I know I'm safe but I
> know there's a chance I could fall. He would be one to
> stand way back and just look at it. [...] I think that to
> live, you have to take those chances. And there's so
> many different, there's a lot of reasons why we're not
> equal in that way because... I'm one to take chances to
> get somewhere in life and he doesn't want to take any
> chances at all. And so therefore he always puts me
> down for being a dreamer and wanting to go to school
> and just doing different stuff, and ... I tell him,
> "That's not equal," and then he says, "Well, we're not
> equal to begin with, we were never equal" [*laughter*].
> So you can't really have equality in a relationship when
> one person doesn't want to work on it.

As with Wayne, it is fairly easy to classify Deborah as interpreting
her marital problems through the domain of power. Both respondents
typified various recurring irritations in their marital lives as indicators of
an imbalance of control, freedom, "say," or some other power-related
concept. The biographical particulars that exemplified the issue, how-

ever, only partially overlapped. For Wayne, the way his wife restricted his ability to visit his children and grandchildren seemed foremost on his mind. For Deborah, the way her husband prevented her from pursuing her educational and occupational goals seemed most central or disturbing. Both mentioned how their spouses spoke: Tonya's domineering tone of voice bothered Wayne and even chased off some of the hotel staff, while Bill's yelling let Deborah know when he was on a "power trip." Power inequality also reportedly affected financial matters, but the details differed. Wayne felt he had little influence over the large purchases he and Tonya made, which were inevitably slanted toward Tonya's expensive tastes. Deborah felt as if she had to ask permission to buy things and disliked the fact that her husband constantly second-guessed her. Finally, while Wayne regretted missing out on numerous recreational activities, Deborah stayed focused on work—she felt confined to doing all the indoor housework, and wanted to do some outdoor "manly" chores instead.[7]

These were not the only respondents to emphasize power; Wayne and Deborah's cases were just two of the more narrowly focused and thoroughly developed tales on the subject. Felicia, a sixty-three-year-old African American woman in a happily egalitarian marriage, also invoked language reminiscent of "power" (along with other domains of relevance) at one point in her interesting narrative. Felicia compared her current marriage to the troubled relationship she had with her first husband, a man who was so controlling he didn't allow her to wear shorts or pants. In contrast, the husband in her second, more egalitarian marriage had encouraged her to pursue all of her goals in life and let her make more (if not most) of the important decisions—even about where they would work and live. Her current husband, she said, exhibited a great deal of "trust" and "respect" in part because "he doesn't tell me what I can't do."

THE DOMAIN OF "THE DIVISION OF LABOR"

Power is certainly a much studied area in the general field of interpersonal relationships. But when scholars think about marital equality, the "division of household labor" is probably what most frequently comes to mind. Hochschild's (1989) landmark book *The Second Shift*, Deutsch's (1999) *Halving It All*, and countless journal articles (e.g., see Shelton and John 1996; Warner 1986) have focused on this domain of relevance. As I discussed earlier, a common way of determining whether or to what degree housework is being shared equally is to compare the number of hours spouses spend on various household "tasks." Usually the types of tasks that researchers inquire about are predetermined by the researcher (e.g., washing the dishes, doing the laundry, playing with the children, mowing the lawn, etc.), but sometimes respondents are asked to keep detailed diaries of the work they do around the house. In either case, researchers frequently (but not always) treat hours as the unit of comparison. "An hour is an hour is an hour" is the implicit assumption underlying many traditional methodologies. Equality is thought to exist if the time husbands and wives spend on housework is determined (by the researcher) to be "close enough" to be classified as equal. Most commonly, husbands are found to contribute less hours per week than their wives.

Some of my respondents focused on the division of household labor as they spoke about equality in their marriages. In this chapter, I will present the narratives of two women, Lucy and Meg, who claimed that their husbands did not put in enough time around the house. While their stories sounded somewhat "familiar" in light of scholarly research, what struck me about their accounts was the different types of tasks that Lucy and Meg treated as essential to their plight. Not all tasks are the same, these women seemed to be saying; an hour of this is not equivalent to an hour of that. Lucy proclaimed that her relationship would have been "close enough" to equal if her husband had merely done the things she couldn't do, the kinds of things he was trained by trade to do; Meg, in contrast, highlighted "the weight of the world" that keeping track of their finances put on her.

Lucy's Story: A House That Needs Work and a Man Who Won't

Lucy showed up slightly late for our appointment at a local restaurant, but with a big smile and an outgoing personality. She described herself as a full-time mom to her two teenage children. She and her husband Sam, a carpenter, had been married fifteen years at the time of the interview. Though she was fairly happy with her marriage, she said that there were some things that frustrated her about it. As the interview began, she told me she was a "very opinionated" person who had "really strong feelings about men and women" and their "jobs and responsibilities." She jokingly asked if I really wanted to talk to her, given her outspoken nature. I assured her that I did.

Lucy: And I'm very opinionated in politics too, so [*laughs*]. But um...I don't know Scott, what do you want to know?

Scott: Well, I wanna, well I'm specifically interested in, in, uh, equality in marriage. And you said yours is pretty unequal, I think you said on the phone-

Lucy: I think it's pretty unequal, and I think, you know, I talk to my- most of my friends, and I get the same kind of feedback. You know, we're all kind of in the same boat going [*makes whining noise*] "Nya nya nya nya nya." Um, my husband works really hard, he's a carpenter. And he's always worked- he has a physical, hard job. And I understand but...I have a physical hard job and uh, an emotionally kinda hard job. When he comes home from work he says "OK I want, I want a little time to myself" to regroup and whatever, and I never get that. It's always- Now I have teenagers. I didn't know that they were gonna be, I thought- I thought, you know, two year olds were bad, you know. And you can't compare, you can't even. With two year olds you can lock in a room and say, you know, "You have a time out" and "Don't talk back to me." But when they're teenagers you can't lock them in their room anymore.

Right away Lucy portrayed the inequality in her marriage as a matter of workloads, in terms of the jobs she and her husband did. Lucy ran the household, Sam earned the money. Both activities were characterized as demanding jobs; however, Lucy implied that hers had an emotional component that Sam's did not. In addition, his job was described as ending when he came home while hers never ended. She got no time to herself.

Lucy seemed aware of a popular belief—one that she apparently had held in the past, and one she espoused herself later in the interview—that raising children gets easier as they grow older. After all, someone might say, teenagers are more self-sufficient than infants; they require less time and attention. Perhaps to counter this interpretation, one that would have undermined her claim of inequality, Lucy suggested that the opposite was the case. Since you can't give teenagers a time out, there's no time out for yourself.

Lucy further suggested that although her job was as hard or harder than her husband's, she received no help at home. She characterized Sam as completely uninvolved with their children.

> Like I don't even know if my husband knows my kids' birthdays. They're his kids, you know. And because we- I do everything, I do *everything*, you know, and what if something happens to me? It's like, "Would you remember their birthdays?" You know, that kind of thing.

The inequality of workloads was not just restricted to special occasions, such as birthdays, but occurred on a daily basis. Lucy continued by describing Sam's lack of effort around the house. She repeatedly said that he put out a great deal of energy at work, but as soon as he returned home he was (following my suggested characterization) "done."

Lucy: So he works really hard. You know

Scott: But when he comes home he's pretty much done-

Lucy: It's like, you know, "I'm done. I've got my CD, my newspaper, and I'll do whatever *I* want to do." And so I make dinner, I have, you know, taken care of homework, making sure the kids have what they need. You know, I take them, my son plays football, so I take him to football practice, I pick him up from football practice. My daughter, to the friend's house, back home. Whatever, you know, and then if things get really hectic I'll say, "Well you have to pick up so-and-so because I've got to pick up so-and-so" and things get, you know, but he just thinks he's just plugging right away, doing what he- has to be done. And I can't remember the last time he made dinner. [. . .] Because if I say "Oh look, I can't, I can't be home for dinner or, you know, I have this planned," he'll just call for a pizza, and that doesn't really count in my eyes as, you know, making dinner. That doesn't count. [*laughs*] And he doesn't do any laundry [OK, yeah], you know.

Lucy presented a few examples when Sam could contribute more around the house: making dinner, helping the kids with their homework, and driving them around. Next she mentioned one area in which one might expect her husband to be especially willing and able to help.

Lucy: And he's a carpenter, but our house is like falling apart. Our house is the very last house on the list. He does this all day long, and I can understand that. But I can't paint the house, you know. I mean I can mow the lawn but I can't paint the house. And... well in fact he started- he started remodeling our bathroom, our downstairs bathroom. I mean it's been two years Scott, two years. And the walls still have that uh, the board up. So I said, "That's it" you know, I said, "That's it. I'm gonna call, um," this guy, actually it's his supervisor he used to work with. I said "I'm gonna call, I'm gonna get [Sam's former supervisor] to come out and finish the wall."

Scott: What did he say?

Lucy: And he's like, "Whatever, I have enough stuff to do," you know. And he doesn't, Scott, you know? I mean, if I could lay around all weekend and watch TV and drink some beer and watch the game and, that's not my idea of fun but, that's not my idea of how I want to spend my weekend. [...] But don't get me wrong, because he does work and he brings home good money, but there's- there's got to be some give and take there because you get resentful after a long time, so. And sometimes I do go on strike. I'm like, whatever, "I'm not mopping the floor. It's your turn." And "When's the last time you cleaned the bathroom?," you know. "Five years ago?" You know?

When I asked Lucy how she would like her marriage to be different, she responded by discussing the futility of making lists of chores and reminding Sam which ones he needed to do. When I pressed her to specify what it would take for her relationship to be equal, Lucy's story again returned to the issue of Sam's refusing to use his special work skills at home.

Scott: Well would you want him to do, you know, the exact same amount of chores pretty much?

Lucy: No, I would want him to do things I can't do.

Scott: Oh, OK-

Lucy: Now he's a skilled carpenter, he's like the best, the best
         in his field. So why is my bathroom unfinished? You
         know, because he doesn't use- we have two bathrooms.
         We have a downstairs bathroom, we have an upstairs
         bathroom. He uses the upstairs bathroom. The kids
         use the upstairs bathroom. Nobody wants to use that
         bathroom, you know? And I'm like... It would proba-
         bly take just a weekend to finish it. A weekend, a full
         weekend of work, you know, of getting it in gear and
         doing it. And there's things that... that I can't do, I
         can't do that. Because I don't know how to put a floor
         in. I mean, I'm not gonna go mess up a floor, put a
         floor in and do it wrong. And, and then the big fight
         comes, "Well I said I would do it! And nnhhh," you
         know. Just stuff that I can't do. Like fixing the bath-
         room. I mean.

Scott: That's where he could really

Lucy: Yeah. [...] I would be really happy if I, if he just did
         those type of jobs I can't do. I mean the daily, the daily
         grind is not that bad. Because the kids are older now,
         and they're pretty self-sufficient and, you know

Scott: Laundry and cooking and things like that

Lucy: The cooking- I make dinner every night. Every single
         night. But, you know...

Scott: You could use a break there too it sounds like

Lucy: Yeah. But um, it's not that bad. If he would just do
         things around the house that I *can't* do.

Scott: Ok. That would be the biggest-

Lucy: Oh that would be, I would be happy. That would be
         it, that would be it, you know?

I started to make a joke about Lucy's wanting the bathroom fixed as a
Christmas present from her husband, and it reminded her of an occasion
when she took a strong stand in order to get Sam to do some carpentry
work on their house.

Scott: That's what you want for Christmas this year is the bath-

Lucy: Well, I did say that one time, it was Thanksgiving and we were remodeling the kitchen and I had this god-awful, really old laminate kind of counter, with the stars and weird stuff from the 60s. And we had the, the new countertop in the garage. I said, "I will not make Thanksgiving dinner until I get my new countertop in and my new sink in. It's not gonna happen." And do you know what? Two days before Thanksgiving, it was in.

Scott: All right!

Lucy: Cause I- you know, he's like, "Well, what about Thanksgiving?" I said, "I'm not cooking it. I'm not doing anything for Thanksgiving." So I got my countertop in and my new sink [*laughs*].

Scott: Kind of gave him an ultimatum or something-

Lucy: Right, you know. Cause I don't want to be a bitch about it, but sometimes you just have to say, "Look. Enough is enough."

Scott: Yeah, OK.

Lucy: Because, you know, I would think that 'cause he's a carpenter, and I've seen his work and he does, oh god, beautiful work—I've seen him do. Well, why doesn't he do that to his own home?

Throughout the interview the tone of our conversation had been fairly jovial, despite the subject matter. Lucy did not sound nearly as bitter as a few other respondents I spoke with, though she clearly was not satisfied with her marriage. When I asked about the inequality's effects on her marriage, it led to a somewhat spontaneous numerical estimation of how the chores were divided up in her household. While Lucy would have liked the ratio to be closer to 50/50 than it was, the emphasis returned again to the potential contribution Sam could have made if only he applied his expertise to their home.

Scott: It sounds like you guys get along OK? I mean it's not like, I mean this inequality isn't completely driving you apart, is it?

Lucy: Nnn nnh. No. No, but I have blowup- we'll have blowups now and then. Mostly with me doing the blowing up. But it took somebody kind of to- to, after fifteen years Scott, you kind of, I mean you know, it hasn't always, you know, we, before the kids we had a life, you know. We had fun, and we went out to dinner, and all that stuff like that. But um, yeah, I- I definitely do more than him. It's probably 80/20.

Scott: In terms of dividing things up-

Lucy: Right

Scott: OK. What would you like to see it at?

Lucy: 60/40 would be. . . . And I'm not saying like, "OK, I'm doing the dishes tonight so you do-" cause you know he does work outside the home, and- and I- I don't work outside the home right now. So that's not, it's not like "OK I did the dishes Tuesday so you have to do them Wednesday." But, so it's not like that.

Scott: OK. More closer-

Lucy: Paint the house, paint the house.

Scott: OK, yeah

Lucy: That kind of stuff.

Scott: OK. Yeah, the things you can't do, like you were saying

Lucy: Right

Scott: Get it closer to 60/40.

Lucy: Uh huh.

Scott: That would be- there'd be less blowups that way.

Lucy: Right.

From start to finish, Lucy's tale seemed oriented to a single major domain of relevance: labor. Her account contrasts nicely with that of Wayne and Deborah, who did discuss workloads, but exhibited much more concern over "Who decides what" than with the ratio of effort that their respective spouses put forth. Lucy's case also contrasts with scholarly research that defines equality as power, status, or some other domain—and even differs from studies that define equality as a fair division of labor. The kinds of tasks that division-of-labor researchers usually collect data about are daily and weekly chores, rather than major home improvements. In Lucy's version of her marriage, however, activities such as "painting the house" and "remodeling the bathroom" were typified as central to the calculus of measuring equality.

Meg's Story: Too Much To Do, with the Weight of the World

A second narrative I heard that sounded reminiscent of the theme of the "division of labor" came from Meg, a certified nurse's aid who sold Mary Kay products (makeup) in her spare time. At the time I met her, Meg had been married to Chuck, a carwash manager, for thirteen years. Between working and raising three children (eleven, seven, and four years old), I got the sense from Meg that she and her spouse were very busy people. Like Lucy, Meg claimed that her husband could do more around the house to make their hectic marriage a more fair one. But in this case, Meg placed the kind of emphasis Lucy gave to home improvement on an entirely different task.

Before the interview formally began, Meg told me that she thought it was "about time" someone wrote a book on marital equality. She appeared genuinely interested in the subject, and appeared to come prepared to talk about the issue. At the outset, she quickly rattled off a list of the unfair aspects in her marriage, all of which (arguably) centered around the division of the household labor. As she did so, Meg confidently depicted her husband's faults as common to men in general and reenacted numerous conversations with her spouse—two strategies that served to bolster her account of the inequality in her marriage.

Scott: I have some things to help guide us along, but I'm more interested in just hearing from you how things are going in your marriage and um, I'm not sure what the best place to start is. You could tell me how long you've been married and things like that maybe?

Meg: Ok. I've been married thirteen years as of July. Let's see. Gosh, how do I describe my relationship? Um, what I think that irritates me the worst, OK, is kids are mutual. My husband's startin' to learn this a little bit, but when I first got married to him he got angry because I wouldn't make his lunch for the day. OK? So

it's like, you know, and I'd always snap back at him-
when I was working at the time, "Well, why don't you
make my lunch?" [*gasps*] "What do you mean?," you
know. And "Nooo," you know, "if I'm gonna make
your lunch, then you can make mine." And he "Well,
I get up earlier than you." "Well, you get up earlier,
so- and I have to get up later for work, so why can't I
get more rest?" "Whatever," you know. So, so that-
that's like- that's not fair.

Scott: Right, OK.

Meg: And the kids' situation. Uh, diaper changing. That's
probably old as hell. If it's wet, that's OK. But if it's a
mess, "You change it. I can't do this, I'm gonna get
sick," you know. And they run off. "I'm gonna get
sick, I can't do this, I can't do this!" And they're holding the kids to the side "I can't to do this!" OK. So
mom changes the dirty diapers. That's not fair.

Scott: Yeah, yeah. That's- that's pretty much steady, that's
how it works?

Meg: Mm hmm. And there's even the sexist thing. The girl
baby, OK, 'cause I have a daughter. You know,
"Honey, she's wet. You change her." But when it was a
little boy, it wasn't hard. OK, he'll change a little boy,
but he doesn't want to change the little girl. "There's
something wrong, you want to look at it?" "OK." So
again, you know, it's- it's the gender. Um, another big
thing, dishes. Men don't like to do dishes...in marriages. I don't care. Sometimes they'll do 'em, but if
they do 'em it takes 'em hours and hours. And I don't
know why.

Scott: Just draggin' their feet or something

Meg: Mmm hmm, mm hmm. Or my husband does a good
thing. It's um, he's- he's the outside cleaner. He cleans
outside, I clean inside. OK, he works- I work Saturday
through Tuesday. That way we only have a babysitter
two days a week because he works Monday through
Friday. And on his- on my days off I keep the house
clean. By the time my four days of work comes- rolls

around, Wednesday comes, I have the day off, the house is a shambles.

Scott: Oh no.

Meg: "Honeeey, why couldn't you keep the house clean? You know, it's just a couple days." "I cleaned the outside! I cleaned the yard!... Well, if you don't want to do the yard- or if you want me to do the house, then you can do the yard." I'm "OK, I'll do the yard." "Uhhh." You know, and it's kinda, yeah, that's how he got outta cleaning the house this week. He did the whole yard.

Scott: Like raking and things like that?

Meg: Raking, hauling things off to the dump, anything but the house. And, you know what's funny is I only asked him to do one thing. I said, "Would you please mop the kitchen floor?" No, he didn't mop the floor. He got the outside of the house cleaned up.

Scott: You narrowed it down to one-

Meg: Yeah, so, and then there's the um, babysitting. . . . It was always my job to find a babysitter. OK. His job came first, mine came second. If we didn't have a babysitter, I either had to stay home or I had to find a babysitter, because his job was first. He made more money, etc. etc. Um, he goes to the store "I'm going to the store. Bye. . . . Um I gotta run over to Darrel's house or my friend's house. Bye." OK, me on the other hand, "Honey can you watch the kids—I'm going to the store." And then I stop and I say, "Well, why am I asking him to watch his own kids?" You know, why? It's like, but it's- I always find myself doing that. You know. But now, we're starting to work on that. He's getting better about that. He's um, he has, he was working at one job, and I was actually making more than him, which was rough. Because he has always been.. making more, he's always made more than I have. But when he went on to management, he had to work on a different schedule which would clash with mine. So he found a babysitter. Which was, I mean after being married for thirteen years that was a first. Cause I asked him, I said, "What are we gonna do about a babysitter?" And he goes, "I've already got it taken care of." And I just felt just floored, it was like "You're kidding me," you know. So he's totally taken on that responsibility, which shocked me. But I still, you know, when I go to the store, "Honey, watch the kids." Or, on his days off it will be "I am so tired of sitting around the house with the kids on my days off. I don't ever get no days off." And I'm like "OK, well, you know, on my days off what am I doing?" "You're at home." "With the kids," you know "it's the same thing." And he's like "No it's not, I need some time-" I said, "Well, so do I."

From making lunches, to changing diapers, to cleaning the house, to finding babysitters and watching the kids, Meg's narrative documented a consistent trend of unfairness. Though she was laughing about it and at times sounded like a stand-up comedian ("What is it with men, anyway?"), her tale seemed clearly centered on the reportedly unequal division of labor in her marriage.

Consider what Meg said would need to happen for her marriage to be more equal. Once again, she focused on daily household chores.

Meg: I'd want him to be more active as far as...Um, let's see. What would be nice, and I've tried to talk with him and instill it in his head, is for him to be more active and more responsible for what goes on in the house. As far as not "What are *you* cooking for dinner?" you know. How 'bout "What are we having for dinner, what can I help you with?" If he has the day off, pull something out of the refrigerator and say, "This is what I've planned for *us* to have for dinner." You know, "us." Not "I've planned for *you* to cook" or...like that. Um, what else. When he goes to the store, go to the store, you know. When I go to the store I don't want to have to say, "Will you watch the kids." You know, or "Take so-and-so with you or take this person with you" it's like No. "I'm going to the store, I'll be right back." Um, he's done the babysitting part pretty good, whereas, you know, cause, he's han-dled that pretty well. But it still sometimes feels like a

burden- I mean not a burden, my kids aren't a burden,
I don't mean to say that but, like if I have to work an
extra shift or something, you know, I'll have to find a
sitter. Which I guess is pretty reasonable because, but
if he has to work an extra shift he still tends to say,
"Well, I have to be gone on this day, I don't know
what you're gonna do." And I'll say, "Nuh uh. I'm
scheduled." You know, "You need to find a sitter."
Then he tones down and goes, "You're right." I've
worked at this job for almost three years, or a little
over three years actually. So he's understanding that
way. Um, just to be more active, more equal parts, you
know, just more active. Cause when I get home from
work I don't stop. I straighten the house out, I'm getting things going. When he gets home he lays down,
plops, and dies. It's like "Come on!" you know?

One way in particular that Chuck could be more active and responsible, Meg told me, was by helping her with the task of managing the
money and paying the bills. While some might view "controlling the
money" as a kind of decision-making privilege, Meg typified it as an
overwhelming responsibility.

Meg: My husband's more [of an] old-fashioned type, I don't
        know if they did it back in those days, but he doesn't
        take responsibility for paying bills. I mean I can be
        irresponsible, I flake off sometimes, we all do. But he
        more or less takes what he needs from his paycheck,
        gives me the rest and says, "Take care of the bills." So I
        pay the rent, I pay the utilities, I do all the, the home-
        work. So. . . .

Scott: OK. He just kinda leaves that up to you. So you feel
        like you're doing a lot of extra work there, is that how
        you kinda see that?

Meg: I feel like I have the weight of the world on my shoul-
        ders.

Scott: Really?

Meg: Yeah. Well because he doesn't see the bills. I see 'em.
        I'm the one who worries about when they get paid-

sure he's helping pay for them, but I'm the one that gets "Oh god, I gotta pay this bill by this date, I gotta pay this." It's just like when he hands over his check, he's handing over all the responsibilities of worrying about what goes where, and how much, and this and that. OK, and not have to think about the next month "Oh, there's this much left on this bill. Are they gonna do this or are they gonna do that." OK, so by handing over the check he's basically lost the responsibility. "She doesn't pay it, that's on her."

Scott: He doesn't even have to think about it anymore.

Meg: No, no. That's where it's unfair. I'd like, I would like to sit down and talk with him and say, "OK, every other month we'll do it this way." You know, let you do one month, I'll do one month. You know, cause it really gets hectic. [...] Because I got all this stuff. You know I've got all the bills, and going and talking to the land-lord, and making sure the car payments and the bills are paid, and then on top of that, "What are we having for dinner?" the kids are "Aaaahh!" [*makes a screaming noise*], you know, it's like "Aaaahh!" [*Meg makes another screaming noise for herself and pulls on her hair.*]

Scott: You've got a million rattling around in your mind I guess-

Meg: Yeah, I got my schedule from work rattling around, then got my Mary Kay business rattling around, you know, who has yet to order and who hasn't paid, and it's just like I want to take it [*makes a gesture as if throwing something away*] and say that's enough. You take over for a while. But I think he would pop.

Scott: Really?

Meg: I personally don't think he could handle the stress of paying all the bills. It scares me. It scares me to-, I would be afraid to death to hand him my paycheck and say "Here. Take care of the bills."

Scott: You'd be too stressed out or something.

Meg: Yes, I would be stressed out, I'd be going "Oh my god,
       are the lights gonna be on tomorrow?"

Meg's narrative thus presented a virtually unsolvable predicament: she experienced paying the bills as an extremely difficult task and would have preferred to share it with Chuck; Chuck, however, was reportedly disinclined and, more important, unable to take care of their finances.

Like Lucy, Meg discussed the inequality in her marriage happily, without sounding overly bitter or angry. This struck me as curious and I asked about it. In response, Meg first confirmed the gist of my rather leading question, then admitted to feeling some frustration and even resentment over the bill-paying task.

Scott: You've been talking about the inequality in your mar-
         riage, but it doesn't sound like you're, I mean these
         things aren't causing you a whole lot of anger and
         resentment and fights and things, it doesn't sound
         like. . . .

Meg: Me-, no um, not really. But I think frustration, frustra-
         tion especially with just the stress of everyday life, you
         know. I just don't- I kinda resent the fact that he can
         hand me a check and say "OK" and not have to worry
         about anything. Maybe he does worry, I don't know.
         But seemingly he doesn't. And that kinda, there's a
         little bit of resentment. You know, it's like, you know,
         'cause I would like that freedom, to be able to just
         come home and sit back and go "Yeah." You know,
         everything's paid for, everything's taken care of. And I
         don't get that. Nn nn.

Over the course of the interview Meg discussed many things: She explained that Chuck wouldn't let her go shopping after dark by herself, but that he was not nearly as controlling or dominating as she had seen some men be to their girlfriends and wives; that a past boyfriend physically abused Meg, but she was happy to know that Chuck would never do that to her; and that she wondered why men feel free to wake up their wives for sex in the middle of the night, but get cranky whenever women do the same to them.

At the end of the interview I asked Meg for advice: What would she ask people about if she were me? How would she go about doing these interviews? After discussing the pros and cons of using detailed questionnaires, Meg brought up the issue of bill paying one last time. In response to my questioning, she portrayed that issue as an enduring source of inequality in her marriage.

Meg: The main thing that sticks out in my head is them bills. "Take them bills. I don't want to see 'em. I don't want to see 'em. None of 'em. You get the mail, you pay the bills, you worry about it for a while-"

Scott: You think that's like the biggest inequality in your marriage or

Meg: I think so, oh definitely. I mean that's just kinda petty, but to me, you know, when you've got numbers in front of you, and you're trying to figure out what he's making, you know, that you got to put it with yours to get it, I'd just- I'd like to just take forty dollars out of my pay check, stick it in my pocket, say, "Here ya go, honey. Take care of the bills for this month." But then again that scares the crap out of me.

Scott: You think he might screw up or something.

Meg: "Oh the phone doesn't work. Honey, why is that?"

Scott: Yeah, that could cause some problems. OK.

Meg: Definitely.

Earlier in this chapter, we saw that for Wayne and Deborah the division of labor was merely one of the many issues through which an inequality of power manifested itself. Taking care of the yard or negotiating employment duties were merely some of the many different kinds of things that they and their spouses might disagree over, creating an opening for a dominant spouse to take control. In contrast, for Meg and Lucy housework stood out more as a crucial domain in its own right. But though these two women arguably defined marital equality in similar ways, a traditional research methodology—one that simply counted and compared the hours spouses spent on housework—would miss the different subjective senses the women give to various household "tasks." In the context of their discussions with me, Lucy and Meg both elevated a single task to the highest level. For Lucy it was the home improvements that her husband was well equipped but not inclined to make. If Sam would just paint the house, fix the bathroom, and so on, things would have been great—or at least, distinctly better. For Meg, paying the bills emerged as the issue that caused her the most stress and resentment. In her narrative, a fair division of this task alone would have signaled a much greater degree of equality in her marriage. Getting their husbands to help out with these tasks was the central dilemma that drove much of the plot in the stories Lucy and Meg constructed about the state of their respective relationships.[8]

THE DOMAIN OF "LOVE"

One of the less researched themes that can be found in qualitative (Kimball 1983; Schwartz 1994) and "how to" (Stapleton and Bright 1976) books on marital equality is the importance of being "best friends" with one's spouse, rather than casual roommates. Along with splitting up chores and decisions, having egalitarian sexual relations, and communicating fairly, to a few authors, "equality in marriage" requires that spouses enjoy each other's company and put each other first—above career and perhaps even family. In my interviews, the theme of being an intimate companion did arise as an important aspect of marital equality, though with different nuances and examples in each case. Moreover, unlike many researchers' conceptions of marital equality, some of my respondents elevated having a close, loving relationship with one's spouse to such importance that other potential aspects of equality paled in comparison. Dividing the labor and making decisions, for example, can be minor or irrelevant concerns to those who are focused on the intimacy they have or lack with their spouse. Eric, whose story I turn to next, was one such respondent.

Eric's Story: It's a Love Thing

When I met Eric for breakfast at a small restaurant, he appeared almost ecstatic about his marriage despite the relatively early hour. A thirty-one-year-old man who described his occupation as "property maintenance," Eric explained to me that he had "won the lottery" because he and his wife Molly were such compatible and loving partners. Early in the interview, Eric explicitly defined marital equality as two people being equally in love and equally committed to each other's happiness. At the very beginning of the conversation, though, he said much about "work." As parents to three young children, he and Molly had their "plate full."

Compounding the situation were two ongoing illnesses that required constant attention: Eric's live-in mother suffered from chronic depression and his son was afflicted with ADD and feelings of anxiousness. As a result, there was plenty of work to do and decisions to be made. But he soon described these equality issues as "little things" in comparison to the commitment and love the two of them felt for each other.

Eric: I think we have an equal marriage. I mean, we.. I mean we, you know by equality, I just mean that- that we both love, each with the same intensity, and we are both, you know, um, equally committed to, to the happiness of the other person. And, you know, so, you know, I mean, yeah, I don't know if I do more dishes than she does, or she has more say over what happens with the money, or I mean, it's like- like, you know, the little things. I don't know that you could parcel them out in equal piles, but, but the foundation of our commitment and our love and- and our vision for the future, you know, we're right there with each other. And, um, you know one of the funny things, or, you know, one of the things that we've talked about is this notion of, I don't know, you hear on TV or in articles or whatever about, you know, How do I explain it? Like "Being in a relationship and- and being married is good, but you have to have your identity. You know, you have to keep your, you know, you have yourself and then your relationship. And you have to keep some individuality, keep some autonomy and not depend-" and from, I mean, I don't know where in the relationship, but there was this time where we went "I am totally dependent on you, and who I am . . . is because of you. I mean without you, I'm not who I am," you know. So, there isn't that, I mean I don't- I don't have, I don't have like this separate part that I just- of myself that I hold- that I hold, you know, as my individual so I don't get lost in the relationship. I'm totally lost in the relationship. I don't, I don't know how to define myself outside of this woman. You know, I wouldn't know how to live. You know, when I had my vasectomy, um, the doctor said "Well, are you sure you want to do this?" And, so one of the questions was, "So if next week your wife and your three kids are on a plane and they crash and die, are you gonna, are you gonna start-, you know, you're gonna be fixed and this is not really a reversible process." And I just looked at him and said, "I'd be so messed up in the head for the rest of my life I couldn't even- I mean the last thing I'm gonna think about is having more kids." You know what I mean?

When I asked Eric if he ever compared his marriage to other marriages, he said he knew only one couple with a relationship similar to his. Though the couple was much older, they reportedly exhibited a closeness that reminded Eric of his intimate bond with Molly.

Scott: I was wondering, Eric, um, do you ever kinda compare yourself to other couples or look at them as having equal or un-

Eric: For the first time, uh, it was maybe a month ago, my, my wife's in a um, graduate uh, writing program. She's getting her MFA in creative writing through um, a college out of state. So she does uh, twice a year she goes there for two weeks. And she met a woman there who became a friend of hers, and blah blah blah blah blah, and they ended up coming to visit us. Her and her husband. And they're like... mid-sixties, early seventies-, I mean they're considerably a different generation than us, but this couple was the first couple I'd ever met who seemed like, you know, had a similar relationship. We, I mean, we've gone through these last eleven years and looked around us and gone "I've never met anybody-," there's no pattern, there's no template, there's, you know, we're not, we're not trying to copy our parents' relationships which were totally fucked up, or, we're not-, I mean, there's, I mean, we've been sort of blazing the trail ever since the get-go. So, no, you know, I don't, I don't know anybody, besides this couple who has ever had a similar relationship.

Scott: Ok, ok. So, um, they seem to have the same sort of equal-

Eric: They did, yeah, I guess it was a love thing, you know.
          But they just... very dependent on each other, I mean
          very close, and very loving, and very appreciative, and
          very, you know, when he, you know, they had their-
          their little jokes with each other, and they- they really
          understood each other.

Next I asked Eric if there was anything that could potentially disrupt
his equal marriage. In response to my question, Eric spoke of his
employment choices and his ego. He portrayed these kinds of issues as
possible obstacles to what he really valued, his close relationship with his
wife. In the end, he used a biological metaphor to try to better explain
that relationship.

Scott: OK.... Are there any specific things you have to look
          our for that might disrupt your relationship, um, espe-
          cially in terms of equality or

Eric: Well,... yeah, I guess. Well, like recently, we just, we
          were living in Wisconsin, well, we were living in
          Eugene let's say. We met in, just outside Eugene in a
          small town, in 1988ish. Moved to Eugene. Lived here
          until 1994, moved to Michigan, and just came back.
          Just got here a month or two ago. And, and I had to
          find work. And, I got two job offers. One that, as we
          were coming here I was saying, "Oh, this is what I
          want to do. I wanna, in the next stage of my life I
          wanna do construction and I wanna work with this
          kinda crew." You know, so I had this whole picture in
          my head. And one job offer that I got, was basically
          exactly what I'd said. And the other job I got was basi-
          cally what I had been doing in Michigan. OK? And
          the one that was the same as what I was doing in
          Michigan, you know, seemed like it would keep me
          around more. I mean like I'd have a company car and,
          and probably a cell phone so that I could, you know,
          get calls or call home or whatever. And the hours
          would be a little bit, it would be a little less travel
          time. You know, maybe fifteen, twenty minutes a day.
          And, and I, inside myself I went, "You know, this
          would keep me closer to home, but the other job is

what I said I wanted to do. For me." And so I made *that* choice. And for me that was the wrong choice. Because what I love, what I am, is- is- is being home. It's being with my wife. Being with my kids. Working on the house. I mean that, that's it. And for me, every decision needs to be made in terms of "What's gonna keep me closer to that?" Not, you know, what-, not this other thing. And so, I guess ego, you know, I mean that's always, in anybody's life, that's, that's a killer. You know, "Well, I'm gonna, I'm gonna, you know, make something of myself. I'm gonna show the world how wonderful I am." You know? And, I mean I think that's something you gotta look out for. Because it's not about ego. It's not about you being the best, or you being needed by your partner, or having some, I mean, there's a difference between dependence and like dependence. You know? I mean, we are dependent on each other, but we're not... I don't know

Scott: It's not like she's maybe financially, like she has no choice, or uh-

Eric: Yeah it's not, it's... it's like a symbiotic relationship rather than, you know, like a, a, a host and a dependent. You know?

When I asked if Eric and Molly ever discussed the issue of equality explicitly, Eric described equality as an unstated element of his marriage. He contrasted his relationship with those involving dominant and abusive husbands. Because he and Molly thought of each other as equals, he said, they were more like companions "traveling along the path of life together" than owner-and-object. Eric also suggested that he and his wife were right for each other because they were intellectual equals of the same age who shared similar goals. Finally, when I commented that Eric and Molly seemed to have a lot in common, and asked if they like to doing things together for fun, Eric claimed that if he had his choice he would spend all day with his wife.

Eric: I mean, we do the basics, we like to go out to eat together, we like to go on walks together, we like to garden. We will, you know, we quilt together. You know, so, so yeah, we do. I mean there's, she writes and I do woodworking, and I don't write and she doesn't do woodworking, you know but, beyond that, I mean, if we could do everything together we would. You know there's those people, haven't you ever heard those people who say, "I like to go to work because it just gives me time to get my head together"? You know, it's like if I had to spend all-day-every-day with her, I would. And if I- if we could have a business at home and just be, you know, do it together? Any day, hands down.

Scott: That's great. You guys really get along. . . .

Eric: So . . . and- and- and I have to say, I don't know if it's divine providence or dumb luck or work. But you know I don't care. I got it, and there it is, you know. I won the lottery.

Eric was not the only respondent to discuss the importance and relevance of having an intimate relationship with one's spouse. Nor was this theme unique to people who felt they had a close, loving marriage. One of my respondents who claimed to have an unequal marriage, for example, defined equality as getting along so well with your partner that "You just click." What he longed for was "someone who you look forward to seeing at the end of the day, or whenever you see each other." Comments such as these reminded me of the "best friends" version of marital equality that I had read about in the self-help and scholarly literature (Kimball 1983; Schwartz 1994; Stapleton and Bright 1976), though my respondents applied the theme to unique circumstances and imbued with it with specific subjective senses.

The case of Eric already has moved us some distance from the more common scholarly definitions of marital equality—primarily power and the division of labor. To me, his story starts us down the road toward the "unfamiliar" end of the familiar/unfamiliar spectrum of stories that I heard in my interviews. In the next chapter, I present four more tales that seemed to fall even further outside the boundaries of conventional scholarly discourse about equality in marriage.

5

Narrating Marital Equality
Unfamiliar Domains of Relevance

The previous chapter presented the stories of respondents whose narratives somewhat resembled the themes that marital scholars have propounded. Here, chapter 5 discusses respondents whose narratives differed more dramatically from mainstream definitions of marital equality. Some of my respondents told tales that, arguably, highlighted idiosyncratic forms of equality that haven't been the subject of mainstream quantitative surveys or qualitative interviews in the marital equality literature. While conventional sociological readers may be tempted to dismiss the following stories as delusional, illogical, or inaccurate, I would argue that these kinds of "aberrant" perspectives deserve attention if scholars want to develop an approach to marital equality that remains sensitive to the experiences and viewpoints of actual married people.

Alicin's Story: The Importance of Intellect

Intelligence has not been a central issue in previous research on marital equality. It does not appear on any scale that measures power or the division of labor. It is simply not a major component in mainstream social science definitions of what constitutes an equal marriage.[1] Nevertheless, "Alicin," a thirty-five-year-old social worker and mother to two children, suggested to me that the major form of inequality in her marriage was her husband's intellectual inferiority. According to her, this inequality had not only been a constant source of dissatisfaction in its own right, it had also been the cause of other problems—including other problematic inequalities—that had plagued her failing marriage with her spouse "Kevin." Intelligence was thus an organizing theme for Alicin, a domain of relevance that shaped the sense of her marital troubles as she explained them to me.

Alicin contacted me in response to a newspaper advertisement soliciting wives in unequal marriages. After a brief phone conversation, we met at a local restaurant where we sat in a booth talking and sipping sodas. I began the interview with a somewhat awkward open-ended question, but that was enough to prompt her to explain the main point of her narrative: her husband was not a smart man.

Alicin: Do you have like questions that you ask or

Scott: No, I'm more interested in hearing kinda, you know, in your own words what's going on in your marriage and um, you know, the inequality you're experiencing and things like that

Alicin: OK. Well-

Scott: I mean you could start- you don't have to- you can tell me a little bit about your relationship if you want first

Alicin: OK. Yeah, um, well I'll tell you first off that I'm separated. [...] So that's um the direction that's taking. And um, we'll probably be getting a divorce before too long.

Scott: How long were you married before

Alicin: Nine years last week. [...] And I'm amazed that it lasted that long. Um, it's probably something that never should have started but you know, you get into it and then you start having kids and it's hard to back out once you get heading down that road but.. um, the inequality that we have is um, ..I think uh, probably it's mostly intellectual inequality, and then everything else just kinda stems from that. Um, because we have earning inequality and.. you know other basic differences but that's something that has caused him insecurity from the beginning, because he's always said, "You're smarter than I am" and, you know, "Are you gonna leave? What's gonna happen?" And so that

I think made him a little bit suspicious sometimes, which would really bother me. You know, if I got home fifteen minutes late, "Where are you?" you know, "Where were you?" And I, and I have to say "You know, fifteen minutes is not a big deal and" you know, I don't question him if he's gone late and, and it came from that insecurity.

Right away Alicin presented the point of her story: the inequality in her marriage is "mostly intellectual inequality, and then everything else just kinda stems from that." She then quickly alluded to other relationship problems that seemed related to Kevin's weaker cognitive skills, especially his "insecurity." While it is easy to imagine that some wives and analysts might interpret Kevin's questioning behavior ("Where were you?") as an exercise of power or control, in Alicin's tale it was cast as the result of Kevin's insecurity due to his knowledge that she was smarter than him.

As Alicin's narrative proceeded, I learned how Kevin's lack of acumen had also caused economic difficulties in their marriage. He not only earned less money than Alicin would have liked, in certain years he actually lost half the money that she made.

Alicin: The year before we got married, he had somehow managed to be in a position where he made pretty decent money for a kid with a high school education, and, but he actually was unemployed when we met. And when we got married he was making minimum wage. [...] He made a lot of changes in his line of work. And eventually he decided that he wanted to be self-employed, which was um, okay, you know, I wanted to be the supportive wife and say "Follow your dream" and all that

Scott: A little bit of a gamble?

Alicin: A big gamble. And he borrowed um, some money partly from my family, you know, and other people but, um, I kind of had, you know, I had this ideal that we had this equal marriage and even though I knew it was unequal I- I always wanted to believe it was more equal than it was. And so I- I think I kind of blinded to my- myself some of his limitations and um. . . . I- I-

> I probably should have put a stop to the self-employ-
> ment early on, because he really didn't have the- the
> knowledge to make it work. And so, um, that was-, he
> had a couple years where . . . I made the money and he
> lost half of it.

When I asked what line of work Kevin had tried to pursue, Alicin's
answer again highlighted Kevin's putative low intelligence (in particular
his deficient math skills) and its negative effect on his businesses.

> In the beginning he did kind of a small contracting
> business. And he had- actually he went and got his
> contracting license and everything but um, he ran into
> problems with that because he- he didn't have enough
> capital to support what he was doing. And- and I
> think looking back part of it was he didn't really know
> how to do accurate estimates. I mean something as
> simple as going in and calculating the area, you know,
> how much stuff he was going to need. He didn't really
> know how to do it. And I didn't realize the- the extent
> of that problem for a long time. And then the next
> thing he tried to do was a carpet cleaning business,
> modeled after his brother-in-law's business, which was
> successful but, again, that same basic math problem
> got in the way.

Alicin next linked the intellectual inequality in their marriage to differences in their familial and educational backgrounds. She and Kevin's
marital inequality, in Alicin's causal account, was thus deeply rooted in
the past. Over the years the inequality produced "most of the problems"
they had experienced, including communication problems.

> I went to college and he, you know, scraped through
> high school. And he's very proud of that, you know.
> He should be. Because he's the only one in his family
> to graduate from high school. So, you know, we had
> very different backgrounds too. My family expects
> everybody to get a master's degree. His family, you
> know, no one goes to finish high school. So . . . big dif-
> ference in that background. . . . Yeah, I think most-
> most of the problems that we have as far as- commu-
> nication problems and everything, you know. I con-

> tinually get frustrated because I want to have a conver-
> sation, you know, that is beyond I think what he is
> interested in and what he can really um, participate in
> very well. I have a hard time following his logic some-
> times because I just don't know where it is [*laughs*].
> Which makes me feel a lot of guilt because I think,
> "Gosh, you know, I'm basically- I-" there's an alcohol
> issue too but I think really, you know, that's kind of
> my front, I can blame everything on his drinking but
> the real underlying problem is um, all that just exacer-
> bates the main thing which is ..I just need somebody I
> can relate to on a better level.

Even Kevin's drinking—potentially a tellable cause of marital dissolution
by itself—was in Alicin's story portrayed as insignificant next to "the real
underlying problem" of the intellectual inequality. Alcohol was merely
(to put it in statistical terms) a moderating variable that strengthened the
trouble-producing power of Kevin's low IQ.

Alicin paused and I asked her if we were covering "the main inequalities" in her marriage or if there was "anything else." She responded to
my prompting by mentioning the more "familiar" issues of decision
making and the division of labor, discussing the latter at greater length.
She described Kevin's contributions to child care and housework as
unequal to hers.

> I mean we're, we tried to contribute equally as far as,
> you know, decision making and that kind of thing.
> But um, you know, and child care- well there's
> another inequality thing also. [*laughs*] He- he's gotten
> much better over the years but in the first few years
> when we had children I was very resentful of what I
> thought of as inequality with child care responsibili-
> ties. Um, . . . pretty much you know he had that idea,
> he grew up with the idea that the mom is in charge of
> the kids. Regardless of the fact that we both worked
> the same number of hours and, you know, that whole
> thing. It's up to me and if I wanted help I had to ask.
> [. . .] And uh, his, his idea of when we earlier got,
> early in the marriage, in the first couple years, he, he
> said "Well you know my contribution is I'll keep the
> cars maintained. And I'll, you know, I'll wash the car,

I'll mow the lawn and, and um, you take care of
kids." Well, I didn't think that was very equal because
how often do you change the oil on the car, you
know? And you don't mow the lawn in the winter
and, [*laughs*], and here I am doing laundry every day.
So, but that eventually evolved into I think a lot
better situation.

Before discussing child care, Alicin had alluded to the issue of power
by mentioning decision making. Next she returned to that issue. She
told a story about power, but one that is incorporated into her larger
story of intellectual inequality. Alicin ultimately would have liked to
share control of their finances, but she was afraid Kevin could not handle
the complexity of the responsibility.

A stressful thing for me was trying to um, trying
to...I don't know, I had this inner idea of how the
power thing ought to be, and this idea of what I
thought he ought to think the power was. You know.
Because I was raised also, you know, that the man
needs to think he's in charge, you know. Really. That's
the idea I got from my family, is even if the woman's
in charge, the man needs to think he's in charge. So I
really struggled to- to get over that and try and be
on...on better terms. It was pretty tough. Because I
felt like I ought to be in charge 'cause I had the ability
to be in charge. [*laughs*] Just, you know, something
not too great for me to say maybe but. [...] For a
while he paid the bills, and he started bouncing checks
and things and I said, "You know, you're under a lot of
stress, and you're working a lot of hours, how about I
take over the bills?" [*laughs*] And so I took them over
and um, and I did that for a long time and then when
our, we started having some other financial problems
partly because of these changes in jobs, the self-
employment and all that. Then I was really stressed
out about paying bills because the money just wasn't
there. And he said, "Oh you're really stressed out.
How about if I take over the bills?" And I-, and then I
thought, "What do I say? Because I am really stressed
out." And that's what I said to him but I didn't want

> to say, "I don't trust you with the money." And so um,
> he did do it for a little while.

Thus, in Alicin's story, housework and child care played a rather insignificant role in her depiction of the inequality in her marriage. Power, in turn, arose as a consequential issue to her, but primarily as a yet another area in which Kevin's intellectual inequality had caused problems. Unlike much conventional research, intelligence took precedence over power and the division of labor. As further evidence, consider what Alicin did when I asked if she ever compared her marriage to other people's marriages, such as family or friends, in terms of how equal or unequal they were. Once again the answer that was given centered around the importance of intellect. Kevin's lack of smarts made for boring conversations and a limited social life, in comparison with other more "egalitarian" relationships Alicin knew of.

> Um, you know, I compared our marriage, for example,
> to some friends that we had. Um, neighbors who had I
> thought a pretty equal marriage. They were really just
> equal in so many ways. And I, and I was envious of
> that. You know. They enjoyed each other's company so
> much more than my husband and I, and so I really did
> envy that. And same thing with my dad, he remarried,
> he remarried somebody who had so many more um,
> things in common with him, and equal in terms of
> education and, you know, the types of jobs that they
> do. [...] And he's really happy in that marriage and I
> wish we had something like that. And honestly I wish I
> had someone I could take and, and... you know, take
> and meet some of my other friends and be able to have
> a group conversation, but instead I-, and I'm kind of
> ashamed of this, but I was- I was embarrassed to have
> him around. [...] Even if some- something as simple
> as, you know, one night we went to some friends to
> play Trivial Pursuit and it was painful to watch him
> play, for everyone in the room. [...] I feel like it really
> limits the types of things that we can do together. And
> so I got really dissatisfied with that. [...] For example,
> like um, we started going to church at this certain
> church, and I was really, you know, I wanted to talk
> about it, and talk about different aspects of what was

going on and the history of it. And he really couldn't
get beyond saying things like "A lot of women go
there." [*laughs*] And so I was really frustrated because I
couldn't, I couldn't have that type of discussion. About
things that were important to me.

When I asked Alicin what it would take for her relationship to be
more egalitarian, a comparison with child care emerged. In contrast to
disparate child care workloads, the intellectual inequality in Alicin's marriage was portrayed as something that probably could not be changed or
at least as something that her husband was reluctant to work on. Kevin's
unwillingness to complete a community college class was described as
"the final straw" in the coming dissolution of their marriage.

Scott: So for it to have, what would have been more like the
          ideal situation, or a more equal relationship? The
          main thing would have been for him to have been,
          maybe if he had been more educated or just generally
          smarter or something?

Alicin: Yeah. And it kinda, I hate to have it sound like it just
          boils down to that but I really think that that was the
          root of most of our problems. [...] And actually, um,
          I had hoped last year that maybe it could change a
          little bit. He got excited about going back to school.
          He was gonna take some classes at [a community col-
          lege], and, and I was so excited for him. And he was
          excited, and I said, "Go for it!" you know. And he
          worried that we couldn't afford it I said, "I don't care,
          we'll find a way to afford it." And um, and he had me
          help him with some of his homework because he
          didn't understand it, they didn't go over it enough in
          class or whatever, and I was willing to do whatever, to
          help him get it. But um, and actually I think this was
          like the final straw for me, and when he dropped out
          of Effective Study Skills because he thought he knew
          more than the teacher and he, I think it was really
          difficult for him. And I said, "I can't, this is just more
          than I can handle."

From virtually beginning to end, intellectual inequality seemed to
dominate Alicin's tale far more than any other issue. Her story of her

marriage differed dramatically from the stories told by Wayne, Deborah, Lucy, and Meg, and it certainly would differ from the kind of analysis a conventional researcher might provide. A curious reader might also wonder what competing interpretations Alicin's husband Kevin would offer. Would he really agree that he was less intelligent than his wife? What might he say (for example) about his unsuccessful businesses? Would he agree that these failures were due to his lack of smarts or would he place the responsibility on external factors out of his control, such as bad luck, a competitive marketplace, or unreasonable customers? Regarding his supposedly poor conversational skills, would Kevin dispute that "fact" by invoking his lack of interest in certain topics or his occasionally "quiet nature," rather than concurring with Alicin that he was not on his wife's "level"?

From a constructionist perspective, it would be interesting, but is not necessary to know whether Kevin would agree with Alicin or not. Kevin cannot serve as a "fact checker" because neither person's account would provide a pure reflection of reality. As I argued in chapter 1, people can only produce selective and constructive *interpretations* of social affairs because of "the principal ambivalence of the meaning of all social phenomena" (Schutz 1964, p. 227). In presenting Alicin's version of her marriage, my main goal is simply to demonstrate the difference between investigating equality-meanings and imposing equality-meanings. On its own, her account is sufficient for that purpose.[2]

Matthew's Story: Modeling the Bible

While most sociologists take a secular view of social life, spirituality does play a significant role in the everyday lives of many laypersons. And if religion is important to the people whose behavior one is trying to understand, then it must be given a place in one's research. This has not been the case with the study of equality in marriage, as in family studies more generally (Daly 2003, p. 776). Sociological articles or books that deal explicitly with marital equality have not tended to include a strong religious element.[3] "Being responsible for the spiritual well-being of the children," for example, has not been a common "household task" or "decision-making privilege" measured in previous studies. In contrast, for a few of my respondents the issue of marital equality was portrayed as inseparable from their religious beliefs.

Matthew, the thirty-five-year-old teacher whose narrative I present next, was one such respondent. He claimed that his equal marriage was based on the model put forward in the Bible: Wives are to submit to their husbands, husbands relinquish their lives to their wives, and each spouse honors and elevates the other. Matthew described the mundane aspects of equality—decision making, housework, child care, and other "nuts and bolts" of living—as mere "offshoots" that stemmed from this deeper "biblical framework."

Matthew started his story rather tentatively, acknowledging that others may have different ideas about equality, even speaking self-consciously as if his faith were something that might shock or alarm some people. He first focused on the way he and his wife, Nancy, made familial decisions: They tried to achieve consensus on all major decisions, but each of them could make unilateral decisions when the situation called for it. He gave an example suggesting that if Nancy had been with the kids all day, she might know more than he would about a problem involving them and thus could better resolve the situation. Soon, however, he decided to "bare his soul" to me and discussed the "deeper" foundation of the equality he perceived in his marriage. Matthew first began to formulate his biblical tale in response to my question asking if their decision-making practices were the major component of equality in his marriage.

> You know, I'm gonna get real honest with you, and I'm gonna bare my soul. Uh, I don't know that- for me that isn't the major component. I think it is an offshoot of something much deeper. [...] I think it has to do with value systems. Both my wife and I are Bible-believing Christians. Ok? And that, you know, that's gonna raise a lot of eyebrows and perk a lot of ears, but the fact of the matter is we came to a marriage both believing the same thing, both um, having the same sort of values, and that lends itself I think to traveling in one direction versus another. So we're both on the same value path, and that makes decision making so much easier. You know what I mean? [...] And that's why, I think, that's where that trust comes in. The ability to say "I relinquish that. Because, you know, I- I trust that you're seeing it the way that I see it. I trust that you're not gonna go half-cocked. That you've researched, you know, the situation. That you've, that you understand what's going on in-" see

it's, so this biblical framework. So I think, to me, that is the core component, that we both, we both have a deep, you know, seek a deeper relationship with God. That brings us toward a deeper relationship with each other.

At this point, I gave Matthew a chance to demur from the concept of equality and to focus perhaps more directly on his biblical framework. In response, he asserted that the biblical model of wives submitting and husbands relinquishing does lead to "a certain equality," an egalitarian-ism that also accords with God's view of men and women being created as equals.

Scott: So um, would you call this a form of equality, a deep form of equality, or is it not related so much to it-

Matthew: You know, I guess, yeah, you know every- I look at it this way. You know, for every belief system, for every way of looking at the world, for every way of behaving, you have to have some standard. You know. That standard can be warped off this way or warped off that way. But some- at some point you have some basis for basing your rationale for all the behaviors and all the decisions that you make. We've decided that the Bible would be that stan-dard for code and conduct of our lives. And uh, particularly, there- I don't know if you're familiar with this, but there's a book in the Bible called Ephesians, OK? Where the Apostle Paul wrote to the church in Ephesians. And he describes some, he described um, man and wife relationships. And this is what he said. He said that the wife should submit to the man, but the man should love the wife as Christ loved the church. And he goes on to explain that in submitting to the man, that doesn't mean she's a doormat. But that the man, in- in loving the- loving the- his wife as the church, well what did Christ do for the church? Well he was willing to die for the Church. He was willing to give up his life. So I as a man, What am I supposed to do with my life? I'm supposed to be willing to give up my

life, which includes time, money, effort. Basically
my life is not my own anymore. See? And so you
get this cyclic thing where she is submitting, but
then I'm giving up everything, everything in my
life. And so, what does that lead to? It leads to certain harmony and certain equality because, again,
this idea of submission isn't one of doormat. This
idea of submission is "OK, you're the head of the
household," but then I come right around and say,
"You know what, Honey, I'm to give up my life
for you." That means time, money, effort. Time
could mean "I'm gonna sit down and listen to
what you have to say. I'm gonna respect what you
have to say. So please tell me what's going on." So
you get this, you know, this thing where it just
generates this sense of helping each other, [...]
that sense of submitting and resubmitting [to each
other] if you will.

With some prompting from me, Matthew elaborated on the different ways that his biblical approach to marriage related to his life. He discussed matters that some scholars might consider to be germane to the
real "core" aspect of equality, the division of labor.

Scott: So there's um, does this model have to do mostly
            with making decisions then? Or it sounds like- I
            think you said that was just one offshoot-

Matthew: That was one offshoot. You know, making decisions,
            there's certainly, there's certainly more to life I think
            than just making decisions. But, you know, maybe
            it has to do with uh, with stuff around the house.
            You know I mean just chores around the house.
            [...] We call ourselves "Team Hayden." And every-
            body [parents and children alike] sort of has a job
            to do, you know. That doesn't mean we always
            function in that one particular area. [...] Those
            chores need to get done by somebody. You know,
            somebody has to step up to the plate. And that's
            where usually the parents should come in and say,
            "OK, you know, this this this needs to get done.

> Who wants to do this?" Kind of distribute it. And
> then the parent takes re- one of the responsibilities
> and then Team Hayden goes to work, you know.
> And that's kind of how we've organized it. Once
> again, the equality part, you know, and that sub-
> mission is, you know, "I'm gonna do this just
> simply because it needs to get done. And I'm not
> gonna hassle about it, I'm not gonna throw a fit,
> I'm just gonna do that."

Earlier in the interview, Matthew alluded to the significance of "elevating" his wife. When I asked him to compare his marriage to other people's
relationships he discussed this "elevating"—respecting, supporting, prais-
ing, and so on— as part of the "job" of following the biblical model.

> Um, it's very disturbing to me when, even in jest,
> even in jest, you know, some of my very good
> friends or people I know, they'll say something even
> in jest about their wife in public that . . . you know,
> all that "My woman and blah blah blah blah blah."
> Um, or "I gotta get all over her for that" and that
> type of thing. I made a pact with myself a long
> time ago that I would never run my wife down in
> public. That doesn't mean we don't have disagree-
> ments or arguments, but that's always in private.
> That's between us. But never in public would I run
> my wife down because my idea is to seek to elevate
> her. I want people to know what a great person she
> is, Ok? Because you know, we all make mistakes.
> But on the average my wife is about the kindest,
> wisest soul you'll ever meet. You know. And I don't
> want- I don't want to run her down. Cause my-,
> you know, my job is to elevate her. Her job is to
> elevate me. Our successes are each others', together.

Matthew's story reminded me of Gubrium's (1993) examination of
nursing home residents' stories about the quality of their lives and the care
they received in their assisted living environments. In his interviews,
Gubrium found that the quality of care that respondents received was often
a minor issue to them. This was especially true for those focused on "lovin'
the Lord." For these particular residents, daily comforts or irritations were

almost irrelevant compared to such otherworldly concerns as everlasting life. The religious respondents whom I spoke with, however, found the issue of marital equality more germane than Gubrium's respondents found the quality of their care. In Matthew's case especially, his spiritual faith provided him with a model for an equal marriage that, in his account, went much deeper than the kinds of concerns one might find in sociological research, such as making everyday decisions and doing housework.

Clearly, my recruitment strategies and interview questions, at least partly, may have helped elicit the responses given to me. Unlike Gubrium, I asked numerous pointed questions about the topic of marital equality, rather than focusing on life in general. Thus, it is important not to treat Matthew's and my other respondents' narratives as static representations of what was "really" in their minds or what was "really" going on in their relationships. My respondents' lengthy descriptions may have resonated better with their own experiences and concerns than, say, a scholarly story generated via a set of fixed-response survey questions; however, my respondents' autobiographical stories were not the only and not necessarily the best tales that could have been told about their lives. A different interview (or an entirely different interactional setting) could have significantly altered the marital accounts I heard even from respondents themselves. Context is intimately connected to the production of descriptions (see Gubrium and Holstein 1995).

I should also point out that although Matthew's story was by far the most thoroughly developed religious narrative I heard, his was not the only spiritual account. One woman, for example, also mentioned the Bible as an important guiding source in her reportedly egalitarian marriage. At one point she referred to a different passage—one about loving your neighbor as yourself—but she managed to make it relevant to her marriage in her own way: "So the closest neighbor that I have is [my husband] right now, so I have to love him with all I have. To support him, to encourage him, to help him. He does the same thing." The lesson for future researchers is to realize that, and study how, married people may creatively draw on religious teachings as they interpret the state of equality in their marriages (see also Bartkowski 2001; Bartkowski and Read 2003).

Courtney's Story: Living Life in Different Styles

As I mentioned in chapters 3 and 4, being close friends is described by some qualitative scholars as an essential feature of egalitarian marriages

(Kimball 1983; Schwartz 1994). While "friendship" itself is an extremely broad theme, for these authors it included matters such as spouses enjoying each other's company and putting each other first—above other relationships and above work. Common interests and perspectives have also been described as an aspect of friendship and hence egalitarian marriages. Schwartz (1994, p. 152), for example, has argued that these shared proclivities are as much *a result* as a cause of being egalitarian: Husbands and wives who share work and child care responsibilities live in overlapping worlds and so think alike and have more to talk about.

For one of my respondents, however, merely "being different"— having different personalities, philosophies, likes, and hobbies—was depicted not as a minor subtheme of friendship but as a major form of inequality in its own right. "Courtney" was a twenty-eight-year-old newlywed (married four months, with a daughter from a previous boyfriend) who responded to my advertisement aimed at wives in equal marriages. She described herself as very happy with her husband Tom, and said that her relationship was equal in several respects. She explained that Tom worked more hours outside the home and made more money, but she did a little more housework and child care. As she put it: "I do more of the house crap and I still go to work, and he does a little house crap and does more of the outside work. So we feel, in that sense, it's pretty equal."

Along with the equality in their marriage, however, there was a large inequality that reportedly caused recurrent arguments between Courtney and Tom. The two of them had very unequal lifestyles, Courtney explained. They made a very unlikely couple: He looked like a "frat boy" and thought and acted like a conservative; she was an open-minded, alternatively dressed recreational drug user. Although I came to the interview expecting to talk about marital equality, Courtney seemed most interested in discussing this putative inequality in her relationship with Tom.

The interview began with Courtney explaining how she and Tom were first introduced. Because of their obvious differences, she did not initially think of him as a romantic possibility, but soon after they started dating they liked each other so much they knew they would get married.

> Courtney: Well we met through a friend at- at my work, where I was working at the time. Um . . . we . . . I didn't even- we didn't start dating right away. Took about a month. He had to talk me into it. [*laughter*] And

he finally had to trick me. He tricked me into going out with him on a double date, and then that was it. After that we started dating. And it was about a month later, two months later, we were like, I mean, he goes "You know we're gonna get married." I was like, "Yeah I know." He's like, "Okay." And that- that was that. [...] I was doing retail at the time, at The Gap.

Scott: And he worked there too?

Courtney: No, actually a friend- this girl that he was friends with worked there. And it was really strange because she- she called him up and said, "I have somebody I want you to meet." But it wasn't me, it was this other girl. And so he came in to meet her but met me before her, and then met her and was like "Oh. Well I want to date her instead." And I was like...he's very- you know, he's very different from me. He's very conservative. He looks like a big frat boy. [...] He's very straight and conservative looking. So it was.. not in my lifestyle at all.

Scott: Really?

Courtney: Mm hmm. So...I think that's probably I think our biggest inequality in our marriage. Our lifestyles are very different. He's never done drugs, he's never smoked a cigarette. He's never even been drunk once in his whole life.

Scott: Oh my gosh, OK.

Courtney: I know! That's just crazy! [...] So, um, that's- that's what we- you know, we don't fight about very many things, we don't fight about money. OK, we get stressed out about money, and we get- we have fights about other things, but we don't fight about money. We fight about um...just about...just about our differences in our- in our- in our opinions and um.. He's very closed-minded.

In the ensuing conversation, Courtney proceeded to explain how the "biggest inequality" in their marriage—her and Tom's divergent attitudes toward dressing, drugs, and alcohol—also carried over to life more generally. She characterized Tom as being "extremely judgmental" compared to her, though he was reportedly "improving" as he grew older and spent more time with her. Then Courtney traced the differences in their personalities back to their childhoods. Tom's upbringing was depicted like a 1950s sitcom taking place in an idyllic small town, while hers was at "the other end of the spectrum." Her familial experiences and big city education, Courtney argued, led her to a different mind-set, especially with regard to drug use.

> Courtney: I mean he had- seriously, he had like the- the Ward-and-June-Cleaver-type household. He had like this perfect childhood. [...] I mean he can count on one hand how many times he was spanked in his whole life. Like three times. [...] And the worst thing that ever happened to him in his whole childhood was that his dad's business...like money was tight for like one year. That was the worst memory he has of growing up. That's it.

> Scott: That's it. Money was tight.

> Courtney: Money was tight for a year....Can you imagine? [...] My childhood was totally different. I mean like the other end of the spectrum. [...] He grew up in this little tiny town, and I grew up in this- in this big city. It was just really weird....Um, but his lifestyle is totally different. Like I said he never smoked, never did drugs. Um.

> Scott: These are all things you've done?

> Courtney: Oh yeah. I still smoke. So. And I mean this is [city], everybody smokes pot....And so I couldn't even believe it when he said he never even tried it, he had no desire to try it. And so he has um...So when I talk about- and I'm pretty open- I'm always open with him. If I went out and like got drunk and did some stuff I'd come home and I told him exactly what I did. I don't care. He hates it. He gets mad, but I'm not gonna keep anything from him. So, it's um, it's been hard for him to deal with that. Cause I mean I did drugs...like all the time when I was in high school. That's all I did. And I told

> him. And he- and he was just like "Well I didn't-"
> you know. In high school everybody I knew was a
> drug dealer and a junkie. You know what I mean?
> It was that kind of school. So he has no idea what
> you're talking about, cause he's never, you know,
> lived through that.

Still unaware of the extent of Courtney's drug use, I tentatively asked about the issue. In response, she reiterated her contention that her and Tom's divergent lifestyles formed the "biggest inequality" in their marriage.

Scott: So, do you still kinda want to do some of those things and it bothers him, or is this just when you talk about the past?

Courtney: Oh, I still go out and do whatever I want. I go out- I only have like- I only have really two friends. My girl- my best friend and her boyfriend. Those are like the only two other people I hang out with. And so, it's usually like me and her, and like we go out and we do what we want. We're responsible. And I told him that. But he still, he still doesn't get it. He still thinks that it's all like bad news or... See that's where the biggest inequality is. Just his conservative thinking and upbringing and stuff.

Courtney next claimed that she tried to limit the negative effects of the inequality in her marriage by withholding some information from him. She then explained—employing her own idiosyncratic version of the myth/reality contrast (cf. Hochschild 1989)—that Tom's concern and disapproval were unfounded since the drugs she took weren't "really" any different than his recreational activities.

> I mean, you know, I thought I would marry a
> grungy musician or an artist. [...] I mean we had-
> we had a lot of adjusting to do. And we still do.
> Sometimes I feel like I can't tell him- like I
> shouldn't tell him certain things. And I shouldn't go
> off and wait to tell him certain things... that I've
> either done or did... because uh... just because I
> know I'll upset and I don't feel like getting into it
> with him. But most- 95% of the time I tell him
> whether he wants to hear it or not. [...] It's on my

time, it's responsible, it's with people that- I mean
it's with my best friend and her boyfriend and like
that's it. I never in my- Oh and one of my sisters
and her friends. We party. And it's like, it's always
responsible. And so I said, "You know, you've got
nothing to complain about." I said, "I'm not out
doing heroin or something. I don't do white drugs."
I said, "I'm not addicted, I'm not crazy, I'm not
spending all the rent money." I said, "It's a minimal
amount" and I said, "And I have fun." And I- and I
said, "And I need it." I said, "This is like my
release. This is my outlet." I said, "You go to the
movies and you work on your- you spit polish your
car." I said, "That's like your therapy." I said,
"Going out and partying and dancing, that's mine."
I said, "I have a great time." Um, it still doesn't
please him though.

When I asked what it would take to reduce the inequality in her
marriage, Courtney responded pessimistically. She and Tom would
always have divergent lifestyles, she asserted, even though she had
decreased her drug use for him.

Scott: So for it to be more equal in that respect, your
            lifestyle differences, what would have to happen?

Courtney: I- I honestly don't know. Cause I don't think there's
          ever gonna be true equality there.

Scott: Really?

Courtney: Well, yeah, it's always gonna be unbalanced. It's
          always gonna be.. there's always gonna be tension
          there, just because- and I'm not saying- and I said-
          you know, his lifestyle is not the most ideal lifestyle.
          I said, "Everything in moderation." He's too severe.
          He's- he's all or nothing. There's never a gray area
          with him. And I'm like that about a lot of things,
          but not everything. And he just doesn't see how you
          can do anything fun and not lose it. So, there's
          always gonna be problems with that. And plus I
          don't kn- I told him in the beginning I have no
          intention of changing my lifestyle. I totally- I laid it

all out. I said, "This is who I am. This is what I do. If you don't like it, get out. I don't need you." And he stuck around anyway. And I said, "Well, you've got nothing to be pissed about." I said, "You knew." [...] I try to respect the fact that uh...he doesn't approve...in that I'm not blatant about it. Given that he respects- respects that I do it and that I'm responsible and I don't do it in front of him. So I guess that's...so we've made progress but it's never gonna be 100% just because he's never gonna love it and I'm never going to...and I'm never going to...I shouldn't say I'm never gonna stop, because at some point I will. But I mean I'm never going to...lay down my convictions. Say "Yeah you were right, it's bad, and I hate it-" you know what I mean?

In some of my interviews, it seemed that personality differences were treated as causes of equal or unequal situations. One respondent claimed that she and her husband were similarly sensitive to each other's emotional needs and, consequently, could be equally "there" for each other. Or, recall Wayne's story from chapter 4. Wayne claimed that his wife's strong desire for expensive material things (alongside his indifference) helped promote unequal decision making about major purchases. In contrast to such cases, Courtney's story shows how a certain personality difference can be portrayed not as a cause or effect but as "a huge inequality, just in and of itself." Different ways of thinking, dressing, acting—all these were typified by Courtney as examples of her and Tom's lifestyle inequality, a serious kink in an otherwise happily egalitarian marriage.

Michael's Story: An Accepting Wife and a Place That Feels Like Home

Many of my respondents (such as Courtney, Wayne, and Lucy) spoke of wanting their partners to change for the better: Equality might be achieved or inequality reduced if only spouses would improve themselves or their conduct in some way. Not all respondents spoke of equality in this manner, however. In my last example of an "unfamiliar" tale,[4] I turn to someone who explicitly defined marital equality as accepting your spouse just as he or she is. To paraphrase Michael (whose story I present next) the desire to change or improve your partner is a sure sign of inequality. As a part-time musician (and teacher and student) who works odd hours for low pay, Michael argued, Kathy's acceptance of his career choice was central to their equal marriage. But there was more to Michael's story than that. Their relationship had a rocky beginning due to a related form of inequality. Michael was sixteen years younger than Kathy and only about five years older than her son from a previous marriage. The strain of being a live-in boyfriend and ambiguous authority figure to Kathy's son created an initial "imbalance" that Kathy and Michael were still recovering from. Establishing equality consequently has involved finding a "turf" that belonged equally to Michael and where Michael felt he equally belonged.

The interview began with Michael explaining somewhat hesitantly (though lightheartedly) how he ended one relationship and began another with Kathy.

> Scott: I give people a lot of free rein in what they want to talk about. I'm interested in equality in marriage, but maybe it's better if you tell me a little bit about you guys in general? Um, what do you think the best place to start is?

> Michael: I would guess I need to tell you about family makeup. We are an interracial couple. Um...I am 28 and...Do you need me to describe myself?

> Scott: Sure, that would be great.

> Michael: Twenty-eight-year-old black male. She is a forty-four-year-old white female. Um, we have a daughter who is eleven months old I think. Um...we dated...I guess I can tell you this stuff. We dated for about a year and a half...and the pregnancy came before the marriage. We were planning on getting married, but...the pregnancy came sooner [*laughs*]. So I said, "Why not? Let's go and do it." And we did it. Um...she's a registered nurse, and I am a school teacher slash musician. So...there's a lot of juggling to deal with...who we are, and who are for each other. Um...Yeah, what else can I tell ya?

Scott: You guys met here in Portland?

Michael: We met here in Portland. Do you want to talk about that, how we met?

Scott: Yeah, that would be great-

Michael: OK. We met at [a coffee shop]. And uh ... I had just gotten out of a relationship ... and, I was still in it actually. I guess I can tell you the dirt.

Scott: [*laughs*]. It's confidential.

Michael: My previous girlfriend and I were living in the same house and had decided we weren't working out. So it was a basically a ... "Let's pay rent, let's pay bills, stay out of my way" sort of thing. And I met Kathy ... uh, going to [restaurant]. And it was strange because ... I'd never- I had never pursued anybody that I had just saw, sitting in a crowd. I just saw her, and I went, "Wow." She was sitting alone and I actually approached her and said, "Hey! Do you mind if I sit with you?" So it was like a movie kind of thing. And it was cool. Um ... I would continue to go to [restaurant], and she would be there. So I kind of picked up ... something was going on. I asked her to uh, dinner and the symphony with me. Turns out she likes classical music, and I'm a classical musician. So that was really nice. And ... about two months into this I saw it was getting serious and ... luckily we had to move out of- I was still living with the other female and ... she was an older female- I like older women by the way. [*laughter*] Um ... we got a notice that we had to leave the place cause the owner was gonna come back in and take over his house. Which was great. I said, "OK, I'm gonna go my way, you go your way" and that was that. Um, I moved into my own apartment. I chose not to move in with Kathy because I was just getting out of one thing and I wanted my own space. Um ... but we continued to date. ... She has ... kids. At that point in time she had a daughter who was nineteen and a son who was twenty-one. That was interesting right there.

In response to my interest in how Michael and Kathy met, Michael focused on *places*: he met Kathy in Starbucks; he was living with someone else until their landlord asked them to leave; he then got his own apartment because he wanted his own space. Location continued to play a pivotal role in Michael's narrative as he discussed why he finally moved in with Kathy and the problems that arose when he did.

> Uh, she owned the house, and the kids lived there. And it got pretty stressful for her because she was spending a lot of time at my apartment, and I said, "There's no way I can move in. Your kids, and just that environment. There's no way." Um . . . and it got really . . . it got even more stressful for her. She really wanted everyone under one roof. And I'm a really easygoing guy. So I said, "OK. I'll do it." We moved in . . . and uh . . . there were problems at the house. Because she'd been a single mom for twelve years. And the kids had kinda- everyone had gotten their roots into that house. And they did things the way they wanted to. And it wasn't really my cup of tea. Um . . . we got married . . . shortly after I moved in. And uh, I struggled to make changes in the house. And it wasn't . . . these weren't changes like uh . . . I want her oldest kid to change his ways completely. I- I saw things that didn't fit the norm. Uh, having a living room where people didn't have to walk through clutter to sit down, etcetera etcetera. So I did that, and then I noticed that it wasn't working. Because the kids were doing their own thing. They just- they'd been so used to living this way. The tension [*laughs*], the tension rose. And I said, "Look. If we're gonna do this, and I'm gonna have my kid- and we're gonna have our baby, I want it to be on neutral ground. I want to move out of here, and I want us to start . . . start from scratch, where it's ours." And these are grown, you know, they're- they're in college and they're doing their own thing. You know? So um, she didn't want to kick her oldest kid out. And I didn't want her to do that. All I really wanted her to do was say, "Hey. You're twenty-one years old. You need to start helping around the house. Uh, at least get a part

time job and support yourself." Cause he was still
under her financial belt. Which kind of bothered me.
I even uh... I paid for some of his tuition, which I
thought, that was really lenient. I don't anymore.

Michael recounted the various characteristics of Kathy's household that
struck him as strange, but most prominent was her son's behavior and
Kathy's response to it.

Michael: It was just a compact house. It was one of those uh,
built-in-the-seventies starter home, every house in
the neighborhood looks just like it. Um... bedrooms
are probably... especially the master bedroom...
could be exaggerating here, six by six, or something
like that. It was small. You got the bed in there and
there was no room

Scott: [*laughs*] Wall-to-wall bed

Michael: The carpet... carpet was orange. It was orange!
[...] So yeah... it was too small, the living room
was too small. Everything was just right there. If
you turned you'd go "Owp!" there was another wall.
And her son, always right there. Always. [*laughter*]
You go to work and you come home and he'd still
be sitting there.

Scott: Oh, playing games or something

Michael: Playing videogames. Um... the part that got me so
much about that guy... was um... she was falling
into- she fell into the trap... and I would kid her, I'd
say, "Do you want me to buy you a collar so he can
lead you around? Cause you know he snaps his fin-
gers and you get it. You got to turn it around some."
That really just... got under my skin. Um...

Scott: Like what would he do?

Michael: Well say- say, for example, the bill for his Internet
service. Of course he's on the Internet. I bought his
last computer. What an idiot! And it was better than
mine! That drove me crazy! Anyway... so his
Internet service got cut off once. It was because
um... they were doing an auto-debit thing, and the

account didn't have enough. So...he'd come in put his hands on his, you know, on his sides, "The damn Internet service is off. What are you gonna do?" And I would just get *mad*! And I'm thinking to myself "No, what are *you* gonna do?" And he- he- he's just been that way for years. And she's been in that mode...What do they call 'em? Is it the enabler?

Scott: Oh yeah, I think so.

Michael: Is that what it's called?

Scott: Sounds right, yeah.

Michael: Man, she's been doing that for years.

Michael didn't approve of what he saw when he moved in with Kathy, and he "struggled to make changes in the house." Michael felt out of place, he seemed to be saying, a guest in a home he disliked. He wanted "to be on neutral ground," to "start from scratch."

Michael: So what we did was we agreed to move out on our own and start our own family. And it's been great ever since. We left the house...He- her son lives in the house now. We rent it to him, our babysitter, and her husband. And it's been a great arrangement ever since then. So, we all live under one roof. Me, Kathy, and my daughter.

Scott: Great.

Michael: Yeah

Scott: Lot less tension now?

Michael: Less tension, less stress.... So now it's equal.

Scott: It is now?

Michael: Yeah. It wasn't at first.

Scott: Yeah. What about it makes you say that?

Michael: Um...there was just that terrible imbalance of me coming into that turf...and I felt it since day one, you know. I thought "It's their stuff. This is the way they do things. And I don't have a right to be here. I don't have the right to come into this house and change things." And um, that's why I had to say,

"Hey, we really need to go somewhere else...." I was even thinking if he was gonna leave- the daughter moved out by the way. She lives in Idaho now. If he was gonna leave, then I'd still like to start over. I mean, we're talking clutter and junk, from uh, twenty, thirty years. And I wanted to start over. I wanted to do wallpaper, and new carpet. I wanted to have the sense of starting from scratch, or some- some fresh ground. But we- that- that wasn't gonna happen. But uh...so all that...going against me, it just- it never would have worked. But now we're setting our own, you know, our own rules, our own groundwork. And it's working out pretty good.

There was much in Michael's narrative that could be interpreted as merely a story about "power." He described his dissatisfaction over his inability to change things in Kathy's old house—especially her son's behavior—and his satisfaction that he had started to co-create the rules with Kathy in their new house. But statements like "I thought... 'I don't have a right to be here'" also suggested that it was just as important for Michael to feel that *he belonged* where he lived as it was for where he lived to belong to him. Twenty or thirty years of clutter, odd carpet and old wallpaper, a generic tract-home design—features such as these made their first residence seem like Kathy's old house rather than their shared home, Michael explained.

Things became more equal once Michael and Kathy had set up new living arrangements. According to Michael, though, he and Kathy were still dealing with the interpersonal ramifications of the "imbalance" he first felt coming into "that turf." Michael reconstructed conversations with his friends and his mother that showed others confirming the problem as an issue of "territory."

We're still repairing from that, you know. Cause I really took a lot of that personal. I mean I talked to.. I have friends who are into the psychology thing. "What's going on here?" "Oh, that kid's doing that on purpose, you know. He's doing that because you're in his territory." I call my mom, "What's going on here, mom?" Oh you're in his territory, you can't expect-" "Oh man!...What did I ever do to this guy?"...So yeah, he's coming over for Thanksgiving. I think that's when we're gonna try to make things better between us. Because uh...my wife's a little upset about that. It's her kid.

Two-thirds through the interview I asked a question that prompted
Michael to give me an explicit definition of marital equality, one that
addressed another element of his marriage. In addition to creating a
more balanced turf, Michael next described marital equality as having a
spouse who accepts you.

Scott: Sometimes I like to get advice on- What would you
be asking if you were me? What should I ask people
if I want to know if they have an equal marriage? . . . Is that too abstract or?

Michael: Sort of.

Scott: OK.

Michael: But . . . I can tell you what *I* think equal is, an equal
marriage. Cause it's gonna vary, couple to couple.
. . . Equal marriage is when . . . two people accept each
other for who they are, and can live with it for the
rest of their lives.

Scott: OK. . . . What do you mean by "accept," like not try
to change 'em?

Michael: Not try to change 'em . . .

Scott: OK.

Michael: And I think it's that simple.

Scott: Is it?

Michael: Yeah. If you start trying to change people, it doesn't
work. And I tried to conform, I mean . . . you know,
sometimes we get- I get down, and I say, "You know,
I wish I was an accountant. Then I could play golf. I
wouldn't do this music crap. [*laughs*] I wish I wasn't
driven to do music cause it's almost like a curse
sometimes. And then she probably wouldn't have
[*laughs*] liked me if I hadn't been this way. It's like
these earrings. I drove into Portland, got my ears
pierced. Didn't tell my wife. Came home. "What do
you think?" "She just goes 'You need bigger ones.'"
[*laughter*] So that was pretty cool.

Scott: That is.

Michael: So she knows I'm gonna always push it a little bit.

When Michael compared his marriage to his fellow musician's relation-ships, he reported feeling extraordinarily lucky.

> She puts up with me. I *am* a musician. Um...I know a lot of people can't deal with that. I'm not saying I'm a bad musician, like the heroin kind. I'm not that kind of musician but...um...Like I'm working on a project. Everything's iffy. It's this big thing for MTV. [...] And it's strange when I tell people, they think I'm full of it. But it's either me or one of two other bands. Which is a big deal. So every bit of spare time I get I'm working on the MTV thing. And she is *so* cool with that. She's so cool with me going to the studio and spending...hours, you know. Some nights she won't even see me. I just call and say, "Yeah I'm at the studio." And she's really cool with that. And uh...I know a lot of- a lot of my friends aren't that lucky.

In addition to supporting his work projects, Michael told me, Kathy had also been accepting about his educational pursuits. Kathy had even expressed a willingness to move near a school in another state.

Michael: Um...she's been cool about my uh...graduate studies. Cause right now we're talking about um...possibly going to another state. Cause I found a school who'll actually just pay my way to finish my degree. And that's like a big deal. It's an OK university, it's not the greatest but...the thing I wanna do is actually go...focus on my degree, rather than...teach a little bit here...kinda half-way do my degree. That's the way it's been since I've been here. Um...

Scott: Is your degree in music too?

Michael: Yeah. It's in music education. And uh, I don't want to go to school forever. Right now this is- like I'll never get it done. I want to go and get it done and um...maybe...go for a college gig or something, I don't know. Right now...um...I mean she sacrifices a lot cause she has put down roots. Oregon's been her life. She grew up in Salem...and she owns a house here. But she's- If I decide to go and finish my degree...and uh...you might say that that's not equal [*laughs*]. She- she has sacrificed a lot for me.

Interestingly, as Michael described his marriage to me, he seemed to become aware that his relationship could be interpreted as unequal. I noticed his embarrassed laughter and asked a follow-up question, which prompted him to provide evidence countering the appearance of inequality.

Scott: Do you feel- it sounds like you might feel guilty a tiny bit that she's willing to give up so much

Michael: Oh yeah.

Scott: OK.

Michael: Um, but she also realizes that...see I'm from the South. 2,000 miles away. And uh.. if I'm lucky I'll see my family once a year. She knows um...we-we've gotta find a- a middle of the road kind of spot [*laughs*] that we can go and visit our families. Cause right now my mom is just really wanting me to move back...cause of her grandkid. This is her first granddaughter.

Location thus came back again to play a crucial role in Michael's story. The potentially inegalitarian implications of Kathy's willingness to move were diminished as Michael strategically suggested that he too had made sacrifices by living where he was.

Though all of my respondents' narratives were at least semi-spontaneous constructions tailored to meet the demands of the interview, the improvisational nature of Michael's story seemed especially pronounced to me as I noticed him adjust his tale in response his own potentially contradictory remarks. The state of equality in his marriage, as in all the narratives I have presented, was constructed in a somewhat ad hoc manner in the course of our conversation. Naturally, the term "improvisation" implies that some "notes" are artfully selected while others are left silent. Some sociologically minded readers will certainly notice that one note that could have been accentuated in Michael's story involves race.

In explaining the "imbalance" he felt when he first moved in with Kathy, Michael seemed to emphasize his outsider status and the small age difference between him and Kathy's son. While he mentioned that his was an interracial relationship, he did not dwell on the any of its possible effects. He might have, though, if *I* had encouraged him to pursue that direction. A different interviewer, or in a different interview with me on a different day, might have resulted in a slightly different story. The point is that the narrative improvisation presented here was a duet, as are all autobiographical tales told in social settings.

CONCLUSION

I began this book by suggesting that traditional approaches to studying equality neglected an important line of inquiry: the meanings things have for people. When researchers define equality, measure its causes and effects, and advocate policies to promote it, there is a tendency to *close down* what the meaning of equality is: "Equality" means *X*; "it" is correlated with *Y* and *Z*; to minimize "inequality," we need to do *A, B,* and *C*. All the while, people's diverse, situated interpretations of putative equal and unequal situations are relegated to the sidelines. I hope I have shown that equality can be treated in a more *opened-ended* manner. By adopting an agnostic pose regarding the real meaning of the equal/unequal dichotomy, one can attend to the variety of subjective senses the concept may acquire as people apply it to the specific circumstances of their lives.

Are there some ways that my study may be applicable beyond the issue of marital equality? Unless the topic of marital relations is somehow unique, there is probably a cornucopia of meanings and measurements of equality throughout every area of social life. If so, then the approach I have outlined and demonstrated here should have parallel implications for all sociological subfields that are concerned with the issue of equality/inequality. I take a closer look at that possibility in the final chapter of this book.

6

The Implications of Constructionism

Most sociologists regularly assume that inequality exists in society and that it is their job to document and explain it. Indeed, the central message of much sociological research is that inequality is ubiquitous and deleterious, and ought to be reduced (see also Cancian 1995). Sociologists are not alone in their concern over inequality and their desire for equality; scholars from related disciplines share the same sentiments. But sociologists, it seems, give inequality more attention than any other social science. Questions such as "Which groups are better off than others?" are at the heart of innumerable sociological studies, and can also be traced back to the field's founders (such as Weber and Marx). A typical introductory sociology textbook not only has chapters on "social stratification" and "global stratification" but also large sections on race, gender, work, education, and families—all of which are pervaded by the issue of inequality (e.g., Anderson and Taylor 2001). Or, for additional institutional evidence of the conventional wisdom, consider the themes of three recent Annual Meetings of the American Sociological Association: "Allocation Processes and Ascription," "Oppression, Domination, and Liberation," and "Inequality and Social Policy."

A second assumption common in sociology is that there are only two major approaches to the study of inequality: functionalism and conflict theory (Marger 1999). To put it simply, the popular belief is that one can treat inequality as a somewhat positive feature of an integrated organic system or one can treat it as a matter of unnecessary exploitation and unfair advantage between groups. Few sociologists claim to be functionalists today. Consequently, Davis and Moore's (1945) article on the importance of inequality to a smoothly functioning society remains the focal statement of the functionalist perspective on inequality, while conflict-related studies of inequality continue to proliferate (e.g., see Shapiro's [1998] edited collection). Textbooks on stratification and introductory sociology often summarize functionalist and conflict perspectives on inequality in tables that provide point-by-point comparisons of the two approaches (Anderson and Taylor 2001, p. 176; Kerbo 1991, p. 92).

What's missing from the conventional picture of the sociology of inequality is an appreciation of what an interactionist, social constructionist approach can contribute and how that contribution differs from other approaches. Certainly, there are many different brands of interactionism and related interpretive traditions that derive from pragmatism, phenomenology, and ethnomethodology.[1] At minimum, though, an interactionist-inspired approach would likely emphasize such issues as meaning, interaction, and the qualitative investigation of real-life experiences. Recently, three attempts have been made to set agendas that would move the sociology of inequality in this general direction: Collins's (2000) "Situational Stratification: A Micro-Macro Theory of Inequality," Chang's (2000) "Symbolic Interaction and Transformation of Class Structure: The Case of China," and Schwalbe et al.'s (2000) "Generic Processes in the Reproduction of Inequality: An Interactionist Analysis." In what follows, I will compare these three statements about the future direction of research on inequality with what I have done in this book. First, I will distill the main points of each publication. Next, I will explore the different ways that each deals with the issues of locating inequality, discerning its forms, documenting examples, and identifying causes.

My goal is to demonstrate that Collins, Chang, and Schwalbe et al. do not make a significant departure from the first assumption of the conventional wisdom; that is, they all presume that it is the sociologists' job to find and explain inequality. By carefully summarizing and critiquing these authors' work, I hope to demonstrate the implications an interpretive, social constructionist approach has for study of equality and inequality in *all* areas of social life, not just marital relations. As I have tried to show in this book, that approach contradicts the conventional wisdom because it focuses on the meanings that "inequality" has *for people*, as well as how those meanings are achieved in everyday life.[2]

SUMMARIZING COLLINS, CHANG, AND SCHWALBE ET AL

Collins on Situational Stratification

Randall Collins is a prolific author who has an encyclopedic knowledge of sociological theory and research (see Collins 1988; 1994). While he is familiar with interactionist work, it would probably be more accurate to describe him as a Weberian conflict scholar who draws eclectically from interactionist-related sources, such as Goffman (1967). His message in "Situational Stratification," however, does echo many interactionist themes. In short, Collins calls for more ethnographic research on people's actual experiences of inequality by systematically observing the interaction that takes place in a wide range of diverse "subjective worlds." Collins couches this argument within his long-standing view of micro-macro linkages and within a historical tale about a fundamental shift in the nature of stratification.

For Collins, macro structures are not so much self-subsistent entities as they are aggregated chains of interaction (Collins 1981). The "state," the "economy," and the "culture" are shorthand ways of referring to patterns of interaction. Large social structures and aggregate statistics are nothing without the ritualistic behaviors that constitute them. Collins argues that "microsituational data"—the kind of data interactionists are usually interested in—take priority over macro data because "Nothing has reality unless it is manifested in a situation somewhere" (Collins 2000, p. 18). Accordingly, the best way to ground theories is through detailed observation and analysis of people's thoughts, words, and actions as they occur in concrete situations. At the same time, though, Collins does not dismiss macrosociologies. Those approaches provide crude but helpful approximations of social life. However, statistical charts and related macro realities must be "microtranslated" by studying the repetitive everyday events that comprise those realities (Collins 1983, p. 187).

While micro events have always formed the basis of macro realities, Collins asserts, there was a closer relationship between the two realms in the past than in recent times. In previous centuries, what sociologists think of as macro inequalities (such as differences in class or power) were highly institutionalized and public. For example, members of the nobility and other status groups not only had more prestige and economic clout; their reputations preceded them. Everybody knew who deserved deference, and it was frequently and ceremoniously expressed in daily encounters. Persons were treated more as manifestations of social cate-gories (e.g., servant or head of the household) than as individuals with individual reputations. The present state of affairs stands in distinct con-trast, Collins (2000, p. 38) argues: "Contemporary social structure gen-erates a life experience in which most individuals have at least intermittent, and sometimes quite extensive, situational distance from macrostructured relationships."

Since approximately the beginning of the twentieth century, stratifi-cation experiences have increasingly been tied to particularized networks. The micro events that constitute stratification operate differently in dif-ferent "circuits" of interaction.[3] As a result, Collins suggests (2000, pp. 17, 27), individuals may rank one way on an abstract occupational pres-tige survey but the opposite way when evaluated by their companions at certain social gatherings. For example, imagine an awkward, overweight surgeon at various kinds of parties. Or, consider how influential scholars may be completely unknown or even disrespected outside of the particu-lar circle of academics who appreciate their work.

Thus, very much in interactionist fashion, Collins doubts that the statistics and graphs so common in sociological textbooks can adequately convey the reality of inequality. In order to better understand people's experiences with inequality, he believes sociologists need to make system-atic ethnographic observations of how and whether people incorporate and act on it. Instead of asking "Who has what?," sociologists should investigate how people may use or fail to use their status (or wealth or power) in everyday life. "We need to undertake a series of studies look-ing at the conversion of abstract macrodistributions...into the actual distribution of advantages in situational practice" (Collins 2000, p. 18).

Chang on Class Transformation

While Collins is interested in the social shaping of diverse stratification experiences in everyday situations, Chang focuses on the role of meaning in the creation of large-scale social classes. Chang's article presents an intricate historical account of the structural changes that have occurred in China over the past several decades. He hopes his article will help ele-vate symbolic interactionism "to the status of a significant competitor and contributor in the club of macro sociology" (Chang 2000, p. 223). Although Marxists and Weberians incorporate some analysis of "mean-ing" in their research, Chang argues, they have not done so to the degree that interactionism can (Chang 2000, pp. 224, 247–48). To demonstrate the contribution interactionism can make, he delineates three kinds of meaning—"motivation-oriented meaning," "action course-oriented meaning," and "justification-oriented meaning" (Chang 2000, p. 228)—and explains the role they played in China's transition from a five-class system to a seven-class system. His analysis specifies many interest groups in China, but centers around the interpretations of the Chinese Communist Party (CCP) and how they provoked, guided, and justified the economic reforms that began in 1978. Chang examined news reports and government documents, but also interviewed 125 Chinese individuals who had undergone a change in their class stratification.

The foil for Chang's article is the Marxist argument that economic changes are generated when the current economic system has depleted (or nearly so) its ability to develop productivity (Chang 2000, p. 228). Chang is not convinced that objective structural strains are what provoke reform. He proposes a trademark interactionist explanation that focuses on actors' cognition–what he calls *perceived relative strain*: "[The] perceived comparative inferiority of an economic structure is more relevant for understanding the basic change of a structure.... This perceived inferiority derives from comparing the given economic structure with one or more alternatives, real or imagined, that are believed to be more capable of promoting productivity" (Chang 2000, p. 229). Chang argues that some Chinese began making such comparisons in the years just before the reforms began. Statements made by leading reformers (Deng and Hu) show that they were aware that capitalist countries appeared to be doing better than China, and that semicapitalist farming was proving more productive than collective farming within China itself. Chang believes that these perceptions, not an objective structural strain, are ultimately what "drove" reformers to act.

To enact changes, reformers needed to get their message to the majority of the Chinese people. It took four or five years to accomplish this. Deng and his followers first needed to acquire positions of power in the CCP; they did so by winning a publicized philosophical debate with entrenched communists about the necessity to test political beliefs against reality. Once in control, reformers publicized the successes of privatized farms and encouraged peasants to follow suit. Subsequent successes, Chang asserts, persuaded the masses that basic economic changes were needed in cities as well.

As reforms were being made, additional meanings were generated. Deng and other leaders defined the economic changes as "ideology-free" experiments rather than as explicit moves toward capitalism. To illustrate, Chang (2000, p. 233) cites Deng's well-known slogan "A cat is a good cat, be it black or white, as long as it captures rats." Still, Chang argues, this "action course-oriented meaning" could not suffice on its own. The changes being made in China conflicted with years of socialization in China. The Chinese people had come to believe deeply in the superiority of socialist economies.

Consequently, reformers used three justifications to promote the legitimacy of the new agenda in order to augment the stated objective of increasing productivity. The first justification argued that new business practices actually adhered to the overarching framework of socialism because (a) they were being conducted on collectively owned land and (b) "the nature of an economic system was determined by the ownership of the means of production, not by how it was used" (Chang 2000, p. 234). The second justification claimed that an economy that included private businesses could still be classified as a socialist system if the majority of the means of production were collectively or state owned. The third justification argued that it was necessary for private businesses to promote economic development until their productivity ran its course and a purer form of socialism resulted.

Although different segments of the population responded differently to these three justifications, most Chinese adopted and acted on the interpretations promoted by the leading reformers. Many intended and unintended consequences resulted. In particular, two new classes—the bourgeoisie and the petty bourgeoisie—have arisen. Also, there has been some shift between (and within) the relative positions of the remaining five classes—the bureaucratic/managerial class, the professional class, the clerical class, the working class, and the farming class.

Chang's conclusion is that mechanistic analyses of social change must be replaced by nonmechanistic ones, and interactionists can best accomplish this task. Economic situations can be interpreted in different ways. The manner in which powerful leaders act, and the way the masses respond, depend on the meanings they give things. Thus, Chang argues, meaning is a "world-constituting force" that must be taken into account when scholars study macro level phenomena such as the class structure of a nation. Although Chang provides no explicit methodological directives, the implication from his study is that these meanings are accessible by examining public statements and interviewing representative members of the population in question.

Schwalbe et al. on the Reproduction of Inequality

Like Collins, Schwalbe et al. (2000) are critical of the vast literature that summarizes inequalities in statistical tables and graphs. However, their criticism is centered less around the diverse experiences that quantitative data gloss. Their main argument is that scholars have not paid enough attention to the question, "How are these inequalities created and reproduced?" (2000, p. 419). While some scholars might respond that there are innumerable causal arguments made in the pages of quantitative books and articles on inequality, Schwalbe et al. are seeking a somewhat different kind of answer than that provided by variable analysis. Through careful ethnographic work, the authors argue, researchers can directly observe the recurrent patterns of behavior that create and reproduce inequality. Because these generic social processes (Prus 1996) may operate in similar ways across innumerable diverse contexts, Schwalbe et al. believe this sort of inquiry can contribute much to understanding how various forms of inequality arise and remain stable.

Actually, they argue (Schwalbe et al. 2000, pp. 421–22), a large amount of this kind of qualitative work has already been done on inequality. In preparing their article, the authors read scores of such studies in order to conceptualize and extract the processes most central to the creation and maintenance of oppressive situations. By treating the previous ethnographic research as data and subjecting it to analytic induction, the authors arrived at the following four concepts: othering, subordinate adaptation, boundary maintenance, and emotion management. These four processes, they argue, are "essential and generative" in that any situation of inequality will inevitably depend on them for its existence.

Schwalbe et al. (2000, p. 422; cf. Fine 1994) refer to othering as "the process whereby a dominant group defines into existence an inferior group." This process underlies race and gender relations, but also myriad other inequalities, such as how temporary workers may be depicted by their employers as unskilled and unmotivated (Schwalbe et al. 2000, p. 423). While othering can be direct and blatant, it can also be subtle. Those in positions of power (e.g., CEOs and politicians) can use their resources to present superior self-images that by implication create and denigrate supposedly inferior others.

Subordinate adaptation refers to the tactics that oppressed persons may employ to deal with the inequalities they face. For example, subordinates may adapt by "hustling," using illegal and or dishonest means to exploit others for financial gain. Because targets are usually the weak, this adaptation helps reinforce inequality. Or, in order to salvage a sense of self, subordinate groups may create alternative subcultures with distinctive systems for attaining prestige. These beliefs and practices, however, can be "debilitating and risky, and diminish chances for mainstream success" (Schwalbe et al. 2000, p. 428).

With the term "boundary maintenance" Schwalbe et al. make the point that the differences between groups, in terms of resources and privileges, are not self-sustaining even after they are in place. It takes interactional work to secure the borders. Boundaries between the haves and have-nots are maintained by (1) the transmission of cultural capital, (2) the operation of networks, and (3) the use (or threat) of interpersonal violence. Thus, men's advantage over women may be reproduced as parents and teachers inculcate different skills and predilections into boys and girls, as gatekeepers exclude potential network members based on gendered criteria, and as husbands physically dominate their wives.

The last inequality-producing process that Schwalbe et al. identify is emotion management. Inequality, though beneficial to some, frequently generates uncomfortable feelings of shame, anger, resentment, and hopelessness in others. These emotions can be destabilizing to the system, and so must be dealt with. One strategy is to regulate the discourse that could arouse emotions and mobilize action. The careful use of metaphors by elites can desensitize subordinates from their negative feelings and encourage them to act to maintain inequality. This is reflected in the way employees are taught methods of emotion work ("think of the customer as a guest in your home") that will earn the most money for their employers, regardless of the long-term effects on workers' sense of self (Hochschild 1983).

In their conclusion, Schwalbe et al. encourage researchers to jettison reifying notions of structure that obscure the way people *do* things together in ways that reproduce inequality. With the four concepts of othering, subordinate adaptation, boundary maintenance, and emotion management, they hope to provide a theoretical framework for subsequent qualitative studies of inequality. Future research, they suggest, could "directly examine" the operation and nuances of these generic social processes through careful ethnographic inquiry. They parallel Collins (2000) by arguing that "the key analytic question is not about resources or their distribution, but about how resources are used, in any given time and place, to create and reproduce patterns of action and experience" (Schwalbe et al. 2000, p. 440).

Harris on Marital Equality

The research that appears in this book, like the articles by Collins, Chang, and Schwalbe et al., has again highlighted the common interactionist themes of meaning and interaction. However, in my opinion, my approach differs from that found the other three publications in some important ways. First, I began with the assumption that inequality is an interpretation rather than an objective condition. Second, I have proposed that scholars should bracket the concept, turn it into a topic rather than a resource, and study how people tell stories that transform ambiguous experiences into coherent narratives about inequality. In so doing, I have attempted to combine Blumer's (1969) formulation of interactionism with compatible constructionist concepts from phenomenology (Schutz 1964), ethnomethodology (Garfinkel 1967; Pollner 1987), and narrative analysis (Gubrium and Holstein 1995, 1997; Maines 1993; Riessman 1993).

Taking marital equality as my point of departure, I have critiqued previous research in order to open a space for a constructionist agenda. In chapters 2 and 3 I argued that in the past four decades, quantitative and qualitative researchers alike have studied the costs, benefits, prerequisites, and impediments of marital equality. They have done so by adopting (implicitly or explicitly) particular definitions of what qualifies as an equal or unequal marriage. There are two big problems, I argued. First, marital scholars do not agree with each other on how to define and measure inequality. Consequently, the same couple may be categorized as equal or unequal depending on which approach is used. Second, it is likely that many of the scholarly meanings and measurement devices do not resonate with the diverse ways that respondents may perceive equalities and inequalities in their marriages—if and when the issue is relevant to them.

With this critique in mind, I have tried to investigate and demonstrate how the issue of equality/inequality might enter the experiences of married people. I did so by soliciting interviews with thirty individuals who defined their own marriages as equal or unequal. Unlike previous scholars who developed interview guides that reflected a preconceived meaning of equality (Deutsch 1999), I asked more open-ended questions that were intended to promote respondents' storytelling. I wanted to encourage respondents to construct narrative accounts about the issues that concerned them, while recognizing that the research setting shaped the production of those accounts (see also Atkinson and Silverman 1997;

Holstein and Gubrium 1995a). I then analyzed and presented the stories I heard through Schutz's (1964) notions of *domains of relevance* and *typifications*. These concepts suggest that forms of inequality can be seen as socially acquired interpretive constructs that people use to make sense of the world. No object has inherent meaning (Blumer 1969). People typify indeterminate things as this or that depending on the purposes they pursue and the perspectives they take as they interact within particular discursive environments (Gubrium and Holstein 2000). These typifications do not break out randomly, but tend to reflect culturally constructed categories and concerns. Thus, I considered the various examples and themes that previous researchers have focused on—such as instances of "power" or "the division of labor"—to be socially acquired typifications and domains of relevance. I then used these Schutzian concepts to compare scholarly research with lay accounts.

In chapters 4 and 5, I presented lengthy excerpts from nine of my respondents' narratives, five of which I portrayed as somewhat "familiar" or similar to scholarly domains of relevance, and four I cast as "unfamiliar." Of the two "familiar" tales, Deborah's was perhaps most memorable. Deborah depicted her relationship as very unequal due to an imbalance of power. She described her husband Bill as a traditional male who liked to be "the man of the house." As examples of "power trips" that her husband went on, she recounted her husband's habit of yelling at her for invading his privacy in the bathroom and failing to anticipate which tool he needed when they worked together in the yard. She also claimed that Bill second-guessed her purchases, and had even prevented her from going back to college.

Though Deborah's story resembled the common scholarly theme of "power," I noted that the "indicators" she relied on were not the same as might be found in many quantitative scales and observational checklists. Moreover, I suggested that her narrative did not merely convey information about objective states of affairs but actively constituted a sense of reality. The experiential particulars she used as examples could each be typified in many different ways. Deborah (and the rest of my respondents) would likely, if questioned in a different context, recast the same biographical events into different narrative patterns. For example, I believe that if my interview had centered on "dysfunctional marriages" or "rude behavior," Deborah might have typified some of the same instances of her marital past as elements within those domains, rather than power inequality.

For the "unfamiliar" tale, the case of Matthew stands out for me. This respondent drew creatively on the Bible as an interpretive resource to craft a portrait of his marriage as thoroughly egalitarian. With the concepts of "submitting," relinquishing," and "elevating," Matthew presented his own analysis of the generic processes that purportedly created and reproduced the equality that existed in his marriage (and the inequality that existed in others' relationships). His religious conception of marital equality is foreign to the secular viewpoints presented in most mainstream scholarly accounts. Nevertheless, I deemed it worthy of consideration for the way it could sensitize researchers to (1) the diverse meanings equality can have and (2) the interpretive practices (e.g., demarcating domains of relevance and typifying examples) that produce those meanings.

The point of my research, then, is that marital researchers have tended to heavy-handedly transform their subjects' experiences into typified elements of *scholarly* tales about inequality. Moreover, I am claiming that stratification research in general tends to overlook the stories of inequality that everyday people live by, as well as the methods through which (and settings within which) people construct those narratives. To remedy this neglect, I have called for more research that attempts to salvage the meanings, however shifting and transitory, that the equality/inequality dichotomy has for people.

COMPARISON AND CRITIQUE

So far this chapter has summarized the main points of four recent proposals (including my own) for the development of a more interpretive, interactionist approach to inequality. I would argue (though others may disagree) that each proposal is interesting and worth considering. Many criss-crossing similarities and differences can be found between these agenda-setting works, depending on readers' purposes and perspectives. My perspective is constructionist, and my goal is to distinguish between traditional and constructionist approaches to studying equality and inequality in social life. In what follows, I will highlight those elements in Collins, Chang, and Schwalbe et al. that—despite the authors' differences—reflect their shared commitment to the conventional wisdom about inequality. In contrast to the approach taken in this book, the authors of the other three publications all assume that it is primarily *the sociologist's* prerogative to find and explain the inequality that exists, factually, in society. This assumption is apparent in their treatment of four central

issues: locating inequality; discerning its forms; documenting its manifestations; and tracing its causes and effects.

Locating Inequality

For Collins, Chang, and Schwalbe et al., inequality clearly does exist in
society. "It" is a thing out there, waiting for sociologists to find it. For
example, at one point Collins (2000, p. 17) cites a reputable source and
states authoritatively "The distribution of income and wealth has
become increasingly unequal since 1970." Similarly, Chang (2000, pp.
242–43) makes statements such as "New dimensions of stratification
have emerged within the working class" and "Cross-region inequality has
also increased significantly." Meanwhile, in their introduction, Schwalbe
et al. (2000, p. 421) make their position abundantly clear: "We take
inequality to be endemic to and pervasive in late capitalist societies."

However, these authors also assert that though inequality does exist,
sometimes it does not present itself clearly. Correctly identifying inequality
is difficult. Much of the uncertainty hinges on the idea that inequality,
while thing-like, also depends (to an unexplored degree) on the way sociologists and laypersons choose to look at it. Unlike in constructionism,
though, the tension between analysts' and members' depictions of inequality is not converted into a full-blown research topic. Rather, it is either
glossed over or dismissed as priority is given to the researcher's perspective.

Consider Collins's critique of quantitative studies of occupational
prestige. He argues that some sociologists treat the statistics produced by
these studies as if they captured the realities of stratification when they
actually may distort those realities. On page 18 he asks, "What is the
real-life standing of construction workers when they display a style of
outdoor muscular activity that receives respect... [and] when the presti-
gious style of automobile is the big, trucklike 'sports utility vehicle'?" But
as Collins develops his argument that quantitative surveys neglect subjective diversity, he simultaneously highlights and minimizes the importance of people's perceptions: "Occupational prestige can only be
realistically understood if *we* can survey situations of occupational
encounters and judge the actual situational stratification that takes place"
(Collins 2000, p. 18; emphasis added). Thus, while Collins describes
inequality as difficult to measure and contingent on members' perspectives, he still characterizes it as a factual, observable phenomenon. He
assumes that there is one real version of inequality—"the actual stratifi-

cation" that is out there. Moreover, it is up to sociologists to observe and decode "it."

I find a similar pattern in Chang's article. Like Collins, Chang also presumes that inequality exists, factually. He does acknowledge, though, that the nature of the inequality that is "there" is shaped both by people's perceptions and by the way *he* defines it:

> I define 'class stratification' as a system of class hierarchy in which the relative position of each class is determined by its location in the power relations between classes, by the direct or indirect returns to the exercise of its power, and by the way it is *perceived* by its own members as well as by the members of the other classes. *Based on this definition,* two distinctive patterns of class stratification *may be identified* on the Chinese mainland. (Chang 2000, p. 237; emphasis added)

Thus, the importance of people's perceptions is built right into Chang's definition. However, it is extremely unclear how these perceptions factor into the "two distinctive patterns" of inequality that "may be identified." Let me also point out Chang's use of the passive tense here. Exactly who is identifying the patterns? That murky issue is what a constructionist approach would focus on, along with other questions related to the representation of reality.[4]

Schwalbe et al., though they take a more interpretive slant than either Collins or Chang, also tend to confound lay and analytical treatments of inequality. For example, recall their description of othering as "the process whereby a dominant group defines into existence a subordinate group" (Schwalbe et al. 2000, p. 422). That is a very curious sentence, when read from a constructionist perspective. In this context, shouldn't there be quote marks around "dominant" and "subordinate"? Exactly who decided that the dominant group is dominant and that the subordinate group is subordinate? Where do researchers' definitions begin and members' definitions end?

In contrast to these authors, I have attempted to treat inequality as entirely dependent on people's interpretive practices. I have tried to remain acutely sensitive to the question, "Who is doing the 'stratifying,' people or the sociologist?" While not denying human suffering and exploitation, I have claimed that experiencing a troubling state of affairs as "unequal" is first and foremost an interpretive accomplishment. From a constructionist perspective, as I argued in chapter 1, equal and unequal states of affairs only exist when members of a setting describe or understand situations in those terms. I then proceeded to demonstrate how my respondents brought equal and unequal states of affairs into being through their storytelling practices.

Discerning Inequality's Forms

If inequality is presumed to exist, then what shapes does it take? Collins, Chang, and Schwalbe et al. have definite ideas about the various forms of inequality that exist out there. Collins (2000, p. 20), following Weber, devotes much attention to the concepts of "class," "status," and "power." He also sets aside a special section devoted to "deference," and delineates two subtypes of power–deference power and efficacy power (Collins 2000, p. 33). Chang, as I mentioned earlier, is concerned mostly with "class" (and China's putative transformation from a five-tier to a seven-tier system), but he also writes much about "power." The subtypes he coins are not precisely the same as Collins, though. He posits three components of "position based power": "power locus," "power sweep," and "power use" (Chang 2000, p. 246). Schwalbe et al., meanwhile, depict the inequalities they discuss as falling under the domains of race, class, gender, and sexuality. They believe each form is crucial, and they chastise previous researchers for not examining all four of these inequalities in the course of their studies: "Even when one form of inequality (e.g., gender) is brought into an analysis, it is not uncommon to see other forms (e.g., race and class) left out or barely mentioned" (Schwalbe et al. 2000, p. 443).

From a constructionist perspective, it would not make sense to cite to a famous sociologist (e.g., Weber) in order to justify why one is focusing on a particular form or forms of inequality. Nor would one assume that there is one, or three, or four forms of inequality, with a predetermined number of subtypes, that merit attention. Rather, the issue of discerning the forms of inequality and ranking their importance would be *members'* practical task. For a constructionist, what merits attention are the forms of inequality that people themselves are concerned with. Thus, the only reason to incorporate Weber's tripartite conceptualization into one's study would be if it were actually used as an interpretive resource by the participants of an interaction that the researcher was investigating. A constructionist scholar would not assume that a particular form of inequality was in play at a certain place and time, or even that the issue of inequality was relevant at all.

This is the approach I have attempted to take in my study. First I tried to investigate, instead of presuming, what forms of inequality mattered to my respondents. Then I used my data to show that not all these forms coincided with the venerable and ready-made concepts of classical sociology, as in the case of Matthew's religious account or Alicin's story about her husband's intellectual inferiority. Moreover, I argued, those persons who do employ familiar sociological concepts may do so in a highly selective or idiosyncratic fashion, as in my respondents' narratives about power and the division of labor.

Documenting Examples

If inequality is presumed to exist and take particular forms, then it makes sense to seek out examples of the inequalities. And that is exactly what Collins, Chang, and Schwalbe et al. do. Recall that Collins was very interested in "power" and "deference." To document instances of these phenomena, he presents a number of examples drawn from his personal experiences. At the beginning of his article, for instance, he asks readers to consider some "typical scenes," one of which involves "a muscular black youth, wearing baggy pants and hat turned backwards and carrying a boom box" who "dominates the sidewalk space...while middle-class whites palpably shrink back in deference" (Collins 2000, p. 17). Later, Collins depicts the nature of contemporary highway driving to bolster his point that macroinequalities (such as class) may be only partially microtranslated into actual experiences in everyday situations.

> [Situational dominance] may be mildly correlated with sheer physical property: an expensive, fast car lords it over ordinary cars by passing them; overt *deference* is displayed as a car captures the dominant trajectory of motion...so that other cars get out of the way when they see it coming.... Here *we* see that economic power translates into situational dominance to some extent. (Collins 2000, p. 40; emphasis added)

A constructionist scholar would note that Collins's characterization of these instances as examples of "deference" and "dominance" is an interpretive accomplishment. These situations could be characterized in many different ways. The documentary method of interpretation is very much in operation as Collins's themes and examples acquire their sense through mutual elaboration (Garfinkel 1967; see also Prus 1999, p. 153; Watson and Goulet 1998).

While Collins draws primarily on personal observations to cast doubt on the veracity of many quantitative measures, Chang makes extensive use of statistics as evidence of China's class transformation. He cites without hesitation the *Statistical Yearbook of China* (*SYC*) and other sources. Notice also Chang's use of the passive voice as he describes the changes that "have stratified" the Chinese people:

> Reform policies have significantly affected the life chances of peas-
> ants. In 1997 China's population was 1.24 billion. About 70 percent
> of the population lived in the countryside (*SYC* 1998:105). But 18.5
> percent of the rural labor force actually worked in village and town-
> ship enterprises (*SYC* 1998:127); 40 million to 80 million people
> migrated to cities, taking temporary jobs as *peasant workers*... 6 mil-
> lion were employed in rural private enterprises (*SYC* 1998:152); and
> a significant proportion were engaged in self-employed businesses.
> Only the remaining rural population constituted the farming class (or
> rural working class).
>
> These changes have stratified the formerly homogenous peasants
> into three broad categories: the rural petty bourgeois, the marginal
> stratum of peasant workers, and the farming class. The emergence of
> the first two categories suggests that the rigid divide between *nongye
> renkou* (rural residents) and *fei nongye renkou* (nonrural residents) has
> blurred (Chang 2000, p. 241; emphasis in original)

Here Chang's evidence for the existence of the Chinese class system is derived from members' systems and procedures for counting and classi-fying people. While constructionist scholars often treat statistics as prod-ucts of and flexible resources for people's agendas (Heritage 1984, pp. 168–76; Kitsuse and Cicourel 1963; Zimmerman and Pollner 1970, p. 83), Chang incorporates them confidently into his account, ignoring all of the hidden interpretive work that goes into producing and employing official statistics. A constructionist would wonder, Do Chinese people use these concepts (e.g., "peasant workers") to characterize their situa-tions as manifestations of class stratification? How, when, and where do they articulate these terms with the messy details of their everyday expe-riences (Gubrium 1988; Miller and Holstein 1989)?

In the article by Schwalbe et al., the authors provide mostly implicit examples of inequality, as they are interested primarily in the four processes that sustain "it." Their data are neither personal observations nor statistics, but the findings (or "makings") of previous ethnographic research. Still, in passages like the following, authors subtly frame as unequal those situations in which some persons have less money than others and/or are victimized for having less money.

> From classic studies of gangs....Gypsies...fortune tellers...and drug dealers...qualitative research has shown how members of subordinate groups, rather than challenge the system or push their way into the mainstream, organize to exploit it from the edge. Usually this means exploiting those who are vulnerable—the jobless, the elderly, the uneducated, the addicted. This kind of hustling exploits the human fallout from extra-local inequalities, and in turn helps to reproduce those inequalities by further debilitating the weak. (Schwalbe et al. 2000, p. 429)

When hustlers take advantage of people with minimal financial resources, Schwalbe et al. argue, they are reinforcing already existing "inequalities" by making the poor even poorer.

As difficult as it may be to contemplate from within mundane reason (Pollner 1987), examples of "economic disparities" are not inherent indicators of inequality. They must be typified as such, rather than being ignored, noticed but considered irrelevant (e.g., compared to spiritual concerns), or taken as indicators of some other problem. It certainly may be demonstrable that some person or group possesses more wealth than another. Nevertheless, affixing the label "unequal" to that state of affairs is an interpretive act. There is nothing in the situation that absolutely necessitates that particular characterization, rather than other possible characterizations. Once applied, though, the label of inequality helps create the meaning of the situation, while the situation gives some sense to the term "unequal."[5] Thus, though it may be difficult for some readers to recognize, in the previous passage Schwalbe et al. are themselves "reproducing inequality" on a deeper level. By juxtaposing the theme of inequality with examples of the poor getting poorer, they are implicitly reproducing a *sense* of inequality with which many sociologists are familiar.

In contrast, the agenda that I have proposed in this book would make the creation of inequality meanings the explicit focus of research. What are examples of inequalities that members of a setting perceive? How do speakers select and transform a set of indeterminate examples in order to accomplish certain interactional objectives? Do people make interpretive connections between "inequalities" in one place/time and another? If so, how? In short, what is missing from traditional scholarly research on inequality is an appreciation of people as interpretive ethno-graphers of their own lives (see also Gubrium and Holstein 1995). This kind of agenda is much different from those proposed by Chang, Collins, and Schwalbe et al., who assume that it is ultimately the sociol-ogist's prerogative to identify and assemble examples of inequality.

Causality and Motive Talk

Once inequality is presumed to exist, take certain forms, and manifest itself in concrete examples, conventional scholars can then attempt to trace the cause-and-effect linkages between the precursors and conse-quences of inequality, including the motivations that drive people to act as they do in relation to inequality. Thus, a fourth major difference between Collins's, Chang's, and Schwalbe et al.'s conventional accounts and my constructionist account has to do with whether the researcher tends to treat causality as a topic or a resource.

Consider Collins. He argues that, in modern times, macroinequali-ties are not always directly microtranslated into everyday experiences. As a result, one's wealth may or may not manifest itself in consumption ability. For the super-rich, he claims, the appeal of money may not be its usefulness for buying things.

> The main attraction of having extremely large amounts of money may be the emotional energies and symbolic membership markers of being on the phone at all hours of night and day, engaging in excit-ing transactions. In terms of sheer consumption power, the extremely wealthy have attained the maximum of what they can get as material benefits; yet most of them continue to work, sometimes obsessively lengthy hours, until advanced ages.... It appears the value of money at this level is all in the microexperience, the activity of wielding money in highly prestigious circuits of exchange. Money here translates into situational power and into nothing else. (Collins 2000, p. 21)

In this extract Collins assigns motives to elites. Emotional energies, sym-bolic membership, excitement, and situational power are offered as rea-sons why the ultrawealthy continue to work hard even when they appear to have no need for additional funds. Certainly, other parties (including wealthy persons themselves) might attribute this behavior to different motives—such as greed, habit, drive, self-fulfillment, duty, neurosis, altruism, or ego—depending in part on the audiences and interactional objectives at hand.

While Collins does not use the term "motivation," Chang does so explicitly. As I summarized earlier, one of Chang's arguments was that China's class transformation should be traced not to the mechanical operation of an objective social structure. Chang treats meaning—the "perceived relative strain" discussed earlier—as the main causal factor behind the reform movement:

> 'Motivation' here refers to the driving force that pushed Chinese soci-
> ety toward a presumably better alternative to its prereform system. The
> dominant social actors (the top reformers, the ruling party, and the
> majority of the public who support the change) share this motivation to
> various degrees as a potent societal impulse. (Chang 2000, p. 228)

Again, a constructionist scholar might ask, What other reasons and motives could be offered for this behavior? By whom? In what contexts?

Schwalbe et al. also confidently posit connections between various causes and effects of inequality. Recall that they defined emotion management as an essential feature of the reproduction of inequality. In their view, inequality causes certain destabilizing emotions (e.g., anger), and this leads dominant groups to regulate societal discourse so those feelings can be muted. In that section the authors further argue that people may actively organize the mundane aspects of public gatherings so that inequality-reinforcing emotions are generated. They cite a previous study to explain:

> Scripted events... reproduce inequality by *encouraging* subordinates
> to ignore inequality and embrace the dominant regime.... For exam-
> ple, Schwalbe (1996) shows how the leaders of men's movement
> gatherings artfully combine simple acts—decorating a room with
> totemic objects, burning incense, playing ethereal music, drumming,
> chanting, invoking spirits, and excluding women—to *induce* a feeling
> of emotional communion that *compelled* men to ignore political con-
> flicts, social class differences, and sexist behavior by other men.
> (Schwalbe et al. 2000, p. 438; emphasis added)

While they carefully skirt the issue of whether people are purposefully inducing feelings in others, Schwalbe et al. nonetheless construct a causal chain of events that characterizes—from an omniscient viewpoint—the putative emotions, behaviors, and settings of the gatherings. A constructionist scholar might wonder whether it is the participants or the authors who have assigned the parts, chosen the props, and set the scene within which all the participants are portrayed as acting.

In contrast to Collins's, Chang's, and Schwalbe et al.'s approaches, a constructionist approach would convert motivations into motive talk and would then proceed to study competing vocabularies of motive and the interactional dynamics of their use (Mills 1940; Potter and Wetherell 1987, ch. 4). The researcher would refrain (as much as possible) from assigning motives and causes in order to study how reasons are proffered, accepted, contested, revised, and so on.[6]

In my research, I have tried to stay more in line with this latter approach. I did not search respondents' speech and behavior for clues to their real motivation. Instead, I have focused on the ways spouses assigned motives (to themselves and others) and identified the causes and effects of inequality. Recall my respondent Deborah, for example. She offered an explanation for her husband's "power trips" that bolstered her larger story about the inequality in her marriage. She suggested that because she "came into the relationship with nothing" and he "put a roof over [her] head," her husband felt justified in not treating her as an equal (see chapter 4). Another one of my respondents, however, mobilized a similar but inverted rags-to-riches plot line in order to explain his wife's reportedly bossy demeanor. Remember that Wayne attributed the source of his wife's personality to a status change that went to her head: When his wife Tonya became his co-manager at a prominent hotel in a small town, her newfound power and prestige slowly turned her into a domineering person (see chapter 4).

What I have attempted to demonstrate with this interview data is a basic point: just as scholars impute motives and make causal linkages that support their larger narratives, so too do people. Their accounts also interpretively constitute conditions of inequality, the reasons behind them, and the victims and villains involved (see also Best 1999; Holstein and Miller 1990; Loseke 1993). Their tales may be as informative and interesting as scholarly versions, and merit close attention.

CONCLUSION

Is it the sociologist's prerogative to identify and explain inequality? I have argued that, to date, that has been the usual assumption among sociologists. The conventional wisdom in sociology is that inequality is "one of the most significant and decisive facts of human societies" (Maines 2000, p. 257) and that it is sociology's charter to document its extent, causes, and consequences. This premise unifies a wide array of "competing" approaches within the general rubrics of conflict theory and functionalism alike.

Recently, symbolic interactionists and other interpretive scholars have attempted to demonstrate the contribution they can make to understanding situations that fall on the "unequal" side of the equal/unequal dichotomy. However, as I have tried to show in this concluding chapter, these scholars have also tended to reproduce the conventional wisdom. In order to develop a more distinctive approach to inequality, perhaps a different premise is needed: Nothing is inherently unequal. This *un*conventional wisdom may provide a useful starting point for studying how individuals and groups construct versions of "inequality" by interpretively documenting (in Garfinkel's [1967] sense) its extent, precursors, and consequences.

The idea that "nothing is inherently unequal" may strike some readers as outrageous, if not silly. However, much interactionist research in the field of deviance has grown out of a similar premise—that no act is inherently deviant. Recall Becker's influential statement that "deviance is *not* a quality of the act the person commits.... The deviant is one to whom that label has successfully been applied" (Becker 1973, p. 9; but also see Pollner 1987). Similarly, the rich tradition of research on the construction of social problems can be traced, among other sources, to Blumer's statement that "social problems are fundamentally products of a process of collective definition instead of existing independently as a set of objective social arrangements with an intrinsic makeup" (Blumer 1971, p. 298; see also Loseke 1999; Miller and Holstein 1989; Spector and Kitsuse 1977). To say that nothing is inherently unequal seems no more bizarre than to claim that nothing is inherently deviant or problematic. Perhaps this unconventional premise will prove no less useful for researchers than those earlier premises have.[7]

But what does it mean to say that inequality is "not inherent"? On what is it contingent? Through what processes is it constructed? Much ambiguity pervades the ideas of contingency and construction. Consequently, scholars have used the same concepts to convey very different points. Researchers who presume the world is "built up" in the daily interactions of people may not necessarily be taking the constructionist viewpoint that it is people's *interpretive* practices that bring a recognizable world into being. For example, Collins (2000, p. 18) asserts that macroinequalities must be "microtranslated" into everyday experience to have any real existence; Chang (2000, p. 246) describes meaning as a "world-constituting force, a major factor that has contributed to China's... change of class structure"; and Schwalbe et al. (2000, p. 440) encourage studies of how people actively use resources "to create and reproduce patterns of action and experience."

The trouble is that a constructionist approach would use nearly the exact same language to say something quite different. Like Collins, a constructionist approach would study how people "microtranslate" inequalities, but it would do so by examining how people employ inequality-related concepts from the larger culture (e.g., "class" or "marital power") as they interpret the indeterminate complexities of their everyday lives (see Miller and Holstein 1989; Loseke 1999, 2001). Like Chang, a constructionist approach would consider interpretation to be a "world-constituting force," but in a less realist sense. For a constructionist "the world" is constituted by the way people "talk it into being" (Blumer 1969, p. 69; Heritage 1984, p. 290; Pollner 1987, p. 7), not by the way a few meanings here or there contribute to the creation of social structures.[8] And, like Schwalbe et al., a constructionist approach would be interested in how people "create patterns of action and experience," but *create* in the sense of selectively linking and transforming ambiguous incidents into comprehensible narrative patterns (Gubrium and Holstein 1997, pp. 146–47).

I don't want to overstate the difference between conventional and constructionist approaches, however. No matter how "strictly constructionist" an interactionist attempts to be, some assumptions must be made about the world out there (Best 1993). At the very least, the constructionist scholar assumes that the "interpretive practices" that constitute the world are demonstrably real. Beyond that, some constructionists have found it helpful to self-consciously incorporate somewhat "realist" observations of the social context in order to explain the differing contents and consequences of interpretations that are made in different settings (e.g., Loseke 1999; Weinberg 2001). However, these observations are limited and cautious, and made with the recognition that they could be subjected to constructionist analysis at any time (Gubrium and Holstein 1997, p. 120; Gubrium and Holstein 1999).

Also, I do not want to give the impression that all claims about inequality, because they are social constructions, are erroneous. To say that a story about inequality is socially constructed doesn't mean it is "false," just that it is not the only potentially useful account that might be given. And to say that inequality is an interpretation is not to argue that the concept or issue should be set aside in favor of more "objective" concerns. If everything is socially constructed, then there is no need to search desperately for rock solid footing. I am not arguing that sociologists should give up on inequality as an overarching theme for their research and advocacy. A large number of people (myself included) have found scholarly narratives about inequality to be particularly applicable and compelling. Undoubtedly they will continue to do so. Ideally, constructionist research on inequality can simply add a dose of clarity and humility (rather than despair) to the study and amelioration of injustice, by explicating the ways in which inequalities (like all social problems) are reflexively constituted by those who think and talk about them (see also Blumer 1971; Loseke 1999; Miller and Holstein 1989; Spector and Kitsuse 1977).

What I *am* arguing is that among the emerging agendas reviewed here, not all of them make a significant departure from the conventional sociological wisdom on inequality. There is another option besides treating inequality as a more or less factual condition that arises out of exploitive relations between groups, the functional requirements of a self-organizing system, or any other scenario. It is this: Researchers can treat inequality as a conceptual tool that people use to create a sense of social order. Not all interactionists need to treat inequality in this way; certainly not all sociologists should do so. Nevertheless, I think it is important that some scholars try to understand the generic *interpretive* processes that make inequality a recognizable, experienced feature of the world. These processes are arguably as "generative and essential" as the generic processes Schwalbe et al. and others are interested in.

The Practical Benefits of Social Constructionism

One final avenue future work could explore is how constructionist insights might actually have some practical benefits to people. Here I return to a subject I discussed in the last section of chapter 1: the moral value and usefulness of the kind of research I am advocating. I return to the issue with some trepidation. Accepting for a moment the dubious distinction between facts and morality, it does seem clear that scholarly versions of "what is" encounter much less resistance and hostility than do scholarly versions of "how to make things better." Perhaps that is one reason why interactionists have frequently avoided discussing the moral implications of their work on an explicit level.

One exception is Joseph Gusfield, a founding proponent of the constructionist approach to social problems. In his article, "On the Side: Practical Action and Social Constructivism in Social Problems Theory," Gusfield (1984) examines the relationship between academic sociology and the concerns of those who want to improve the world. Traditional sociologists, he argues, often set themselves up as experts on one or more social problems; policy makers, activists, college students, and others may look to such sociologists for information regarding the seriousness of certain problems and the effectiveness of potential solutions. Constructionists can't offer that kind of advice, Gusfield says, since they study "problems" and "solutions" as *interpretations*, not factual properties of the real world.

> A constructivist approach…drives a wedge between the elite in the know…and the practical people who attempt to achieve programmatic and personal victories. The sense of reflecting a natural, science-validated view of real conditions is undermined by a focus which brackets out the reality of the conditions around which the problem exists. It takes the affective starch—the driving sense of mission—out of social problems by viewing them as matters of partisan or professional *choice* rather than conclusions forced upon us by the nature of things. (Gusfield 1984, p. 45)

Thus, Gusfield describes the constructionist perspective as incompatible with being a social problems expert—or at least as the sort of expert whose opinion is likely to be sought—because it relativizes any and all statements of fact about issues like alcoholism, child abuse, and inequality. Moreover, Gusfield contends, constructionism necessarily reduces the sense of urgency that people feel about problems. "Serious problems" become *states of affairs <u>defined</u> as serious problems by some people, at a particular place and time, by selectively interpreting available data.*

Though social constructionism cannot offer certainty about the "facts" of social problems, Gusfield does believe it has something positive to contribute: it can make us less naïve, less likely to take descriptions as apolitical statements of fact. "Its social value lies in widening our understandings of self and others and in revealing the many alternatives from which to make choices and interpret events" (Gusfield 1984, p. 48). Constructionism makes us aware of our many interpretive options, but it does not elevate some of those options over others. Consequently, Gusfield claims, constructionist scholars are best thought of as being "on the side." Rather than taking sides, the proper role for constructionists is to sit out disputes—to conduct studies that broaden our understanding of social-problem-interpretation without offering anything in the way of social-problem-resolution.

Gusfield's paper concludes on this point and takes "understanding" as a satisfactory justification for pursuing constructionist research agendas. I'm not sure I want to end there. While I agree that better "understanding" is the main goal of constructionism, and agree further that such a goal is a laudable one, I disagree that practical action need be severed from constructionist research. Although constructionism doesn't begin with the sociological premise "Inequality exists and it is bad," studies conducted from that perspective *can* have practical benefits. Certainly, it is easy to point out the foibles of social science and to doubt the feasibility of improving the world in a rational manner (Gusfield 1984, p. 46). The difficult thing—what I earlier referred to as Dewey's challenge to us—is to take seriously the interpretive aspects of equality while still trying to collaboratively build a just social world. Rather than *removing* the affective starch from social problems, constructionism can, for instance, *add* a measure of humility to accompany the outrage with which sociologists and others tell stories about inequality. I believe constructionism can enrich affect, rather than merely reduce it, as long as people choose to seek the "working harmony among diverse desires" that Dewey advocates (see chapter 1). In what follows, I will briefly mention three areas in which constructionist insights on marital equality might be useful to practical actors who adopt a Deweyan orientation.

First, married persons themselves could benefit from constructionist research. There are many ways this could be so, but here I am thinking of those respondents who looked to me for validation—asking at the end of our interview together, "Now what do *you* think? Do I have an equal marriage or not?" The ideal of marital equality can be at once vague and difficult to attain. The pursuit of it sometimes causes people distress. Well-intended books on marital equality (e.g., Stapleton and Bright 1976; Kimball 1983; Schwartz 1994) provide goals for people to shoot for, but they also set standards by which people measure their successes. A constructionist perspective may reduce the shame or disappointment people feel if they are not able to establish an egalitarian marriage where breadwinning, chores, decisions, child care, sex, respect, communication, and so on, are all "equally shared." For example, a couple might self-consciously decide to try to be equal only in ways that matter to them—such as equality of love or respect. On the other hand, rather than redefining expectations to a more achievable level, a responsible reader of constructionist work like mine might try to apply a *higher* standard to their marriage. New domains of potential equality and inequality may become apparent to them, leading to greater vigilance in the pursuit of equality. The point is that—whether married couples wanted to adjust their equality standards upwards or downwards—constructionist research might "empower" them to do so in a more self-conscious manner.

Second, marital counselors could benefit from constructionist research. They might, for instance, become more sensitive to spouses' potentially divergent definitions of marital equality; such divergences could be a factor in some marital disputes. At the same time, therapists informed by constructionist work might also be less likely to impose their own definitions on their clients in a heavy-handed manner. In fact, the postmodern turn in academia has already led to the development of two new brands of therapy—"solution-focused brief therapy" and "narrative therapy"—both of which, in part, aim to encourage patients to construct more workable stories to live by (Miller 2001; Freedman and Combs 1996; Parry and Doan 1994). Such professionals may well appreciate reading the kind of work I have undertaken here. It might help them imagine different possible ways to re-story married lives.

A third group to whom future research could be helpful is social movement organizations (SMOs). Those associations that desire to effect large-scale social change by framing issues in terms of equality could benefit from a constructionist understanding of that concept. For example, SMOs could more self-consciously assess whether the domains and typifications they employ in identifying inequalities resonate with the interpreted realities of "the public." Mobilizing support often requires establishing a bridge between social movement frames and the diverse interpretive frames of potential recruits (Snow et al. 1986). SMO leaders might ask themselves, "How well do the domains and typifications we talk about match up with the domains and typifications that are commonly used by our target audiences? What can we do to produce a better alignment?" Not only could constructionism help SMOs develop more persuasive arguments, it could also help such groups deconstruct the arguments of their opponents. For example, white supremacists make claims about the supposed "inequality of the races," claims that might be better attacked with the help of constructionist conceptual armament.

These are just three possible ideas for the development of the practical uses of a constructionist perspective on equality. This discussion has been, of course, extremely sketchy. It would require several books to give the topic its due.[9] However, even this brief treatment is enough to make my point—that it *is* possible to use kinds of understandings developed here to try to improve the world in some way. I encourage readers and future researchers to consider such possibilities.

The main goal for this book, however, has not been to effect demonstrable change in the world. It has been more modest: to critique traditional perspectives on (marital) equality and inequality and propose an alternative. My sights were set in particular on improving academic sociology, a discipline that is virtually entombed within its own conceptions of equality and inequality. What's missing is a detailed appreciation of equality as it is experienced by actual persons in everyday life. In the end, the contribution that I have tried to make to the study of equality, in marriage and beyond, is to illustrate how one can respect and inquire about the interpretations made by the people whose lives comprise our "data." If similar studies with similar intentions are not conducted in the future, then the tales scholars tell about equality might forever take precedence over the stories that people live by. And that is a poor position from which to pursue a social science or improve the social world.

Notes

PREFACE

1. In fact, in one friendly critique of the tradition spawned by Spector and Kitsuse's book, Miller and Holstein (1989; Holstein and Miller 2003) have argued that the mundane application of social problems categories is just as important an issue as the creation of those categories by large-scale social movements. I agree with them, and so emphasize local usage of the terms "equality" and "inequality" in my book (see also Harris 2000a, pp. 136–37; Emerson and Messinger 1977; Loseke 1987, 2001).

CHAPTER 1

1. The relatively recent work by Barber (1991) was the only extended discussion of Schutz's (1957) paper that I could find.

2. Of course, mutual understanding is demonstrated only "for all practical purposes," and people rarely attempt to investigate "fully" whether they have communicated precisely, completely, without a doubt, what they mean. It is also possible for people to have only the vaguest sense of what they mean before, as, or after they say something.

3. This paragraph should make it clear that I am not turning to Dewey "as an independent source to decide what constitutes equality," as McKenzie (2003, p. 487) suggests in his brief comment on an earlier version of this chapter (Harris 2000b). Rather, I turn to Dewey to develop one kind of answer to the questions "What is constructionist research on equality good for? Why might people want to read it?" In addition to this footnoted paragraph within my larger section on Dewey, I also attempt to answer these questions in the conclusion of this book.

4. I do not mean to imply that Dewey thinks reason is superior to (or even separable from) emotion. Rather, Dewey recommends the expansion and integration of meanings and emotions in the process of moral problem solving:

> The conclusion is not that the emotional, passionate phase of action can be or should be eliminated in behalf of a bloodless reason. More "passions," not fewer, is the answer. To check the influence of hate there must be sympathy, while to rationalize sympathy there are needed emotions of curiosity, caution,

respect for the freedom of others.... Rationality... is the attainment of a working harmony among diverse desires. (Dewey 1983, p. 136)

Chapter 2

1. For example, along with the other publications I cite in chapters 3 and 4, see Blood and Wolfe (1960), Berheide (1984), Blumstein and Schwartz (1983), Deutsch (1999), Gillespie (1971), Gray-Little and Burks (1983), Hatfield, Traupmann, and Walster (1979), Hochschild (1989), Nock (1987), Ross, Mirowsky, and Huber (1983), Steil and Turetsky (1987), Schwartz (1994), Richardson (1979), and Smits, Ultee, and Lammers (1996).

2. See Rosenbluth, Steil, and Whitcomb (1998) for a conventional quantitative response to the difficulty of conceptualizing and operationalizing equality. After a relatively superficial treatment of inter-researcher discontinuity and researcher–subject divergence, they (Rosenbluth, Steil, Whitcomb 1998, p. 242; emphasis added) conclude that "traditional methods of assessing marital equality through measures of task division and decision-making say are not sufficiently inclusive. As empiricists, *we* must operationalize relationship equality as a multidimensional construct, using behavioral outcome measures in conjunction with measures of attitudes, affect, and interpersonal processes." The agenda I am proposing focuses on the problematic "we."

Another strand of research also addresses the issue of different interpretations of equality, in particular by focusing on perceptions of fairness in the division of labor (e.g., Blair and Johnson 1992; Hawkins, Marshall, and Meiners 1995; Lennon and Rosenfield 1994; Thompson 1991). Though these studies overlap somewhat with a constructionist approach, they differ in some significant ways. For example, the "perceptions of fairness" studies tend to (1) presume that equality consists of sharing the labor and (2) confidently compare spouses' interpretations with objective reality. In the beginning of an influential article Thompson (1991, p. 182) asks, "Why do so many wives and husbands profess egalitarianism, but not practice it? Why do most wives see the lopsided division of domestic work in their families as fair?" A thoroughly constructionist approach would avoid such confident comparisons, since all claims about marital equality would be bracketed and treated as data. Instead, a radical constructionist would treat the (interpretive) creation of these spouses and their situations as the topic of inquiry (see Loseke 1993, 2001).

Finally, I also encourage readers to see Hendrix (1994), who provides a critical evaluation of inter-researcher discontinuity in cross-cultural research on sexual equality, yet concludes with a conventional approach to "remedying" the problem.

Chapter 3

1. Gubrium and Holstein (1997) recommend that qualitative scholars remain aware of the tension between naturalism and constructionism, in order to make conscious choices about which facets of experience will be bracketed and which will remain

taken for granted (for current practical purposes) as observably real. They argue that in this way the irremediable tension between the two perspectives can be utilized as a source of inspiration.

2. Naturally, Kimball's and Schwartz's treatments of marital equality are not identical. For example, while Kimball (1983, pp. 29–30) explicitly mentions wives keeping their own last names as a potentially significant issue, Schwartz does not. Or, compare Schwartz's (1994, pp. 69–110) lengthy treatment of sexual relations to Kimball's (1983, pp. 80–81, 154) brief remarks. The authors give very different impressions about the relative importance of sexuality to equality in marriage.

Inconsistency also can be found when one looks to other sorts of authors. Consider two marital therapists' definition of the perfect egalitarian relationship: "To achieve this would be: (1) never letting . . . 'irrational shoulds' get in the way, (2) never trying to win even when each has a big stake in the situation, and (3) never using negative emotion or anger to solve problems" (Tuites and Tuites 1986, p. 194). Also, see Lynch (1992, pp. 13–15), a therapist with a contrasting perspective on power and the division of labor.

3. For contrasting perspectives on the "tasks" of housework, see Valadez and Clignet (1984), Shaw (1988), Coleman (1988), and Ahlander and Bahr (1995). It is also interesting to note that one of my respondents, "Deborah," relayed an anecdote somewhat similar to Barbara's. Deborah also spoke of a situation involving opened doors and invaded privacy (see chapter 4), but Deborah cast the incident as part of a larger pattern of power inequality, not "communicating about irritations."

4. Kimball (1983) is an exception in that she includes an appendix containing full transcriptions of three of her interviews. I am grateful to her for that, because otherwise I would not have been able to see or convey some of the differences between naturalist and constructionist interviewing.

5. Even "lies" create a sense of social order and must be told in an intelligible way.

6. Through a simple post-interview questionnaire, I was able to track my sample's diversity along the following dimensions and arrive at the following distribution:

Age: Seven were in their twenties, thirteen in their thirties, five in their forties, four in their fifties, and one in her sixties.

Time married: With respect to the time married (or for the three cohabiting, length doing so), ten had been together for 0–3 years, three for 4–6 years, four for 7–10 years, eight for 10–15 years, three for 16–20 years, and two for more than 21 years.

First marriage: For twenty-three of my respondents this was their first marriage (or first time cohabiting). Seven had at least one prior marriage (or prior cohabiting experience).

Children at home: Nineteen respondents still had children, of any age, step or otherwise, living in the home.

Education: Regarding their highest degree attained, almost half (thirteen) had a bachelors degree, five had a masters or teaching certificate, eleven completed high school, and one left high school after the ninth grade.

Combined income: Combined incomes of respondents and their partners ranged from $0–10,000 (3), $11,000–30,000 (3), $31,000–50,000 (12), $51,000–70,000 (6), $71,000–100,000 (4), and $101,000–130,000 (2).

Occupation: My respondents were employed in extremely diverse ways that defy easy summarization: three described themselves as "students," three as "teachers," two as "homemakers" and one as "momma." The rest gave fairly unique responses: grocery clerk, office worker, excavator/drain layer, service coordinator, counselor/self-employed contractor, primary parent/aid/writer/dance, property maintenance, tax accountant/social worker, motel manager, software producer, insurance agent, direct care nurse, case manager, unemployed, janitor, disability analyst, business owner, student/janitor, disabled/mechanic/counselor/unemployed, car salesperson, facial technician.

Race/ethnicity: In response to my "race/ethnicity" prompt, eighteen respondents described themselves as white or Caucasian, two as African American. Nine individuals each provided a unique response: Asian, Asian/Caucasian, Asian/American, Presumably White/One-Quarter Native American, Black/Native American, Indian/Hispanic, Mexican/American, White/Jewish, and Celtic. The remaining individual, whom I would label as white, described his race/ethnicity as "Nothin'."

Religion: Responses to my "religion" prompt were also fairly diverse. Four described themselves as Catholic, one said she was "Raised Catholic, now spiritual science," and one reported being "Influenced by Catholicism, but don't practice." Three simply wrote "Christian," one wrote "Christian who happens to attend a Baptist Church," another put "Southern Baptist." One answered "Jewish," another "Jewish/Buddhist," another "Buddhism." There was one Episcopalian, two Protestants, three Unitarian. One responded with "Abibical" and another "Islamic." Seven individuals did not describe themselves as adhering to a specific organized religious belief system; they wrote "none," "nonpracticing," "still forming," "open," "believe there's something going on we don't quite understand," "Earth," and "believe in God and Karma." One preferred not to answer that particular question on my questionnaire, though during the interview he discussed receiving some kind of religious marital counseling with his wife.

7. To what degree Sally's story is malleable and transient is an empirical matter, one that would have to be studied by comparing the tales she told in different circumstances about "the same" marital relationship. It seems likely that Sally would not make up a *completely* new account for each new occasion. The idea of "taking turns," for example, could be very important to her; it could be a narrative resource that she frequently incorporates into the stories she tells about her personal life. But a constructionist per-

spective suggests that the "taking turns" theme will be worked out in diverse ways from one storytelling occasion to another, as new examples are activated and new linkages are created in response to new situations.

However, it is important to note that even if *all* of Sally's themes and examples were constantly changing and completely context-specific, a constructionist approach would still dignify them as worthy of study. Constructionists seek to study the meanings of everyday life, and if those meanings are fleeting, then so be it. Moreover, from a constructionist perspective, it is wrong to think of research interviews as separate from the real world; an interview is a social interaction within the social world, and, as such, merits inquiry (see Baker 2002; Holstein and Gubrium 1995a). Even if the particular tales a person tells don't recur, the interpretive processes that created them probably will. The dynamics of storytelling might remain the same, regardless of whether the stories people live by are undergoing constant revision.

8. See also Spector and Kitsuse's (1977) constructionist critique of functionalist approaches to the identification and analysis of social problems. Occasionally, some naturalists' stories (Kimball's 1983, p. 177; Hochschild 1989, p. 12) are reminiscent of the functionalist idea that uneven social change can lead to disequilibrium (Ogburn 1957).

9. On the one hand, there is a sense in which this chapter has gone too far. I have reviewed the qualitative literature with an eye toward making a discernible contrast. Consequently, it is possible I have overdrawn the distinction between naturalist and constructionist approaches. It is likely that different scholars could purposefully search for commonalities and produce a complementary review highlighting the convergences that I have neglected. For example, Hochschild's (1989) concept of the "economy of gratitude" is somewhat constructionist in that it portrays spouses' perceptions of fairness as being a highly interpretive matter: A husband's workload at home may seem "large" in comparison to what his friends do or what his own father once did, but "small" in comparison to what his wife currently does. Divergent depictions of fairness may result, depending on which frame of reference a spouse employs. Ideas such as these might be incorporated into a constructionist account, once they were separated from their naturalist assumptions—in this case, that a fair division of labor is the correct definition or most germane aspect of marital equality, that household activities can be clearly categorized into "tasks" and "non-tasks," and that an equal relationship involves a 45/55 split in three categories of household labor (Hochschild 1989, p. 282). Future research could thus attempt to extract and refine the "embryonic" constructionist insights that already exist within naturalistic work on marital equality.

On the other hand, there is a sense in which my review did not go far enough. Why focus solely on the field of marital equality? Don't most social scientists take the meaning of equality and inequality for granted? In other subfields, even the most interpretive, qualitative scholars appear to repeat the sorts of naturalist tendencies I have discussed here: assuming an explicit or implicit definition, confidently discounting interpretations by employing a myth/reality distinction, and constructing causal accounts instead of studying how storytellers emplot their own narratives (e.g., see Chang 2000; Collins 2000; Holden 1997; Hollander and Howard 2000; Horowitz 1997; Schwalbe et al. 2000). I will return to this issue in the concluding chapter.

Chapter 4

1. As I attempt to demonstrate some of the diverse meanings that marital equality can have, I do not want to give the impression that I believe my classification of respondents' stories—for example "familiar" versus "unfamiliar" or as domains of "power" versus "lifestyles"—to be the only interpretation possible. After all, how could a constructionist claim that? A different analyst operating from a different standpoint might categorize my interview data very differently. Broad concepts such as "power" (or "labor," etc.) can be stretched to cover a huge range of behavior and situations; scholars who are especially interested in particular concepts may be able to use them to re-cast my "nonfamiliar" domains as "familiar" after all. This is not necessarily a weakness in my study, though. In fact, one could argue that the way I have presented my findings (through extended excerpts of interview talk) is "empowering" in the sense that it enables readers to pose alternative interpretations and to draw their own conclusions. I have done my best to keep my analysis both minimalist and well-grounded in the stories told to me by my respondents. However, I recognize that some readers might view the same stories very differently. If my analysis is "shown" to be faulty by one or more scholars, then I hope I have at least provided a bit of data useful for advancing the sociological dialogue about marital equality. (I would ask readers to compare how difficult it is to argue with, e.g., Hochschild's [1989] and Schwartz's [1994] interpretations of their respondents' marriages, given the minimal amount of direct quotation that those authors include in their books.)

2. See chapter 3, including note 6, for further description of my sample and other aspects of my methodology. While I made an effort to speak with a diverse group of respondents, I don't claim to have assembled a "representative sample." I believe that the small number of individuals I spoke with were diverse enough to give me some indication of the incredibly wide array of meanings that married people can assign to the concept of "equality." But the point of my research is not to create a comprehensive list of possible domains of relevance, or to discover the most popular domains. I think those goals would tend to *close down* what marital equality means. Instead, the point of my book is to *open up* the concept of equality; that is, I want to encourage readers to develop the inclination and ability to imagine (and investigate) what equality might mean to specific individuals in specific situations. I believe that my sample, and the stories I have chosen to present from it, are both sufficient for these purposes.

3. I included many of the hesitations and pauses (e.g., "um," "you know," and "…") in my excerpts of respondents' stories in part to convey this point.

4. Gubrium (1993) served as inspiration for the way I have chosen to present my respondents' narratives.

5. See Gray-Little and Burks (1983); McDonald (1980); Mizan (1994); Safilios-Rothschild (1970); Straus and Yodanis (1995); Turk and Bell (1972).

6. A constructionist approach to power in close relationships (and in all other areas of social life) takes people's definitional practices seriously. I agree with Robert Prus's premise that power is an interpretation, even though Prus and I disagree somewhat on how to conduct research based on this premise:

Rather than positing that power inheres in some situation..., we begin with the recognition that... power is a quality attributed to a situation by some audience. This means that the essential starting point for any analysis of power hinges on the definitions that people make, however tentatively, of specific situations in reference to matters of influence, control, domination, and the like. In the absence of definitions implying power dimensions, the interchanges or situations in question may be defined in other ways, such as play, fun, fascinating, work, frustrating, confusing, boring, instructive, educational, challenging, cooperative, helpful, and so forth. (Prus 1999, p. 153)

7. Another similarity bears mentioning. Though Wayne and Deborah both discussed the negative effects of the inequality, they also described themselves as having reached a point when they would not take it anymore. As if to counter the negative implications of appearing as powerless victims (Holstein and Miller 1990, p. 119), Wayne and Deborah (perhaps dramaturgically) highlighted their strength by proclaiming their newfound ability to stand up to their partners.

8. It is important to note that the division of labor was not an issue that only female respondents were concerned with or felt was an area of unfairness. My respondent "Larry," for example, complained that his stay-at-home wife made him drive the kids to school "Because she's not a morning person," even though he worked long hours (often until one or two o'clock in the morning) in the food service industry. For him, this issue seemed to be a higher concern than home improvement or handling the finances—providing another point of comparison to the cases of Lucy and Meg.

CHAPTER 5

1. Readers might recall that intelligence has appeared in a minor way in the "equity" literature I reviewed in chapter 2. One equity scale includes "having an intelligent partner" as one of twenty-four possible costs and benefits a person might derive from a close relationship (Walster, Walster, and Berscheid 1978). Brief mention of intelligence can also be found in Stapleton and Bright's (1976, p. 27) journalistic "how to" book, where the authors inform dissatisfied husbands that "A more equal marriage could make your wife a more equal person." The rare woman who is intellectually inferior to her husband, Stapleton and Bright advise, may simply suffer from the lack of intellectual stimulation that accompanies housework and child care.

Hence, the line between "familiar" and "unfamiliar" domains is obviously not absolute, nor do I intend it to be. But these kinds of minor exceptions do not suggest (at least to me) that the familiar/unfamiliar dichotomy is not a useful distinction for the purposes of this book, or that Alicin's case cannot justifiably be placed on the unfamiliar side of the spectrum.

2. Future constructionist researchers certainly could, and probably should, attempt to interview both spouses in a sample of marriages, in order to study the differences between (and the interactional production of) competing versions of the same marriages. Needless to say, that kind of project would pose the added difficulty of assembling a sample of willing partners, and might face an elevated risk of creating or aggravating marital discord.

3. However, in a manner similar to my comments in footnote 1, I should note that some sociological research on religious subcultures has included a concern with the issue of equality in marriage (Bartkowski 2001; Bartkowski and Read 2003).

4. I should note that I detected other fairly unfamiliar domains in addition to those of Alicin, Matthew, Courtney, and Michael. For example, one graduate student mentioned an "equality of space" that was lacking in his relationship because of the way bookshelves were allocated in his apartment. Another respondent claimed to notice an emerging equality of "voice" in her relationship, and suggested that over time she had come to feel she had as much right as her partner to speak and be heard in the world. Finally, one man appeared so happy and confident about his equal marriage that near the end of our interview he claimed, "This is like an equal marriage right down the middle." He virtually challenged me to think up domains of relevance for him to apply to his relationship by adding, "And that's with every subject you can possibly think of." The number of possible domains and typifications seemed limited only by people's abilities to carve out distinct areas of their lives as they used the conceptual resources provided by the larger culture and the interactional context.

CHAPTER 6

1. For example, see Blumer (1969), Denzin (1989), Prus (1996), Psathas (1980), and Reynolds (1993).

2. Despite the textbook formulations that ignore interactionism, there are interactionist-related publications (current and classic) that deal with inequality in some way—though not, I would argue, in a thoroughly interpretive or constructionist fashion (e.g., see Anderson and Snow 2001; Horowitz 1997; Maines and McCallion 2000; Mehan 1992; Shibutani and Kwan 1965; Whyte 1943). In this chapter I have chosen to limit my focus to *recent programmatic articles* that move the study of inequality in the general direction of Blumer's (1969) fundamental premises of interactionism. I do this principally to facilitate a detailed comparison of ongoing research agendas that are attempting to build on past traditions and conceptualize new paths for future inquiry. My choice of articles is also justified by the reactions the papers have received. Chang's article has been characterized as "a very ambitious analysis, even awesome in scope... [that] well deserves our careful and considered attention" (Maines 2000, p. 253). Schwalbe et al.'s article has been described as a "milestone essay" (Anderson 2001, pp. 392–93). Although I have not seen any immediate response to Collins's paper, I feel confident that a programmatic article by this well-known scholar will be influential and that it is worthy of my attention here.

3. Here Collins cites Zelizer (1994) for the concept of interactional circuits, but the point being made sounds somewhat reminiscent of Shibutani's (1961) interactionist treatment of status ladders and social worlds.

4. In his commentary on Chang's article, Maines (2000, p. 255) asserts that stratification in China is actually much more messy and complicated than Chang lets on, and that more research would be needed to get it right. A constructionist approach, in contrast, would set aside the goal of getting it right. Instead, the goal would be to study the

interpretive processes involved with assembling a coherent story about class stratification, as well as the different meanings that competing stories convey.

5. The ethnomethodological notions of indexicality and the etcetera principle (Heritage 1984) suggest that an unresolved swarm of potential meanings will always remain around the concept of inequality, and readers or listeners will need to search the context in order to comprehend (but never "fully") the practical implications of the term. For example, is the inequality just a mathematical difference? Is it a problem? Is it a fixable problem? Is it immoral? Who is to blame? What is to be done? What is the person's reason for telling me about this? (See Garfinkel 1967, pp. 38–41)

6. There is a tension between Blumer's first premise of interactionism and the interactionist approach to motive talk that can be difficult to resolve. When researchers use the notion that "Human beings act toward things on the basis of the meanings that the things have for them" (Blumer 1969, p. 2) as an explanatory resource, it can conflict with another interactionist idea—that the avowal and imputation of motives creates order out of chaos (Hopper 1993). In my view, the constructionist approach would accept Blumer's premise as largely true, but still would be extremely cautious about relying on that principle as a warrant to impute motives at will—as Collins, Chang, and Schwalbe et al. appear to do. Here it is worth noting that Chang refers repeatedly to "justifications" without acknowledging Scott and Lyman's (1968) special use of that term.

7. By invoking this premise, I do not intend to imply that large disparities in wealth are "really" no big deal, or that slavery is "really" equal after all, or anything of the sort. However, what I am suggesting is that social actors have considerable interpretive latitude when identifying equalities and inequalities in their social relationships and everyday lives. Interactionists and social constructionists have long argued that people can define problematic situations in many ways, and that different definitions can have a large impact on how they act (Blumer 1971; Loseke 1999; Miller and Holstein 1989; Spector and Kitsuse 1977). For an interactionist, the point of invoking the idea that "meaning is not inherent" is not to argue with the claims made by lay persons, activists, or mainstream sociologists—for example, claims that there are (or are not) real inequalities with real effects. Rather, the main purpose is to encourage researchers *to investigate* (1) the different inequality objects that may exist in diverse social worlds, as well as (2) the contingent interpretive processes that bring those experienced objects into existence.

8. I believe this critique also applies to scholars such as Lamont and Fournier (1992, pp. 6-7) who combine an interest in culture and inequality while still confidently making statements such as "social inequality is growing rapidly."

9. See Miller (2003) for more thoughts on the possibility of an applied constructionism.

References

Ahlander, N. R. and K. S. Bahr. 1995. "Beyond Drudgery, Power, and Equity: Toward an Expanded Discourse on the Moral Dimensions of Housework in Families." *Journal of Marriage and the Family* 57:54–68.

Anderson, L. 2001. "Editor's Introduction." *Symbolic Interaction* 24:391–394.

Anderson, L. and D. A. Snow. 2001. "Inequality and the Self: Exploring Connections from an Interactionist Perspective." *Symbolic Interaction* 24:395–406.

Anderson, M. L. and H. F. Taylor. 2001. *Sociology: The Essentials*. Belmont, CA: Wadsworth.

Atkinson, P. and A. Coffey. 2002. "Revisiting the Relationship between Participant Observation and Interviewing." Pp. 801–814 in *Handbook of Interview Research: Context and Method*, edited by J. F. Gubrium and J. A. Holstein. Thousand Oaks, CA: Sage.

Atkinson, P. and D. Silverman. 1997. "Kundera's *Immortality*: The Interview Society and the Invention of the Self." *Qualitative Inquiry* 3:304–325.

Baker, C. D. 2002. "Ethnomethodological Analyses of Interviews." Pp. 777–795 in *Handbook of Interview Research: Context and Method*, edited by J. F. Gubrium and J. A. Holstein. Thousand Oaks, CA: Sage.

Barber, M. 1991. "The Ethics Behind the Absence of Ethics in Alfred Schutz's Thought." *Human Studies* 14:129–140.

Bartkowski, J. P. 2001. *Remaking the Godly Marriage: Gender Negotiation in Evangelical Families*. New Brunswick, NJ: Rutgers.

Bartkowski, J. P. and J. G. Read. 2003. "Veiled Submission: Gender, Power, and Identity Among Evangelical and Muslim Women." *Qualitative Sociology* 26:71–92.

Bartley, M. 2003. *Health Inequality: An Introduction to Concepts, Theories, and Methods*. Cambridge: Polity Press.

Becker, H. 1973 [1963]. *Outsiders: Studies in the Sociology of Deviance*. New York: Free Press.

Benin, M. H. and J. Agostinelli. 1988. "Husbands' and Wives' Satisfaction with the Division of Labor." *Journal of Marriage and the Family* 50:349–361.

Berger, A. A. 1997. *Narratives in Popular Culture, Media, and Everyday Life*. Thousand Oaks, CA: Sage.

Berger, P. 1963. *Invitation to Sociology.* Garden City, NY: Anchor Books.

Berger, P. and H. Kellner. 1981. *Sociology Reinterpreted: An Essay on Method and Vocation.* Garden City, NY: Anchor.

Berger, P. L. and T. Luckmann. 1966. *The Social Construction of Reality: A Treatise in the Sociology of Knowledge.* Garden City, NY: Doubleday.

Berheide, C. W. 1984. "Women's Work in the Home: Seems Like Old Times." *Marriage and Family Review* 7:37–55.

Best, J. 1993. "But Seriously Folks: The Limitations of the Strict Constructionist Interpretation of Social Problems." Pp. 129–47 in *Reconsidering Social Constructionism: Debates in Social Problems Theory*, edited by J. A. Holstein and G. Miller. New York: Aldine de Gruyter.

———. 1999. *Random Violence: How We Talk About New Crimes and New Victims.* Berkeley: University of California Press.

———. 2000. "The Apparently Innocuous 'Just,' the Law of Levity, and the Social Problems of Social Construction." Pp. 3–14 in *Perspectives on Social Problems*, Vol. 12, edited by J. A. Holstein and G. Miller. Stamford, CT: JAI Press.

———. 2004. "Why Don't They Listen To US? Fashion Notes on the Imperial Wardrobe." *Social Problems* 51: 154–160.

Bird, G. W., G. A. Bird, and M. Scruggs. 1984. "Determinants of Family Task Sharing: A Study of Husbands and Wives." *Journal of Marriage and the Family* 46:345–355.

Bjorklund, D. 1998. *Interpreting the Self: Two Hundred Years of American Autobiography.* Chicago: University of Chicago Press.

Blair, S. L. and M. P. Johnson. 1992. "Wives Perceptions of the Fairness of the Division of Household Labor: The Intersection of Housework and Ideology." *Journal of Marriage and the Family* 54:570–581.

Blair, S. L. and D. T. Lichter. 1991. "Measuring the Division of Household Labor: Gender Segregation of Housework Among American Couples." *Journal of Family Issues* 12:91–113.

Blaisure, K. R. and K. R. Allen. 1995. "Feminists and the Ideology and Practice of Marital Equality." *Journal of Marriage and the Family* 57:5–19.

Blau, P. M. 1964. *Exchange and Power in Social Life.* New York: Wiley.

Blood, R. O. and D. M. Wolfe. 1960. *Husbands and Wives.* Glencoe, IL: The Free Press.

Blumer, H. 1937. "Social Psychology." Pp. 144–198 in *Man and Society*, edited by E. P. Schmidt. New York: Prentice-Hall.

———. 1969. *Symbolic Interactionism.* Englewood Cliffs, NJ: Prentice-Hall.

———. 1971. "Social Problems as Collective Behavior." *Social Problems* 18:298–306.

Blumstein, P. and P. Schwartz. 1983. *American Couples.* New York: Pocket Books.

Bruner, J. 1987. "Life as Narrative." *Social Research* 54:11–32.

Cancian, F. 1995. "Truth and Goodness: Does the Sociology of Inequality Promote Social Betterment?" *Sociological Perspectives* 38:339–356.

Cate, R. M., S. A. Lloyd, and J. M. Henton. 1985. "The Effect of Equity, Equality, and Reward Level on the Stability of Students' Premarital Relationships." *Journal of Social Psychology* 125:715–721.

Cate, R. M., S. A. Lloyd, J. M. Henton, and J. H. Larson. 1982. "Fairness and Reward Level as Predictors of Relationship Satisfaction." *Social Psychology Quarterly* 45:177–181.

Cate, R. M., S. A. Lloyd, and E. Long. 1988. "The Role of Rewards and Fairness in Developing Premarital Relationships." *Journal of Marriage and the Family* 50:443–452.

Centers, R. and B. H. Raven. 1971. "Conjugal Power Structure: A Re-Examination." *American Sociological Review* 36:264–278.

Chang, J. H-Y. 2000. "Symbolic Interaction and Transformation of Class Structure: The Case of China." *Symbolic Interaction* 23:223–251.

Coleman, M. T. 1988. "The Division of Household Labor: Suggestions for Future Empirical Consideration and Theoretical Development." *Journal of Family Issues* 9:132–148.

Coltrane, S. 1989. "Household Labor and the Routine Production of Gender." *Social Problems* 36:473–490.

Collins, R. 1981. "On the Micro-Foundations of Macro-Sociology." *American Journal of Sociology* 86:964–1014.

———. 1983. "Micromethods as a Basis for Macrosociology." *Urban Life* 12:84–202.

———. 1988. *Theoretical Sociology*. San Diego, CA: Harcourt Brace Jovanovich.

———. 1994. *Four Sociological Traditions*. New York: Oxford University Press.

———. 2000. "Situational Stratification: A Micro-Macro Theory of Inequality." *Sociological Theory* 18:17–43.

Collins, S. 1996. *Let Them Eat Ketchup! The Politics of Poverty and Inequality*. New York: Monthly Review Press.

Condit, C. M. and J. L. Lucaites. 1993. *Crafting Equality: America's Anglo-African Word*. Chicago: University of Chicago Press.

Cooney, R. S., L. H. Rogler, R. M. Hurrell, and V. Ortiz. 1982. "Decision Making in Intergenerational Puerto Rican Families." *Journal of Marriage and the Family* 44:621–631.

Cortazzi, M. 2001. "Narrative Analysis in Ethnography." Pp. 384–394 in *Handbook of Ethnography*, edited by P. Atkinson, A. Coffey, S. Delamont, J. Lofland, and L. Lofland. Thousand Oaks, CA: Sage.

Coulon, A. 1995. *Ethnomethodology*. Thousand Oaks, CA: Sage.

Cronon, W. 1992. "A Place for Stories: Nature, History, and Narrative." *Journal of American History* 78:1347–1376.

Daly, K. 2003. "Family Theory Versus the Theories Families Live By." *Journal of Marriage and Family* 65:771–784.

Davis, K. and W. Moore. 1945. "Some Principles of Stratification." *American Sociological Review* 10:242–249.

Denzin, N. K. 1989. *Interpretive Interactionism*. Newbury Park, CA: Sage.

Deutsch, F. M. 1999. *Halving It All: How Equally Shared Parenting Works*. Cambridge: Harvard University Press.

Devault, M. 1991. *Feeding the Family*. Chicago: University of Chicago Press.

Dewey, J. 1929. *Experience and Nature*. Peru, IL: Open Court.

———. 1983 [1922]. *Human Nature and Conduct*. In *The Middle Works*, Vol. 14, edited by Jo Ann Boydston. Carbondale: Southern Illinois University Press.

———. 1988 [1929]. *The Quest for Certainty*. In *The Later Works*, Vol. 4, edited by Jo Ann Boydston. Carbondale: Southern Illinois University Press.

———. 1989 [1932]. *Ethics*. In *The Later Works*, Vol. 7, edited by Jo Ann Boydston. Carbondale: Southern Illinois University Press.

Emerson, R. M. and S. L. Messinger. 1977. "The Micro-Politics of Trouble." *Social Problems* 25:121–134.

Erickson, R. J. 1993. "Reconceptualizing Family Work: The Effect of Emotion Work on Perceptions of Marital Quality." *Journal of Marriage and the Family* 55:888–900.

Flaherty, M. G. 1987. "The Neglected Dimension of Temporality in Social Psychology." Pp. 143–155 in *Studies in Symbolic Interaction*, edited by N. K. Denzin. Greenwich, CT: JAI Press.

Foa, U. G. and E. G. Foa. 1974. *Societal Structures of the Mind*. Springfield, IL: Charles C. Thomas.

Foster, J. 1999. *The Vulnerable Planet: A Short Economic History of the Environment*. New York: Monthly Review.

Fox, B. J. and D. Fumia. 2001. "Pathbreakers: Unconventional Families of the Nineties." Pp. 458–469 in *Family Patterns, Gender Relations*, edited by B. J. Fox. New York: Oxford University Press.

Freedman, J. and G. Combs. 1996. *Narrative Therapy: The Social Construction of Preferred Realities*. New York: W. W. Norton.

Fuller, R. and R. Myers. 1941. "The Natural History of a Social Problem." *American Sociological Review* 6:320–328.

Garfinkel, H. 1967. *Studies in Ethnomethodology*. Englewood Cliffs, NJ: Prentice-Hall.

Garfinkel, H. and H. Sacks. 1970. "On the Formal Structures of Practical Actions." Pp. 337–366 in *Theoretical Sociology: Perspectives and Developments*, edited by J. C. McKinney and E. A. Tiryakian. New York: Appleton-Century-Crofts.

Gerson, K. 1993. *No Man's Land: Men's Changing Commitments to Family and Work*. New York: Basic Books.

Gillespie, D. L. 1971. "Who Has the Power? The Marital Struggle." *Journal of Marriage and the Family* 33:445–458.

Glaser, B. G. and A. L. Strauss. 1967. *The Discovery of Grounded Theory*. New York: Aldine De Gruyter.

Goffman, E. 1967. *Interaction Ritual*. New York: Doubleday.

Goode, E. 1994. *Deviant Behavior*, 4th ed. Englewood Cliffs, NJ: Prentice-Hall.

Gray-Little, B. 1982. "Marital Quality and Power Processes Among Black Couples." *Journal of Marriage and the Family* 44:633–646.

Gray-Little, B. and N. Burks. 1983. "Power and Satisfaction in Marriage: A Review and Critique." *Psychological Bulletin* 93:513–538.

Gubrium, J. F. 1988. *Analyzing Field Reality*. Newbury Park, CA: Sage.

———. 1993. *Speaking of Life*. New York: Aldine De Gruyter.

Gubrium, J. F. and J. A. Holstein. 1990. *What Is Family?* Mountain View, CA: Mayfield.

———. 1995. "Biographical Work and New Ethnography." Pp. 45–58 in *The Narrative Study of Lives*, Vol. 3, edited by R. Josselson and A. Lieblich. Thousand Oaks, CA: Sage.

———. 1997. *The New Language of Qualitative Method*. New York: Oxford University Press.

———. 1998. "Narrative Practice and the Coherence of Personal Stories." *Sociological Quarterly* 39:163–187.

———. 1999. "At the Border of Narrative and Ethnography." *Journal of Contemporary Ethnography* 28:561–573.

———. 2000. "The Self in a World of Going Concerns." *Symbolic Interaction* 23:95–115.

Gusfield, J. R. 1984. "On the Side: Practical Action and Social Constructivism in Social Problems Theory." Pp. 31–51 in *Studies in the Sociology of Social Problems*, edited by J.W. Schneider and J. I. Kitsuse. Noorwood, NJ: Ablex.

Haas, L. 1980. "Role-Sharing Couples: A Study of Egalitarian Marriages." *Family Relations* 29:289–296.

———. 1982. "Determinants of Role-Sharing Behavior: A Study of Egalitarian Couples." *Sex Roles* 8:747–760.

Hagan, J. and R. D. Peterson (editors). 1995. *Crime and Inequality*. Stanford, CA: Stanford University Press.

Hall, L. D. and A. M. Zvonkovic. 1996. "Egalitarianism and Oppression in Marriage: The Effects of Research on Researchers." *Marriage and Family Review* 24:89–104.

Harris, S. R. 1997. "Status Inequality and Close Relationships: An Integrative Typology of Bond-Saving Strategies." *Symbolic Interaction* 20:1–20.

———. 2000a. "Meanings and Measurements of Equality in Marriage: A Study of the Social Construction of Equality." Pp. 111–145 in *Perspectives on Social Problems*, Vol. 12, edited by J. A. Holstein and G. Miller. Stamford, CT: JAI Press.

————. 2000b. "The Social Construction of Equality in Everyday Life." *Human Studies* 23: 371–393.

————. 2001. "What Can Interactionism Contribute to the Study of Inequality? The Case of Marriage and Beyond." *Symbolic Interaction* 24:455–480.

————. 2003. "Studying Equality/Inequality: Naturalist and Constructionist Approaches to Equality in Marriage." *Journal of Contemporary Ethnography* 32:200–232.

————. 2004. "Challenging the Conventional Wisdom: Recent Proposals for the Interpretive Study of Inequality." *Human Studies* 27:113–136.

Hatfield, E., D. Greenberger, J. Traupmann, and P. Lambert. 1982. "Equity and Sexual Satisfaction in Recently Married Couples." *Journal of Sex Research* 18:18–32.

Hatfield, E., J. Traupmann, S. Sprecher, M. Utne, and J. Hay. 1985. "Equity and Intimate Relations: Recent Research." Pp. 91–117 in *Compatible and Incompatible Relationships*, edited by W. Ickes. New York: Springer Verlag.

Hatfield, E. J. Traupmann, and G. W. Walster. 1979. "Equity and Extramarital Sex." Pp. 309–321 in *Love and Attraction*, edited by M. Cook and G. Wilson. Oxford: Pergamon.

Hatfield, E., M. K. Utne, and J. Traupmann. 1979. "Equity Theory and Intimate Relationships." Pp. 99–133 in *Social Exchange in Developing Relationships*, edited by R. L. Burgess and T. L. Huston. New York: Academic Press.

Hatfield, E., G. W. Walster, and J. Traupmann. 1979. "Equity and Premarital Sex." Pp. 323–334 in *Love and Attraction*, edited by M. Cook and G. Wilson. Oxford: Pergamon.

Hawkins, A. J., C. M. Marshall, and K. M. Meiners. 1995. "Exploring Wives' Sense of Fairness About Family Work." *Journal of Family Issues* 16:693–721.

Hendrix, L. 1994. "What Is Sexual Inequality: On the Definition and Range of Variation." *Cross-Cultural Research* 28:287–307.

Heritage, J. 1984. *Garfinkel and Ethnomethodology.* Cambridge: Polity Press.

Hiller, D. V. and W. W. Philliber. 1980. "Necessity, Compatibility and Status Attainment as Factors in the Labor-Force Participation of Married Women." *Journal of Marriage and the Family* 42:347–354.

Hochschild, A. R. 1983. *The Managed Heart: Commercialization of Human Feeling.* Berkeley: University of California Press.

Hochschild, A. with A. Machung. 1989. *The Second Shift.* New York: Avon Books.

Holden, D. 1997. "On Equal Ground: Sustaining Virtue among Volunteers in a Homeless Shelter." *Journal of Contemporary Ethnography* 26:117–145.

Hollander, J. and J. Howard. 2000. "Social Psychological Theories on Social Inequalities." *Social Psychology Quarterly* 63:338–351.

Holstein, J. A. and J. F. Gubrium. 1995a. *The Active Interview.* Thousand Oaks, CA: Sage.

————. 1995b. "Deprivatization and the Construction of Domestic Life." *Journal of Marriage and the Family* 57:894–908.

Holstein, J. A. and G. Miller. 1990. "Rethinking Victimization: An Interactional Approach to Victimology." *Symbolic Interaction* 13:103–122.

Holstein, J. A. and G. Miller (editors). 1993. *Reconsidering Social Constructionism: Debates in Social Problems Theory.* New York: Aldine de Gruyter.

———. 2003. "Social Constructionism and Social Problems Work." Pp. 70–91 in *Challenges and Choices: Constructionist Perspectives on Social Problems,* edited by J. A. Holstein and G. Miller. New York: Aldine de Gruyter.

Homans, G. C. 1958. "Social Behavior as Exchange." *American Journal of Sociology* 63:597–606.

———. 1974. *Social Behavior.* New York: Harcourt Brace Jovanovich.

Hopper, J. 1993. "The Rhetoric of Motives in Divorce." *Journal of Marriage and the Family* 55:801–813.

Horowitz, R. 1997. "Barriers and Bridges to Class Mobility and Formation: Ethnographies of Stratification." *Sociological Methods and Research* 25:495–538.

Ibarra, P. R. and J. I. Kitsuse. 1993. "Vernacular Constituents of Moral Discourse: An Interactionist Proposal for the Study of Social Problems." Pp. 25–58 in *Reconsidering Social Constructionism: Debates in Social Problems Theory,* edited by J. A. Holstein and G. Miller. New York: Aldine de Gruyter.

James, W. 1890. *The Principles of Psychology,* Vol. 1. New York: Henry Holt.

Kamo, Y. 1988. "Determinants of Household Division of Labor: Resources, Power, and Ideology." *Journal of Family Issues* 9:177–200.

Kerbo, H. R. 1991. *Social Stratification and Inequality: Class Conflict in Historical and Comparative Perspective* (2nd edition). New York: McGraw-Hill.

Kimball, G. 1983. *The 50/50 Marriage.* Boston: Beacon.

Kingston, P. W. 2000. *The Classless Society.* Stanford, CA: Stanford University Press.

Kitsuse, J. I. and A. V. Cicourel. 1963. "A Note on the Uses of Official Statistics." *Social Problems* 11:131–139.

Knudson-Martin, C. and A. R. Mahoney. 1998. "Language Processes in the Construction of Equality in New Marriages." *Family Relations* 47:81–91.

Komarovsky, M. 1946. "Cultural Contradictions and Sex Roles." *American Journal of Sociology* 52:184–189.

Kranichfeld, M. L. 1987. "Rethinking Family Power." *Journal of Family Issues* 8:42–56.

Lamont, M. and M. Fournier. 1992. "Introduction." Pp. 1–17 in *Cultivating Differences: Symbolic Boundaries and the Making of Inequality,* edited by M. Lamont and M. Fournier. Chicago: University of Chicago Press.

Lareau, A. 2002. "Invisible Inequality: Social Class and Childrearing in Black and White Families." *American Sociological Review* 67:747–776.

Lennon, M. C. and S. Rosenfield. 1994. "Relative Fairness and the Division of Housework: The Importance of Options." *American Journal of Sociology* 100:506–531.

Levinson, D. (editor). 1995. *Encyclopedia of Marriage and the Family*, Vol. 1–2. New York: Macmillan.

Liberman, K. 1980. "Ambiguity and Gratuitous Concurrence in Inter-Cultural Communication." *Human Studies* 3:65–85.

Lorber, J. 2001. *Gender Inequality: Feminist Theories and Politics*. Los Angeles: Roxbury Publishing Co.

Loseke, D. R. 1987. "Lived Realities and the Construction of Social Problems: The Case of Wife Abuse." *Symbolic Interaction* 10:229–243.

———. 1993. "Constructing Conditions, People, Morality, and Emotion: Expanding the Agenda of Constructionism." Pp. 207–216 in *Constructionist Controversies: Issues in Social Problems Theory*, edited by G. Miller and J. A. Holstein. New York: Aldine de Gruyter.

———. 1999. *Thinking About Social Problems: An Introduction to Constructionist Perspectives*. New York: Aldine de Gruyter.

———. 2001. "Lived Realities and Formula Stories of 'Battered Women.'" Pp. 107–126 in *Institutional Selves: Troubled Identities in a Postmodern World*, edited by J. F. Gubrium and J. A. Holstein. New York: Oxford University Press.

Lynch, B. J. 1992. "Partnership and Ego Equality in the Marital System." Pp. 11–24 in *Equal Partnering: A Feminine Perspective*, edited by B. J. Brothers. Binghamton, NY: Harrington Park Press.

Mainardi, P. 1970. "The Politics of Housework." Pp. 447–454 in *Sisterhood Is Powerful*, edited by R. Morgan. New York: Random House.

Maines, D. R. 1993. "Narrative's Moment and Sociology's Phenomena: Toward a Narrative Sociology." *Sociological Quarterly* 34:17–38.

———. 2000. "Some Thoughts on the Interactionist Analysis of Class Stratification: A Commentary." *Symbolic Interaction* 23:253–258.

Maines, D. R. and M. J. McCallion. 2000. "Urban Inequality and the Possibilities of Church-Based Intervention." Pp. 43–53 in *Studies in Symbolic Interaction*, Vol. 3, edited by N. K. Denzin. Greenwich, CT: JAI Press.

Marger, M. N. 1999. *Social Inequality: Patterns and Processes*. Mountain View, CA: Mayfield Publishing Co.

Martin, M. W. 1985. "Satisfaction with Intimate Exchange: Gender Role Differences and the Impact of Equity, Equality, and Rewards." *Sex Roles* 13:597–605.

Maso, I. 2001. "Phenomenology and Ethnography." Pp. 136–144 in *Handbook of Ethnography*, edited by P. Atkinson, A. Coffey, S. Delamont, J. Lofland, and L. Lofland. Thousand Oaks, CA: Sage.

Maynard, D. W. and S. E. Clayman. 1991. "The Diversity of Ethnomethodology." *Annual Review of Sociology* 17:385–418.

McDonald, G. W. 1980. "Family Power: The Assessment of a Decade of Theory and Research, 1970–1979." *Journal of Marriage and the Family* 42:841–854.

McKenzie, K. 2003. "Discursive Psychology and the 'New Racism.'" *Human Studies* 26:461–491.

Mead, G. H. 1934. *Mind, Self, and Society.* Chicago: University of Chicago.

Mehan, H. 1992. "Understanding Inequality in Schools: The Contribution of Interpretive Studies." *Sociology of Education* 65:1–20.

Michaels, J. W., J. N. Edwards, and A. C. Acock. 1984. "Satisfaction in Intimate Relationships as a Function of Inequality, Inequity, and Outcomes." *Social Psychology Quarterly* 47:347–357.

Miller, G. 2001. "Changing the Subject: Self-Construction in Brief Therapy." Pp. 64–83 in *Institutional Selves: Troubled Identities in a Postmodern World*, edited by J. F. Gubrium and J. A. Holstein. New York: Oxford University Press.

———. 2003. "Getting Serious About an Applied Constructionism of Social Problems." Pp. 236–254 in *Challenges and Choices: Constructionist Perspectives on Social Problems*, edited by J. A. Holstein and G. Miller. New York: Aldine de Gruyter.

Miller, G. and J. A. Holstein. 1989. "On the Sociology of Social Problems." Pp. 1–16 in *Perspectives on Social Problems*, Vol. 1, edited by J. A. Holstein and G. Miller. Greenwich, CT: JAI Press.

Mills, C. W. 1940. "Situated Actions and Vocabularies of Motive." *American Sociological Review* 6:904–913.

Mizan, A. N. 1994. "Family Power Studies: Some Major Methodological Issues." *International Journal of Sociology of the Family* 24:85–91.

Model, S. 1981. "Housework by Husbands: Determinants and Implications." *Journal of Family Issues* 2:225–237.

Morris, M. and B. Western. 1999. "Inequality in Earnings at the Close of the Twentieth Century." *Annual Review of Sociology* 25:623–657.

Nock, S. L. 1987. *Sociology of the Family.* Englewood Cliffs, NJ: Prentice-Hall.

O'Brien, R. M. 1985. *Crime and Victimization Data.* Beverly Hills, CA: Sage.

O'Brien, R. M. and D. Jacobs. 1998. "The Determinants of Deadly Force: A Structural Analysis of Police Violence." *American Journal of Sociology* 103:837–862.

Ochberg, R. L. 1994. "Life Stories and Storied Lives." Pp. 113–144 in *The Narrative Study of Lives*, Vol. 2, edited by A. Lieblich and R. Josselson. Thousand Oaks, CA: Sage.

Ochs, E. and L. Capps. 1996. "Narrating the Self." *Annual Review of Anthropology* 25:19–43.

Ogburn, W. F. 1957. "Cultural Lag as Theory." *Sociology and Social Research* 41:167–174.

Olson, D. H. and R. E. Cromwell. 1975. "Methodological Issues in Family Power." Pp. 131–150 in *Power in Families*, edited by R. E. Cromwell and D. H. Olson. New York: John Wiley.

Oppenheimer, V. K. 1977. "The Sociology of Women's Economic Role in the Family." *American Sociological Review* 42:387–406.

Parry, A. and R. E. Doan. 1994. *Story Re-Visions: Narrative Therapy in the Postmodern World.* New York: The Guilford Press.

Parsons, T. 1940. "An Analytic Approach to the Theory of Social Stratification." *American Journal of Sociology* 45:841–862.

———. 1954. "The Kinship System of the Contemporary United States." Pp. 177–196 in *Essays in Sociological Theory.* New York: The Free Press.

———. 1959. "The Social Structure of the Family." Pp. 241–274 in *The Family* (revised edition), edited by R. N. Anshen. New York: Harper and Brothers.

Philliber, W. W. and D. V. Hiller. 1983. "Relative Occupational Attainments of Spouses and Later Changes in Marriage and Wife's Work Experience." *Journal of Marriage and the Family* 45:161–170.

Piña, D. L. and V. L. Bengtson. 1993. "The Division of Labor and Wives' Happiness: Ideology, Employment, and Perceptions of Support." *Journal of Marriage and the Family* 55:901–912.

Pleck, J. H. 1985. *Working Wives/Working Husbands.* Beverly Hills, CA: Sage.

Plummer, K. 2001. "The Call of Life Stories in Ethnographic Research." Pp. 395–406 in *Handbook of Ethnography*, edited by P. Atkinson, A. Coffey, S. Delamont, J. Lofland, and L. Lofland. Thousand Oaks, CA: Sage.

Polkinghorne, D. E. 1988. *Narrative Knowing and the Human Sciences.* Albany: State University of New York Press.

Pollner, M. 1987. *Mundane Reason: Reality in Everyday and Sociological Discourse.* New York: Cambridge University Press.

———. 1991. "Left of Ethnomethodology." *American Sociological Review* 56:370–380.

Pollner, M. and R. M. Emerson. 2001. "Ethnomethodology and Ethnography." Pp. 118–135 in *Handbook of Ethnography*, edited by P. Atkinson, A. Coffey, S. Delamont, J. Lofland, and L. Lofland. Thousand Oaks, CA: Sage.

Potter, J. and M. Wetherell. 1987. *Discourse and Social Psychology: Beyond Attitudes and Behaviour.* London: Sage.

Prus, R. 1987. "Generic Social Processes: Maximizing Conceptual Development in Ethnographic Research." *Journal of Contemporary Ethnography* 16:250–291.

———. 1996. *Symbolic Interaction and Ethnographic Research.* Albany: State University of New York Press.

———. 1999. *Beyond the Power Mystique.* Albany: State University of New York Press.

Psathas, G. 1980. "Approaches to the Study of the World of Everyday Life." *Human Studies* 3:3–17.

Reynolds, W., R. Remer, and M. Johnson. 1995. "Marital Satisfaction in Later Life: An Examination of Equity, Equality, and Reward Theories." *International Journal of Aging and Human Development* 40:155–173.

Richardson, J. G. 1979. "Wife Occupational Superiority and Marital Troubles: An Examination of the Hypothesis." *Journal of Marriage and the Family* 41:63–72.

Richardson, L. 1990. "Narrative and Sociology." *Journal of Contemporary Ethnography* 19:116–135.

Riessman, C. K. 1990. *Divorce Talk: Women and Men Make Sense of Personal Relationships*. New Brunswick, NJ: Rutgers University Press.

———. 1993. *Narrative Analysis*. Newbury Park, CA: Sage.

———. 2002. "Analysis of Personal Narratives." Pp. 695–710 in *Handbook of Interview Research: Context and Method*, edited by J. F. Gubrium and J. A. Holstein. Thousand Oaks, CA: Sage.

Risman, B. J. 1998. *Gender Vertigo*. New Haven, CT: Yale University Press.

Rodman, H. 1967. "Marital Power in France, Greece, Yugoslavia, and the United States: A Cross-National Discussion." *Journal of Marriage and the Family* 29:320–324.

———. 1972. "Marital Power and the Theory of Resources in Cultural Context." *Journal of Comparative Family Studies* 3:50–67.

Rosenbluth, S. C., J. M. Steil, and J. H. Whitcomb. 1998. "Marital Equality: What Does It Mean?" *Journal of Family Issues* 19:227–244.

Ross, C. E., J. Mirowsky and J. Huber. 1983. "Diving Work, Sharing Work, and In-Between: Marriage Patterns and Depression." *American Sociological Review* 48:809–823.

Safilios-Rothschild, C. 1967. "A Comparison of Power Structure and Marital Satisfaction in Urban Greek and French Families." *Journal of Marriage and the Family* 29:345–352.

———. 1970. "The Story of Family Power: A Review, 1960–69." *Journal of Marriage and the Family* 32:539–552.

Schneider, J. W. 1985. "Social Problems Theory: The Constructionist View." *Annual Review of Sociology* 11:209–229.

Schutz, A. 1957. "Equality and the Meaning Structure of the Social World." Pp. 33–78 in *Aspects of Human Equality*, edited by L. Bryson, C. H. Faust, L. Finkelstein, and R. M. MacIver. New York: Harper & Brothers.

———. 1964. "Equality and the Meaning Structure of the Social World." Pp. 226–273 in *Collected Papers*, Vol. 2. The Hague, Netherlands: Martinus Nijhoff.

———. 1970. *On Phenomenology and Social Relations*. Chicago: University of Chicago Press.

———. 1973. "Commonsense and Scientific Interpretation of Human Action." Pp. 3–47 in *Collected Papers*, Vol. 1. The Hague, Netherlands: Martinus Nijhoff.

Schwalbe, M., S. Godwin, D. Holden, D. Schrock, S. Thompson, and M. Wolkomir. 2000. "Generic Processes in the Reproduction of Inequality: An Interactionist Analysis." *Social Forces* 79:419–452.

Schwartz, P. 1994. *Peer Marriage: How Love Between Equals Really Works*. New York: The Free Press.

Scott, M. B. and S. M. Lyman. 1968. "Accounts." *American Sociological Review* 33:46–62.

Shapiro, T. M. 1998. *Great Divides: Readings in Social Inequality in the United States.* Mountain View, CA: Mayfield.

Shaw, S. M. 1988. "Gender Differences in the Definition and Perception of Household Labor." *Family Relations* 37:333–337.

Shelton, B. A. and D. John. 1996. "The Division of Household Labor." *Annual Review of Sociology* 22:299–322.

Shibutani, T. 1955. "Reference Groups as Perspectives." *American Journal of Sociology* 60:562–569.

———. 1961. *Society and Personality: An Interactionist Approach to Social Psychology.* Englewood Cliffs, NJ: Prentice-Hall.

Shibutani, T. and K. M. Kwan. 1965. *Ethnic Stratification: A Comparative Approach.* New York: Macmillan.

Shukla, A. 1987. "Decision Making in Single- and Dual-Career Families in India." *Journal of Marriage and the Family* 49:621–629.

Simmel, G. 1971. *On Individuality and Social Forms.* Edited by D. N. Levine. Chicago: University of Chicago.

Simpson, I. H. and P. England. 1981. "Conjugal Work Roles and Marital Solidarity." *Journal of Family Issues* 2:180–204.

Smith, A. D. and W. J. Reid. 1986. *Role-Sharing Marriage.* New York: Columbia University.

Smits, J., W. Ultee, and J. Lammers. 1996. "Effects of Occupational Status Differences Between Spouses on the Wife's Labor Force Participation and Occupational Achievement: Findings from 12 European Countries." *Journal of Marriage and the Family* 58:101–115.

Snow, D. A., E. B. Rochford, Jr., S. K. Worden, and R. D. Benford. 1986. "Frame Alignment Processes, Micromobilization, and Movement Participation." *American Sociological Review* 51:464–481.

Spector, M. and J. I. Kitsuse. 1977. *Constructing Social Problems.* Menlo Park, CA: Cummings.

Spencer, J. W. 2000. "Appropriating Cultural Discourses: Notes on a Framework for Constructionist Analyses of the Language of Claims-Making." Pp. 25–40 in *Perspectives on Social Problems,* Vol. 12, edited by J. A. Holstein and G. Miller. Stamford, CT: JAI Press.

Sprecher, S. 1995. "Equity and Close Relationships." Pp. 221–227 in *Encyclopedia of Marriage and the Family,* Vol. 1, edited by D. Levinson. New York: Macmillan.

Sprey, J. 1972. "Family Power Structure: A Critical Comment." *Journal of Marriage and the Family* 34:235–238.

Stapleton, J. and R. Bright. 1976. *Equal Marriage*. Nashville, TN: Abingdon.

Steil, J. M. and B. A. Turetsky. 1987. "Is Equal Better? The Relationship Between Marital Equality and Psychological Symptomatology." *Applied Social Psychology Annual* 7:73–97.

Straus, M. A. and I. Tallman. 1971. "SIMFAM: A Technique for Observational Measurement and Experimental Study of Families." Pp. 381–438 in *Family Problem Solving*, edited by J. Aldous, T. Condon, R. Hill, M. Straus, and I. Tallman. Hinsdale, IL: Dryden.

Straus, M. A. and C. L. Yodanis. 1995. "Marital Power." Pp. 437–442 in *Encyclopedia of Marriage and the Family*, Vol. 2, edited by D. Levinson. New York: MacMillan.

Strauss, A. 1995. "Identity, Biography, History, and Symbolic Representations." *Social Psychology Quarterly* 58:4–12.

Thibaut, J. W. and H. H. Kelley. 1959. *The Social Psychology of Groups*. New York: Wiley.

Thompson, L. 1991. "Family Work: Women's Sense of Fairness." *Journal of Family Issues* 12:181–196.

Traupmann, J., R. Petersen, M. Utne, and E. Hatfield. 1981. "Measuring Equity in Intimate Relations." *Applied Psychological Measurement* 5:467–480.

Trumbach, R. 1978. *The Rise of the Egalitarian Family: Aristocratic Kinship and Domestic Relations in Eighteenth-Century England*. New York: Academic Press.

Tuites, A. H. and D. E. Tuites. 1986. "Equality in Male/Female Relationships." *Individual Psychology: The Journal of Alderian Theory, Research, and Practice.* 42:191–200.

Turk, J. L. 1975. "Uses and Abuses of Family Power." Pp. 80–94 in *Power in Families*, edited by R. E. Cromwell and D. H. Olson. New York: John Wiley.

Turk, J. L. and N. W. Bell. 1972. "Measuring Family Power." *Journal of Marriage and the Family* 34:215–222.

Twiggs, J. E, J. McQuillan, and M. M. Ferree. 1998. "Meaning and Measurement: Reconceptualizing Measures of the Division of Household Labor." *Journal of Marriage and the Family* 61:712–724.

Utne, M. K., E. Hatfield, J. Traupmann, and D. Greenberger. 1984. "Equity, Marital Satisfaction, and Stability." *Journal of Social and Personal Relationships* 1:323–332.

Valadez, J. J. and R. Clignet. 1984. "Housework as Ordeal: Culture of Standards versus Standardization of Culture." *American Journal of Sociology* 89:812–835.

Walster, E., G. W. Walster, and E. Berscheid. 1978. *Equity: Theory and Research*. Boston: Allyn and Bacon.

Warner, R. L. 1986. "Alternative Strategies for Measuring Household Division of Labor." *Journal of Family Issues* 7:179–195.

Watson, G. and J. G. Goulet. 1998. "What Can Ethnomethodology Say About Power?" *Qualitative Inquiry* 4:96–113.

Weinberg, D. 2001. "Self-Empowerment in Two Therapeutic Communities." Pp. 84–104 in *Institutional Selves: Troubled Identities in a Postmodern World*, edited by J. F. Gubrium and J. A. Holstein. New York: Oxford University Press.

Whyte, W. F. 1943. *Street Corner Society*. Chicago: University of Chicago Press.

Woolgar, S. and D. Pawluch. 1985. "Ontological Gerrymandering: The Anatomy of Social Problems Explanations." *Social Problems* 32:214–227.

Zimmerman, D. H. and M. Pollner. 1970. "The Everyday World as a Phenomenon." Pp. 80–103 in *Understanding Everyday Life*, edited by J. D. Douglas. Chicago: Aldine.

Index